Praise for Steve Dorff

"Heart, humor, and, above all, authenticity are part of the audible art created by Steve Dorff. His iconic songs are born in the center of his chest, where 'clever' never gets in the way of 'touching' . . . or 'honest.' From Kenny Rogers's 'Through the Years' to Eddie Rabbitt's 'Every Which Way but Loose,' Steve's Grammy- and Emmy-winning work is an American treasure. I'm proud to call him friend. Enjoy his story."

—Paul Williams

"As many people are, I have always been a sucker for a good love song. Steve Dorff is a master of writing them, so it was a natural fit. I have recorded seven of his songs, one of which was 'I Just Fall in Love Again,' which was one of the biggest records of my career. I shall be forever grateful to Steve for sharing his talent with me."

—Anne Murray

"Whether it's a movie score, a television theme song, or a hit song on the radio, Steve Dorff crafts music that is the background of our lives. I have been lucky enough to be one of the artists that Steve has chosen to sing his songs. From the upbeat 'As Long as We Got Each Other' from the hit television theme 'Growing Pains' to 'We Almost Had It All,' a song that describes a once-in-a-lifetime love that slips away, Steve Dorff remains one of the top musical influences of our day. I am so proud to have been able to work with such a creative writer and good friend."

—B. J. Thomas

I Wrote That One, Too...

I Wrote That One, Too...

A LIFE IN SONGWRITING
FROM WILLIE TO WHITNEY

STEVE DORFF

with Colette Freedman

Backbeat
Books

AN IMPRINT OF HAL LEONARD LLC

Published in 2017 by Backbeat Books
An Imprint of Hal Leonard LLC
7777 West Bluemound Road
Milwaukee, WI 53213

Trade Book Division Editorial Offices
33 Plymouth St., Montclair, NJ 07042

Printed in the United States of America

Book design by Michael Kellner

All photos are from the author's collection.

Library of Congress Cataloging-in-Publication Data

Names: Dorff, Steve. | Freedman, Colette.
Title: I wrote that one, too : a life in songwriting from Willie to Whitney /
  Steve Dorff with Colette Freedman.
Description: Montclair, NJ : Backbeat Books, 2017.
Identifiers: LCCN 2017017452 | ISBN 9781495077296
Subjects: LCSH: Dorff, Steve. | Composers--United States--Biography.
Classification: LCC ML410.D79 A3 2017 | DDC 782.42164092 [B] --dc23

LC record available at https://lccn.loc.gov/2017017452

www.backbeatbooks.com

Andrew, your bright light will shine in my heart for all my days . . . I love you!
—STEVE DORFF

Devon, the world is yours to conquer.
—COLETTE FREEDMAN

CONTENTS

___

CONTENTS

FOREWORD

————

Do you like good music? Do you like good stories, and rare facts that you find nowhere else? Do you like love? Do you love life? Family and friends, heart and soul, treble clefs and bass clefs, piano, guitars and drums, horns and strings, Broadway, television, film, and radio? If you do, then we're on the same page. Pun intended.

You don't usually come across many people who offer all of those things and touch people's lives on a daily basis. Be it through the speakers in your car, in your living room, on your television, or in a cinema on a Friday night, I'm quite sure you will be familiar with the music of Steve Dorff.

It's all too often you hear the phrase, "You never want to meet your heroes," because invariably, when you do, you're disappointed. In this case, I did get to meet my hero at a very young age. He rocked me to sleep as a newborn. He taught me to catch and hit off a tee, and he coached my Little League teams. He helped me with my homework. As an adult, I don't talk to anyone every single day but him. It's music. It's life. It's love. It's friends. It's family.

Are you excited to skip this foreword and get started reading about this man yet? I would be if I were you . . . I can promise this: there is no "Backword" at the end of the book. Undoubtedly, I believe you will want to read these stories over and over again. To laugh again, to cry again, to feel that burst of inspiration again. My feelings won't be

————

hurt if you skip my foreword before the second read. I probably would as well.

I can promise you this . . . you will be on iTunes or YouTube by Chapter 3, discovering some rare musical gems that you will listen to for the rest of your life. You will be in awe of a New York–bred UGA alumni, a dog-loving, (recently-allergic-to) oyster-loving, dreamer and believer, people's mentor, people's friend. What you will learn, reading this book, is that it's not just about music and songs; it's about the underlying theme of everything that makes up the difficulties of life, and the challenges that arise from them. Learning to pick yourself up and dust yourself off, and learning to keep going strong.

It's music. It's life. It's love. It's friends. It's family. It's highs. It's lows. It's heart. It's soul. It's a rare genius of a man.

If you're into inspiration and creativity, turn the pages, and read about the man I like to call my friend, and my dad . . . Steve Dorff.

Andrew Dorff

Nashville, Tennessee
November 10, 2016

INTRODUCTION

————

THE STORY OF MY LIFE can be summed up in one extraordinarily ordinary evening at the Sheraton Universal's happy hour.

My friend Steve "Buck" Buckingham was in town, and he asked me if I could pop by the hotel, have a drink, and meet some people. That is always code for "please don't make me entertain by myself. I need backup."

Buck was my lifelong buddy, and the hotel was close to my house, so I drove over to meet him. The place was packed. Buck and his group had commandeered a front table close to the band. It was a decent little three-piece combo with a female singer; they were playing covers for the happy-hour crowd.

Buck introduced me to three of his friends who weren't in the music business, and about five minutes into our conversation, the band began to play a version of "I Just Fall in Love Again," one of my songs, which had been recorded by the Carpenters, Dusty Springfield, and Anne Murray.

After they finished, Buck leaned over to the singer and said, "My buddy Steve here wrote that song you guys just did."

Intrigued, she smiled and graciously told me how much she loved the song. People never know the guy behind the curtain, and it felt good to be called out. I thanked her for her kind words and went back to my drink and conversation.

————

The band immediately jumped into their next song. It was "I Cross My Heart," one of my songs, which had been recorded by George Strait. As soon as the song was finished, Buck smiled and told the band, "Steve wrote that song as well."

This time they nodded politely and exchanged a few awkward looks between them. They obviously thought we were fucking with them. Any hint of admiration or chance of me getting the singer's phone number was gone.

As the band started to play the first few notes of their next song, I groaned. By sheer coincidence, it was "Through the Years." When they finished the song, Buck was grinning ear to ear.

"He wrote that one, too!" he shouted.

It was true. It was one of my most successful songs, as recorded by Kenny Rogers.

At this point, I'm completely embarrassed; the band is convinced we are lying to them, and I am ready to get the hell out of there.

When they started to play the Beatles' "Michelle" next, Buck yelled out, "Hey, this is amazing, he wrote that one, too." Of course I hadn't, but it was too funny for Buck to pass that one up. The band then took a short ten-minute break and the singer came by our table, leaned in and said, "You guys are so full of shit."

She gave us a dirty look and walked off.

Driving home, I was chuckling to myself about the scenario, and then it hit me. Songwriters like me—who aren't the performers who make these songs famous on the radio—are relatively unknown. I sometimes think the famed quote from *The Wizard of Oz*, "Pay no attention to the man behind the curtain," was meant for songwriters like me. We are the invisibles, the men and women who write the soundtracks of people's lives while often remaining completely anonymous to the public. Sure, the band knew that Lennon and McCartney wrote all of the Beatles' songs, but they had no idea who wrote the Anne Murray, George Strait, or Kenny Rogers hits that they were playing.

If there's a single word to describe my career's journey, I suppose it would be "versatility." This has been both a blessing and a curse: I have not been pigeonholed, but I also don't fit neatly into any boxes, like most songwriters or composers. Writing music for songs, records, television, feature films, and theater, as well as arranging and producing for countless recording artists, has all added up to the reason why I was asked to write this book in the first place. Because why settle on just one thing, when you want to do many?

As a teenager who locked himself in his room for hours listening to records over and over, I always gravitated to composers and songwriters like Henry Mancini, Burt Bacharach, Dave Grusin, and John Barry. They were my musical heroes, and they were all extremely melodic composers who could do both orchestral scoring and write contemporary hit songs. I suppose it's not any wonder that I ended up going in that direction as I set out to follow my dream.

What I hadn't counted on in that dream was the occasional nightmare of discovering the discipline of picking myself up and dusting myself off from the weekly rejections and bitter disappointments that go hand in hand with the journey. It's not an easy business, but if you love it and are good at it, if you are persistent and have a bit of luck, then it can be unbelievably rewarding.

Fortunately, the journey of my dream has been sprinkled with amazing excitement and successes: happy accidents in the studio, incredible friendships forged, tremendous creative satisfaction, and sometimes just plain being at the right place at the right time with the right song in hand.

It all adds up to fulfilling the dream I've had as far back as I can remember:

To write music.

I have intentionally decided not to tell my story in a linear fashion . . . as I believe artists don't necessarily live from A to Z, and I didn't want to tell my stories that way. Oftentimes, when there was a lull in my television scoring work, a movie project would pop up . . . and when movies went cold, theater projects or special opportunities would present themselves. The songwriting was always there, sort of the glue that kept the music within me flowing. Life's ups and downs, twists and turns, joys and sorrows, were the constant inspiration for what I've been blessed to have written. My stories and recollections connect the dots in this little thing I call a career.

I Wrote That One, Too . . .

1

BARBRA MADE ME CRY

———

THERE ARE STARS, there are megastars, and then there are Barbra Streisand, Frank Sinatra, and the Beatles.

I did get a cut on Ringo. Frank Sinatra had put one of my songs on hold, but a hold and $1.95 will barely get you a tall coffee at Starbucks. One of the proudest moments of my life was when I was able to call up my mom and say, "Barbra Streisand is recording one of my songs!"

The first time I met Barbra was when I went to the studio to hear a mix of one of my songs, "Higher Ground." Her executive producer, Jay Landers, had invited me down to Village Recorders in Santa Monica to have a listen and say hello. He told me that Barbra really cares about the songwriters and has always valued their opinions.

I got to the studio and was both excited and a bit nervous to meet her. I had been such a huge fan from the first moment I heard "People," from *Funny Girl*. I am fairly certain I've seen that movie one hundred times, possibly more.

Jay and I met outside the control room. He gave me a few ground rules and then brought me in.

Meeting Barbra was like meeting royalty, only better, because she had perfect pitch and a three-plus-octave range.

I walked over to her, looked her directly in the eye, and told her how honored I was to meet her. Barbra couldn't have been more beautiful

———

and sweet in person. She told me how much she loved the song, and how it had been a bit of an ordeal to "get it just right."

A little backstory . . . George Green, a talented lyricist from Indiana, and I had met over the phone through a mutual publisher friend. George, who had grown up with and written many hit songs with John Cougar Mellencamp, was looking to expand his catalog by writing with some new composers.

We spoke for about an hour during that first phone call. George was a soft-spoken poetic genius who liked to write lyrics first and have music written to them later. Having done this so many times with two of my longtime collaborators, Milton Brown and Marty Panzer, this was not going to be a problem. As he lived in Bloomington, Indiana, George asked if it would be okay to just fax me over things when he had some good song ideas. I told him I was excited to try to write one with him.

It was about two weeks later that I got a call from George. He had been asked by Tommy Mottola, the longtime manager of John Mellencamp, and now chairman of Sony Music, to write a meaningful song for a new artist on the label, Mariah Carey. George thought he had a "really nice lyric" that he wanted me to take a look at and hopefully want to write the music for.

Five minutes later, my fax machine started to print "Higher Ground."

As I pulled the paper out of the fax machine and began to read, I got chills—enormous goose bumps that viscerally told me this was going to be a meaningful and great song. From the first line of the song, I was completely hooked, and by the time I had read it all the way through, I was starting to hear what the tune would eventually be. I didn't leave my office until the song was completely written . . . about an hour later.

It is hard to explain, but the really good songs have always come fast for me. Always. The music has always just fallen out of the sky when I needed it most, and this was one of those times.

This song pretty much wrote itself.

I told George how excited I was about this song when I got him on the line. He was elated and a bit surprised that I liked it so much, and said he couldn't wait to hear it. I booked a basic demo session two days later at my friend Bo Goldsen's Criterion studio, where I had been doing most of my demos. The demo consisted of three of us: I played a Fender Rhodes, Dean Parks played acoustic guitar, and Susie Benson crushed the vocals. It was one of those rare, spectacular sessions where everything just perfectly flowed.

I sent it to George overnight, and he loved it. George sent it to Tommy for Mariah to hear. We waited a long, excruciating week until we finally heard back from Tommy, who told us that it was a "beautiful, beautiful song," but not really right for the direction he wanted to take with Mariah. He went on to tell George that "this would be a monumental song for someone like Barbra Streisand," and that we should get it to her.

It only took seven years, but somehow it eventually landed on Jay Landers's desk and we had a shot.

Jay is a consummate "song man" and a great A&R person in the classic tradition of that position. He impeccably knows his every artist's musical taste and how to create an entire album with song choices that flow beautifully together in a meaningful arc and are never disjointed. He's also a tough customer when it comes to getting a song just right.

Jay called me and explained that he was putting together material for an "inspirational" album for Barbra, and that he thought "Higher

Ground" would be a great song for her and the project. He also wanted to know if we would we consider changing a line or two of the lyric. I think George stuck to his guns on the opening line, but we did change another one for Jay.

Barbra heard the song and wanted to do it. With Barbra singing and Arif Mardin producing, it was getting pretty impossible to not be excited.

I'm not totally sure how many times Arif tried tracking the song—at least twice, as I remember. He called me one day from New York and said Barbra was unhappy with two of the arrangements that he had started. He asked me who played on the demo, because Barbra was adamant about following the simplicity of the demo recording.

I confessed that it was just Dean and me who played on the demo, and Arif asked if I wanted to play on the recording to recreate the exact voicings. I was flattered, but I suggested he use either Randy Kerber or Randy Waldman, who were both gifted musicians and far better piano players than I was. They had also done so many sessions with me that they would know exactly what I had done on the demo. Dean Parks on guitar was a no-brainer as well, since he was on the original with me.

The final track was beautifully arranged and produced, and with that the first song George and I had written together was recorded by the legendary Barbra Streisand. What an incredible way to start a collaboration.

George Green and I went on to write a total of ten wonderful songs together over the next several years, five of them recorded by B. J. Thomas, Vanessa Williams, and Christopher Cross. George passed away at the young age of fifty-nine, way too soon. He was a lovely man, a friend, and a brilliant poet.

Back to Barbra.

As far as I can remember, I've only cried in the studio three times, and all three were related to Barbra Streisand projects.

The first time was in the studio, listening to Barbra's vocal for the first time, with her standing three feet in front of me. It was an overwhelming feeling, knowing that it really doesn't get any better than this. I savored the moment as I unsuccessfully tried to hide my tears, not wanting to look like a complete idiot in front of everybody.

The ultimate icing on the cake was when the album was released and they decided to title it *Higher Ground*. When I proudly gave a CD to my mom, and I saw her tear up, her tears were contagious. She was bursting with pride, and I was so humbled and happy that I had made my mom proud that I cried as well.

A couple of years later, Jay would play another one of my songs for Barbra's beautiful *A Love Like Ours* project. This was a collection of love songs dedicated to her husband, James Brolin. She recorded a song of mine called "It Must Be You," cowritten with Stephony Smith, which thankfully made the album.

It was twelve years later that I got to cry for the third time in relation to a Barbra Streisand project. Barbra was getting ready to start an ambitious project called *Partners*, an album of duets with some of the greatest male duet partners on the planet. All but two of the songs were remakes of her biggest hits, which were all done with all-new arrangements: "People" with Stevie Wonder, "The Way We Were" with Lionel Richie, and "Somewhere" with Josh Groban were just a few of the amazing tracks included.

It was an unbelievable project, and I absolutely wanted to be a part of it.

Jay called and told me that Barbra had always wanted to duet with Willie Nelson, and Jay and Barbra were interested in using one of my songs. However, Jay wanted the song to be rewritten in more of a "friendship" tone, as opposed to the traditional love song that it initially was intended to be.

I was up for the challenge, as I wanted to be on the album. I also didn't feel as if I was compromising my integrity, because I definitely could not visualize Willie and Barbra doing a love song together. Plus, Jay's rewrite ideas for the song were really good ones. He had some great thoughts as to how to tailor it specifically for them.

Bobby Tomberlin and I finished the song, "I'd Want It to Be You." I did a fairly elaborate mockup demo, with Kellie Coffey and Troy Johnson singing the duet. The harmonies were totally mapped out, Barbra loved it, and it was a go.

The problem was, Willie couldn't sing it—at least not in the way we had imagined the duet.

It was too much of a stretch, musically, and in fairness to Willie, not really the kind of song that's in his wheelhouse. Also, when he was paired with Barbra, it was clear that there was no way the duet was going to work.

I was heartbroken. We were in jeopardy of losing the song altogether from the project.

Jay asked me if I knew someone else who could sing it with Barbra.

He suggested Garth Brooks, George Strait, or Keith Urban.

I tried Garth and George. I had good relationships with people who could easily get in touch with both of them. Unfortunately, it didn't fit into their respective recording plans, as both were in semi-retirement at the time.

I called Jay to report the bad news. While we were talking, I thought of someone else who would be fantastic to sing the song with Barbra: Blake Shelton.

There was a brief dead silence over the phone. Finally, Jay said, "Who?"

"Blake Shelton, from *The Voice*. He's on fire. The show's hotter than *American Idol*. He's a great-looking country singer with a big voice to match. And women love him. He'd sing the doors off this song, and it'd be the perfect marriage with Barbra's voice."

Jay resisted a bit, giving me the list of partners already on the album, including Stevie Wonder, Michael Bublé, Billy Joel, and Lionel Richie. He wanted a bigger name.

He had to hang up at that point as Barbra was calling on the other line. Ten minutes later, he called me back and asked me, "Do you know Blake Shelton?"

"I do actually. What made you change your mind?"

He told me that he mentioned Blake Shelton to Barbra and that she loves *The Voice* . . . and she especially loves Blake Shelton.

I got the song to Blake through Narvel Blackstock, Blake's manager and Reba McEntire's longtime husband and manager. I had known Narvel for quite some time, having worked with Reba before.

Blake loved the song and was both excited and honored to be involved in the project. First we had to rewrite a few of the Willie-specific lyric lines to fit Blake, and then we scheduled the session. Blake was in Los Angeles, filming *The Voice*, and he came in to sing his parts to Barbra's partially prerecorded vocal.

We did his vocals at Walter Afanasieff's home studio, which coincidentally used to be my house, two owners previous to Walter owning it. It was like being home again. Blake did a remarkable job, and Barbra ended up resinging some of her vocals to better match with him.

"Partners" was produced by Walter A. and Kenny "Babyface" Edmonds, and it shipped #1 the first week, making Barbra the first recording artist in history to have #1 albums spanning six decades—a record unlikely ever to be broken.

Sitting at the orchestra sweetening session, off to the side of the huge control room at Fox Studios, I cried unapologetic tears as I watched Bill Ross conducting this incredible orchestra, including so many of my friends, sweetening our song.

Once again, I was reflecting back to the beginning of both my lifelong love of music and my career, and feeling so overwhelmingly appreciative of how and where the road had taken me.

2

What's Wrong with Our Son?

———

I was not your typical toddler.

The first time I heard music, I was a baby, banging my head against the lead-painted crib and making guttural noises. While my parents were worrying about how to pay for the long years of therapy I was going to need, I was hearing a full-scale orchestra. For hours, I would bang, sing, and visualize. Clearly, I didn't know what an oboe or clarinet or violin was. I had never heard music, but I was definitely hearing something and I was visualizing it as colorful plasmic bubbles.

At this point, you're probably thinking, "Steve Dorff is crazy. I've picked up this book and it's written by a nut job." Bear with me. The bubbles were real. It's difficult to explain, and to this day I'm still not sure I truly understand it myself.

The first conscious memory I have of hearing music was when I was still in the crib. I was laying on my stomach and making noises that my parents swore was me either humming or singing.

I know that few adults can remember anything that happened to them before the age of three; however, I do vaguely remember the head banging. The brain, as we've all been told, is this mysterious center, most of which is untapped. Sometimes I can't remember what I did last Thursday, but somehow I can vividly recall things I did half a century ago. I admit it doesn't make a lot of sense.

———

Back to the plasmic bubbles.

I remember seeing them as a baby. I know this because I still see them. Whenever I hear music—as an infant, a child, a teen, or even sometimes still today—it is often accompanied by shapes of color that I see if I close my eyes. The best way I can describe these shapes is that they move in depth, as opposed to left to right. The first time I ever saw a lava lamp as a teenager, I remember thinking, "Ah, someone else figured out how to bottle these crazy things!"

These shapes, these plasmic bubbles, represented intervals, tones, or notes; musical pictures that went along with what I was hearing.

When I tried to describe what I had experienced as a kid, a psychologist friend of mine told me, "It sounds as if you've experienced the phenomenon of synesthesia."

There are people who see numbers as colors in their heads, sounds as smells—all sorts of crossover of the senses. It is not completely understood because few people actually, truly experience it. This would maybe explain those crazy-shaped plasma bubbles that I would see when closing my eyes while either listening or dreaming up music. I only know that it was an experience that came to me as naturally as breathing.

I often still wonder if it explains, in some way, the reasons why I was able to identify chord structures, intervals, and time signatures without having taken formal training. Don't get me wrong: there is so much I wish I had learned formally. It would have saved me countless hours of banging that same head against a wall, trying to figure out what a great studio musician easily figures out in twenty seconds. At any rate, that is where my musical journey began.

Bubbles became my toddler mind's version of notes.

My sister was nine years older than me, and she took piano lessons.

As soon as I could walk, I would trudge over to the rented piano; first I'd bang on the low notes, then I'd bang on the high notes. My parents, who by this time were probably wondering what planet I came from, assumed I was having a musical seizure . . . but I was telling a story. To me, the low keys were a bear and the high keys were birds.

Eventually, the pounding took shape, and my parents realized there was something there.

I was trying to communicate. The trouble was, no one was listening.

My parents should probably never have been married. They were both alcoholics, with a strong penchant for vodka, and in the evenings, when I was a little boy, I was kept awake by horrific arguing, glass breaking, cries, and screams.

So I kept retreating into my mind. Into my bubbles.

I grew up in Queens, New York, in a middle-class family. My parents divorced when I was four, so I didn't have the most functional upbringing. The closest thing to a male figure in my life was Uncle Phil. As you may well guess, "Uncle" Phil was not a proper blood-relative uncle but my mother's favorite suitor. The minute dad exited the front door of our apartment, Uncle Phil entered. He was like a surrogate dad to me. I was too young to realize he was banging my mom, so I took him at face value. There was probably an Uncle Bill and an Uncle Pete and an Uncle Bob around, too, but Uncle Phil was around the most. And he was a good guy. He was someone I could count on, he loved my mom and my sister, and, most importantly, he used to buy me albums. The second a new Beatles album came out, I would lock myself in my room and not leave until I knew every note of every song.

Dad still visited quite often, maybe once a month for a day or two, but he was more of a stranger to me. When Dad came back to visit, Uncle Phil would disappear and everyone would play nice. My sister, my mother, and I would all be on our best behavior, and everything would play out functionally until dinnertime, when the booze came out and the arguing began. My sanctuary was my little bedroom, where I'd put a pillow over my head . . . and retreat to the orchestra in my head.

It was the only thing that would drown out the dysfunction that was screaming through the door from the other side of the small apartment.

The plasmic bubbles stayed with me, and I continued to orchestrate in my head, often to everyday activities. When I was eight, I was in a snowball fight with a bunch of friends in my neighborhood of Fresh Meadows, Queens. The point of a snowball fight is generally not to get hit in the face by flying ice, but I found myself standing still in the middle of the crossfire as snow was being hurled at my head from every direction on the compass. I stayed still, however, because I was musicalizing each impact: each crash, thrash, swish, plink, and plunk.

I musicalized each new snowball as it slammed into me, adding it to the symphony in my head. I didn't duck. And that was the moment, while I was purposefully being pummeled, when I think I realized that I was different.

Everyone has that moment in their life when they know. When they know what they're supposed to do. When they realize what they are meant to do. For most people it doesn't usually come until they are in college; for many, it happens somewhere midlife when they realize they are destined to do something even though the trajectory of their life has navigated them in a different direction.

Mine happened when I was eight. When I was getting beaned in the head.

Yes, it hurt and yes, it was cold. But it was a small price to pay for discovering my destiny.

I knew I wanted to learn as much as I could about the music I was hearing, I just didn't know that the traditional route that most musicians took would not be my particular road. I don't think I took either of Frost's two roads that diverged into a wood; instead, I think I managed to find the unpaved, unmarked path and determinedly followed that one.

KICKED OUT OF MUSIC CLASS

I NEVER TOOK traditional piano lessons because I kept insulting the teachers.

It wasn't on purpose. I didn't mean to insult them. I just heard things differently than they did. I did it my own way, and music teachers seem to like to do it their own way.

Apparently, if you want to pass a class, you shouldn't correct the teacher.

The biggest problem with hearing music in your head is that a) you think that you can do it better than everyone else, and b) you usually can.

It started with my sister Sherry's piano teacher, Mr. Teitlebaum. He loved my sister because my sister was the perfect student. She did exactly what she was told: practice scales, learn a song, repeat. She was nine years older than I was, and she started taking piano lessons when she was twelve and a half. At four years old, I remember listening to her practice the same song over and over and over again. Not knowing any better, I would crawl up on the piano bench and could somehow play the song she had been laboring over for weeks, better than she could.

I've always wondered why she didn't try to break all of my fingers. My mother thought it best to get my sister's piano teacher to give me some lessons.

That turned out to be a small disaster.

When it came time to teach me, Mr. Teitlebaum told my parents that I was unteachable. This was because I played songs the way I heard them in my head rather than in the cookie-cutter way he tried to teach them to me. He told my mom I was undisciplined, insolent, and insubordinate. I told him he was pitchy when he tried to sing along, and that he didn't really play in the pocket. Of course I didn't know that music terminology at that age, but he had terrible time, and I sensed it.

He kindly requested that I stop being his student.

When I was ten, my sister got the part of Miss Adelaide in her college production of *Guys and Dolls*. Listening to Frank Loesser's music made a huge impression on me. I loved the songs, and I loved the magic of the theater. After the show, my sister rushed out, expecting adulation. Instead, I gave her a perfunctory hug, said how much I loved the show, and told her that she was great even though she was a quartertone flat most of the time when she sang.

I wasn't trying to be an asshole; I was a kid and she was hurting my ears.

Yes, I think I recognized early on that I didn't listen to music in the traditional way that most people do. My ears would always focus in on what the instruments of the orchestra were doing, as opposed to just listening to the vocalist singing the song. I was far more interested in what countermelodies the strings or brass might be playing, the use and registers of the woodwinds, and little things like orchestra bells, timpani, and harp glisses. For me, the real emotion of a record came from these backing elements.

The actual words to a song were secondary.

Even as a young teenager, there were three great orchestrators I loved listening to: Peter Matz, Don Sebesky, and Herb Bernstein. It was important to me to read the liner notes and see who was putting these records together. Instinctively, I always heard what they were doing. I listened to all those counter lines and the way they used the instruments to complement the singer and not get in the way.

Listening to and studying them became the beginnings of my musical education.

I didn't know how to sit down and write, but I understood why they were doing it, and by listening to them I began to learn how to do what they were doing. I translated what I was hearing into the orchestra in my head and somehow began to visualize how to do that as well.

It was a comprehensive, if not bizarre, way of listening for a young kid who didn't even know what a music note looked like, let alone a cello, oboe, flute, or violin. I didn't know the terminology of woodwinds, brass, percussion, and strings. I just knew that I wanted to be a part of this world. This early recognition and love for orchestral music served as the foundation for everything I've done as a composer and arranger, and was significant to why and how I was able to instinctively understand the mechanics of orchestration and song structure without any formal training.

Most kids have imaginary friends; I just had a huge orchestra playing 24/7 in my head. Just about every aspect of my daily life became connected to this orchestra that was always on call. Whether it was a snowball fight with friends, a home run in a Little League game, or the simple slapping of the windshield wipers in my mother's car on a rainy day, I was always accompanying these visions and sounds of my everyday life with my imaginary orchestra. I literally was underscoring everything I did.

My head was filled with musical onomatopoeias.

Everything was part of my orchestra: the thwack of a ball, the rustle of the leaves, the whisper of the wind. As my friends guzzled soda, my parents clinked glasses, my sister's heels click-clacked. It was symphonic.

When I would ask my mom or my friends, "How did you hear that?" I would get a strange look or expression that undoubtedly meant, "Are you nuts?" I guess I just assumed that, like seeing colors, smelling, tasting, and touching, everybody musicalized their every step like I did.

But my orchestra stayed with me, and I knew that one day I would hopefully be able to actualize the everyday sounds into symphonies.

Jump to 1985 and I am in London, scoring the movie *Rustler's Rhapsody* and standing in front of ninety pieces, conducting the London Symphony Orchestra. The entire London Symphony was staring at me, and all of a sudden I thought, "How the fuck did I get here and how in the world am I going to pull this off?"

And then a brief panic attack took place, and I wondered what I was supposed to do next. I took a deep breath and thought about Burt Bacharach, Leonard Bernstein, Peter Matz, Don Sebesky, Herb Bernstein—all the people I had ever seen conduct on television . . . and this time it was me.

I took another deep breath and raised the baton. I heard the first chord that all ninety of these musicians were playing at once, and it almost blew me off the podium. Tears streamed down my face, and I wondered if I was in a dream or if this was really happening.

That feeling has happened to me repeatedly over the course of the last forty years.

Manifesting dreams became a reality for me. I truly never really believed that someone could just become something because they simply wanted to be. Yet, in many respects, that actually did happen for me.

I manifested a dream I had when I was six years old watching Leonard Bernstein and the New York Philharmonic on a black-and-white TV and said, "This is what I want to do and this is what I'm gonna do, I just don't know how I'm quite going to do it."

I've been kicked out of every music class I've ever sat in. My piano teacher told my mother I was hopeless . . . and yet, here I was conducting the London Symphony Orchestra.

It just doesn't get any better than that.

On a side note: I also watched Mickey Mantle and Roger Maris hit 535-foot home runs out of Yankee Stadium, and I wanted to manifest that dream, too . . . but it wasn't in the cards.

4

MELISSA MANCHESTER SANG MY FIRST DEMO

———

MOST MUSICIANS START in a bad junior-high-school band. I was no exception.

In junior high, my friends and I were determined to be the next Beatles. It was a great idea, except we had a bit of an issue . . . no one knew how to play an instrument, except for me and Herbie Goldberg.

And Herbie Goldberg had a basement where we could practice.

We were all pimply prepubescent thirteen-year-olds, and what we lacked in talent we made up for in determination. Herbie had been taking drum lessons and was pretty good; my best friend Mark Jerome quickly learned guitar; and I taught Steve McDevitt everything I knew about the bass, which wasn't much. By the time we were all on the same page, playing songs with three or four chords, we were sounding pretty good and having some fun. I was desperate to get a Vox Continental organ, like Mike Smith of the Dave Clark 5, but instead my Dad bought me a weird little keyboard that sounded like crap. It came in a small case with four long legs that had to be screwed in before I could stand it up. It was all he could afford—plus he didn't really think our band would amount to anything in the first place.

But I had lofty aspirations.

Mark and I wrote a few songs, which in retrospect were pretty awful, but we were ambitious, and we rehearsed every chance we could in

Herbie's basement. Our biggest dilemma was what to call ourselves. We spent weeks trying to brainstorm the perfect name. Finally, Mark came up with the genius idea of calling us the Four People. We loved it.

Ah, the folly of youth.

In our minds, we became Queens' answer to the Beatles. Only, we weren't asked to play on *The Ed Sullivan Show*. Our biggest gigs were our classmates' bar- and bat-mitzvahs, junior-high and high-school battles of the bands, and the 1965 World's Fair in Flushing Meadows, which we happened to have actually won. It was in the "Singer Bowl," and of course first prize was a brand new Singer sewing machine . . . not exactly an ideal prize for teenaged boys. I still don't remember who actually took it home. I know it wasn't me.

Despite our illustrious track record, my father still wouldn't buy me the Vox Continental organ.

We continued to get a few random gigs for Fresh Meadows Jews who wanted to entertain at their kids' apartment parties—without breaking the bank. And it was fun . . . for a while. Eventually, Herbie and McDevitt threw Mark and me out of the band. My band. The band I created.

I was stunned. I was heartbroken. I was relieved.

I would become the first in a series of musicians who were kicked out of the bands they started: Brian Jones from the Rolling Stones, Steven Adler from Guns N' Roses, Glen Matlock from the Sex Pistols, Dave Mustaine from Metallica, and Steve Dorff from the Four People.

It was probably for the best. They really only wanted to play covers like "Wipe Out" and make some money. I didn't want to play covers— I wanted to write my own songs. They were comfortable playing gigs and singing other people's music. I wasn't . . . I wanted more. A lot more.

After being unceremoniously dumped from my band, I tried playing with another one called the Clyde Hartley 5, but my heart just wasn't into performing. I also hated schlepping instruments around, loading and unloading, and the whole general idea of being in a band. I just wanted to write music. I started to write songs by myself with this dream of making that my future. One evening, I played a few songs of mine for my sister, and she was impressed. Not impressed in the obligatory big sister way, but genuinely impressed.

There are a lot of advantages to having a much older sister, the first of which is that while I was still a stumbling teenager, Sherry was already heavily entrenched in the workforce. Ever since playing Miss Adelaide in her college production of *Guys and Dolls*, she too had the music bug, albeit her interest was behind the scenes. She worked at an advertising agency that often worked with Mark Brown Associates, a music house that serviced advertising agencies, mostly dealing with jingles for commercials. Sherry produced television and radio commercials for Wells, Rich, and Green, one of the top advertising agencies in New York City, and she carried some weight with the various music houses that would bid to do the jingles for those commercials.

She was so impressed with my songs; there was one in particular that she told me she would mention me to a man named Steve Cagan, who was one of the jingle company's talented young composer/producers.

Sherry kept her promise, and the following week she boasted to Steve about her prodigal brother. Humored, he told her he wanted to meet me because his teenage sister-in-law was also a prodigy. He explained that she was an incredible singer who simply needed some good material.

Sherry set up an appointment for me with Steve, and because I didn't have the means to do any demos—hell, I didn't even know what a demo was—I played a few songs for him right at the piano in his office. He heard my stuff and genuinely flipped out.

Steve's sister-in-law's name was Melissa Manchester. He recorded a demo of my song "Moving On," which Melissa sang. It was my first time in a real recording studio. Melissa and I were both kids, barely sixteen years old.

Amazingly, that would be the first of many times that we would be musically connected throughout our careers.

It was late in 1979 when I next saw Melissa. Her recording career had broken, big time, with "Don't Cry Out Loud," as well as some great hit songs of her own. Steve Buckingham was getting ready to produce an album of hers. He was out in L.A. working, and at lunch one afternoon he asked me if I had anything new that I'd like to play for him. I played him a song that I had recently finished with Larry Herbstritt and Gary Harju called "Fire in the Morning." Buck loved it, thought it would be good for Melissa, and asked if he could play it for Clive Davis, who was overseeing the project for his label, Arista Records. Both Clive and Melissa agreed with Buck, and they went in to record it.

Melissa gave a powerful performance of our song. Buck asked me to do the string arrangement, which we recorded in L.A. It was great to reconnect with Melissa after all those years—and actually have a Top 10 record together. On her next album, Melissa would cut another one of my songs, "Any Kind of Fool."

Some fifteen years later, Melissa and I would get back together in the studio once again. I was producing a studio cast album for *Lunch*, a stage musical I had written with John Bettis and Rick Hawkins. Our idea was to record the eleven key songs from the show with some amazing voices from the theater and pop-music worlds. We lined up such stars as Carol Burnett, Faith Prince, Kim Carnes, B. J. Thomas, Davis Gaines, Brian Stokes Mitchell, and a host of others all onboard.

John and I were trying to decide who could sing a beautiful ballad called "Why Fall At All." Almost at the same identical moment, we looked at each other and said, "Melissa!"

I called her, and she graciously accepted our invitation to sing on the project. It is one of my favorite tracks on that album.

Although we've known each other practically all of our lives, Melissa and I have never had the opportunity to write a song together . . . yet. The world of collaboration, and how various people come in and out of your life to share in your musical creations, is a fascinating process. Sometimes it's a complete crapshoot . . . some relationships work, others do not. Many people whom I've had the pleasure of working with, and have written good songs with, have remained in touch throughout the years. Just as many have moved on to other collaborations, or, in some cases, other endeavors entirely. Finding those few "special creative partners" is one of the most challenging yet most rewarding parts of collaboration.

5

HEROES, COLLABORATORS, AND ADVICE

THE QUESTION I GET ASKED most often is, "Which comes first, music or lyrics?"

The answer is that it's different every time, depending on whom I am working with.

Ninety percent of my career has been about cowriting. Like most songwriters, I wrote all of my own songs from the time I was twelve years old through my late teens. My lyrics were universally shitty, stupid, and cliché. Like most beginning writers, I tried to rhyme ridiculous subjects. My first song was called "The Family Grocer," and it was about . . . wait for it . . . the family grocer. It was basically a repetitive clusterfuck of lyrics like these:

> *Why, no sir, yes sir, I don't really know sir*
> *That's okay, sir, cuz I'm the family grocer.*

Yes. It was that bad.

When I started to work at Lowery Music in Atlanta, I was introduced to Milton Brown, a guy with a Southern accent so thick I was absolutely convinced he was a backward hillbilly in overalls. Instead, he was a quiet Jewish man from Mobile, Alabama. We were exclusive as a writing team until I came to California in 1974. That's when other opportunities opened up and I started working with a number of collaborators.

I have been extremely fortunate to collaborate with songwriters whom I admire as people as much as I admire their work. There are far too many to mention, but I couldn't be prouder of the songs I've written with Paul Williams, Linda Thompson, Allan Rich, Cynthia Weil, Joe Henry, Gerry Goffin, Christopher Cross, Gloria Sklerov, Maribeth Derry, and George Green. And while I've certainly experienced a certain magic that can come from a brand new, first-time collaboration, I am best known from my collaborative work with my "big four": Milton Brown, Marty Panzer, Eric Kaz, and John Bettis.

A little introduction to these brilliant masters of words and rhyme . . .

Like I said, I misjudged Milton Brown from the moment I heard his thick drawl. Growing up in New York City, I myopically envisioned a stereotypical redneck sitting on a tractor with a long piece of hay sticking out from his teeth. Never judge a book by its cover . . . or a voice on the phone, as the case may be.

The week before I met Milton, I actually asked him on the phone, "You gonna ride the tractor from Mobile to Atlanta?" Yet as I walked into the restaurant that evening to meet him in person for the first time, he was exactly the opposite of what I had envisioned. He was Jewish, educated, polite, and whip-smart. He looked me up and down and said, in his lower-Alabama drawl, "Well, I thought you'd look different." We have been best friends ever since, and have written hundreds of songs together. He's undoubtedly the greatest lyricist that nobody's ever heard of.

Compared to Milton, Marty Panzer's songwriting process is a bit unusual, as he likes to write a lyric, type it out, hand it to me in a brown legal-sized envelope, and before he lets me even read it, he prefers to dramatically recite it to me. It is quite an experience to watch Marty recite one of his lyrics. It was a new and unique way for me to be drawn into a lyric. It was not unusual for Marty to spend weeks or months agonizing over a word or a comma, and by the time he would give me a finished lyric, he was certain it was finished. It was a rare occasion when I would dare ask him to maybe change a word or add a phrase, since I was basically musicalizing to a set-in-stone lyric.

After handing me the lyric to "I Want a Son," one of my favorite songs that I've ever written, Marty emphatically announced, "I am not changing a comma." He rarely had to. His lyrics roll off the tongue; they have a natural rhythm that jumps off the page at me when I read them, and they speak totally from the heart.

Eric Kaz is a real character. He might have been the lovechild of Woody Allen and Dustin Hoffman's character in *Rain Man*. Kaz has a sharp and sarcastic wit, is crazy funny when he's not trying to be, and is an absolutely brilliant self-contained songwriter. Unlike me, he doesn't need anyone else to write a song.

Eric and I met each other in the mid-eighties in Los Angeles. Randy Talmadge, a publisher at Warner Tamerlane Music, introduced us. I think that one of the reasons we became great songwriting partners is because we had similar journeys. We were both raised primarily by our Jewish mothers, he in Brooklyn and me in Queens. We both gravitated to California at roughly the same time. We were both married for an excess of twenty years, and we both lost our ex-wives to cancer. Both of our moms died within a year of each other. Both of our ex-wives died within a year of each other. Our paths were unbelievably similar, and, perhaps because of that, we were likeminded when it came to collaborating.

Eric is one of my best friends from either side of the piano, and a brilliant songwriter with whom I've written some of my favorite songs. One has to know and love Eric to really appreciate his quick wit and the quirky and unexpected truisms that he often comes up with. One day he said to me, out of nowhere, "You know, only about 20 percent of an iceberg is above water. The other 80 percent is hidden below and almost never seen."

"And that has something to do with the song we're writing?"

"No, not really. But if you count all of the songs in our catalogs that we've written, I bet only about 20 percent of them will ever be heard, let alone be recorded or become hits. So, really, a songwriter's career is like an iceberg."

His analogy is a little esoteric, but it's pretty much right on point. It makes me think about all those special songs that are, without question, some of the best things I've ever written, and why they might have fallen through the cracks and not have become the successes that some of my other songs have.

The perpetual optimist, I still have hope that some of them still have a chance to get above the waterline.

Of my "big four" writing partners, I think I've spent more hours in writing rooms, studios, theaters, and hotel meetings with John Bettis than I have with anybody . . . maybe my own kids. I often tease John that he knows more "stuff" about any and every subject known to modern man than anyone I've ever met. His genius is unlike that of anyone I've ever known. I would have to say there's definitely a yin and yang aspect to the way we've always worked together.

We have often joked that I'm the eternal optimist who sees the glass three-quarters full, and John sometimes can't even find the glass.

Truth be told, I'm too trusting; John questions everything. If I question a line of a lyric, he'll immediately throw it out. Or, if I don't understand where he's coming from—because it might be a little over my head—he'll give me a sixty-minute dissertation on why the line works coming out of the singer's mouth.

While we are writing, he is methodical while I am off to the races.

I met John right after I left Snuff Garrett to sign a deal with Chuck Kaye over at Warner/Chappell. We had known of each other's work for years, and we had met a few times casually on the A&M lot through Ed Sulzer. John had written many mega-hits with Richard Carpenter. When Chuck left Irving/Almo to head up Warners, John followed him. One day, Chuck called me and suggested I get together with John to formally meet and possibly write some songs together.

Write we did . . . for the last forty years.

Not only have we written songs for pop, country, and R&B artists, but John and I have written the themes for hit TV shows like *Growing Pains, My Sister Sam, Murphy Brown,* and *Just the 10 of Us,* and songs for film like *The Last Boy Scout, Pure Country,* and *Curly Sue,* among many others. John's versatility as a lyricist is unparalleled. He can write about anything in his own unique voice and style and possesses that rare ability to either write to an existing melody or come up with a lyric idea first. I had gotten so used to working "lyric first" with both Milton and Marty that working with John gave me the musical freedom to go to more unusual places with both melody and time signatures, rather than keep within the framework of a finished lyric.

The truth is, I love writing both ways, and that's been the beauty of working with all of these guys, but when it came to writing for the theater, which is the direction in which I saw myself inevitably heading, it was John's flexibility for writing anything in any shape that made him the perfect choice to write the lyrics for any show I was approached to write.

The real magic of a successful collaboration is that unique musical miracle that comes from each of them. In every cowriting situation I've had, I've found the chemistry between myself and the person I'm working with to be unique. Fortunately, I've gotten to write with some of the most wonderfully talented people on the planet. I am forever grateful that they shared their time and talents with me over the years, and my deepest admiration goes to them. Unlike the mostly "exclusive" songwriting teams, like Bacharach and David, Elton and Bernie, Bricusse and Newley, and of course, Lennon and McCartney, most of my major successes were written with a select group of four songwriting partners, or the occasional cut or hit from a first-time write with a new collaborator.

It doesn't matter what comes first, music or lyrics. What matters is that you have a symbiotic relationship with your collaborator. The value of working with a cowriter, especially one who is strong lyrically and can turn a phrase and come up with fresh approaches to well-worn stories, is that it makes it fun to cowrite.

At the end of the day, we're usually all just singing or writing about either love found or love lost.

At least that's what I'm usually writing about.

6

KNOCKING ON DOORS 1

Herb Bernstein

I WAS TRUDGING THROUGH HIGH SCHOOL with no band, not much money, and a small stack of some pretty good songs that I had no idea what to do with. I was still unhappy at home, and all I really wanted to do was to run away and join the circus.

But since I was afraid of heights and allergic to elephants, I knew I had to follow a different destiny. I took the subway from Queens to Manhattan and met with a publisher. It was all about chutzpah—instilled by my mom, no doubt. It was about having the guts to follow your dream.

I went directly to the Brill Building, because I heard that's where the publishers were, and I started knocking on doors. The problem was, the Brill Building was not really the happening place anymore. Most of the great writers and publishers had moved on from there.

I wasn't daunted. My endgame was getting into Herb Bernstein's office. He was a man whose work I really loved, and I was determined to try and charm him with my talent.

I was prepared: I studied every record Herb had arranged or produced, and was surprised at how easy it was to find his office address. It was actually listed in the phone book.

So, I knocked on his door.

His office was at 39 West 55th Street. As I walked in, there was a gentleman seated at a desk who asked if he could help me. Gathering my courage, I told him that I had written a few songs I wanted Herb to hear. I didn't know I was talking to Herb's assistant, Bud Rehak.

Bud grinned at me, amused by the audacity of a sixteen-year-old kid, and asked me if I had some demo tapes I could leave for Herb, because he wasn't in the office. I couldn't. I was unprepared and I didn't know I had to leave behind a demo.

"No, not really," I stammered. "I thought I could just play for him."

Bud kindly told me that I could play something for him instead.

So I sat down and played. Bud must have been impressed, because he told me to hang out and wait for Herb. We chatted for a while, and Bud had told me he was a lyricist as well as being Herb's assistant and office manager. About forty-five minutes later, we heard the door open, and it was Herb Bernstein.

I was awestruck.

Herb was one of the hottest arrangers in town, having done many charts for the Four Seasons, the Tokens, Brooklyn Bridge, Laura Nyro, and so many others. Bud introduced us, and Herb asked me to play him what I thought was my best song.

I guessed that meant I probably was only going to get one shot off. I took a deep breath to steel my jittery nerves and played him a song. He listened all the way through.

He asked me if I had another one. About halfway through the second song, he held up his hand, signaling me to stop. I thought he hated it, but it was the exact opposite.

"I'd like to sign you to a publishing agreement," he said, matter-of-factly. "How old are you?"

"I'm sixteen."

Herb sighed and said, "Well, your parents are going to have to sign for you."

I knew that might be a problem.

My dad had returned after a ten-year absence spent making another woman fairly miserable, and the minute he returned, mom kicked out Uncle Phil and pretended we were a normal family again. I was in the middle of hormonal rebellion, and my father and I were not exactly seeing eye-to-eye. Any and every choice I wanted to make for my life was always accompanied by a three-hour dissertation from my father about the pros and cons of making that choice. I only cared about music. I couldn't give a rat's ass about school at that point. I just wanted to write songs.

After having me sit through another one of these long-winded orations, my father surprised me and signed the contract. I guess he figured it would keep me focused until I went to college.

Herb paid me thirty-five dollars a week, which was a lot of money back then—especially for a sixteen-year-old. Within a month of signing my first official songwriting agreement, Herb recorded my first commercial record, a song called "Infinity Blue," released as an instrumental by Al Caiola and his orchestra on United Artists Records.

There was my name, in parentheses, underneath the title.

I was way beyond cloud nine. I was also introduced to my first professional collaborator, Myles Chase, who was from Brooklyn. He was also signed to Herb as a writer, and was a killer piano player. Herb recorded four or five of my songs in the two years I was writing for him, as well as giving me a crash course education in the recording studio and demo process.

Even then, I got involved, and was somewhat adamant about, how and what the players played and what I was hearing. These guys were the top session players of the day in New York, but if I heard something musically that didn't jibe with what I had envisioned for my song, I would quickly give Herb my opinion.

Surprisingly, Herb would often listen to me and make the necessary adjustments to satisfy me. As much as I might have appreciated that gesture then, I find that I appreciate it more now, as it was a valuable first lesson to me in how to collaborate in the studio with great musicians.

Fifty years later, I'm still friends with Herb, who is still working and looking great in his mid-eighties.

As excited as I was to feel like I was finally on the trajectory of doing what I was supposed to be doing, the reality always hit on the subway ride heading back to Queens: I was still a teenager who lived with my parents, and I still had to take chemistry, geometry, world history, and gym. Every time I left the city, I dreaded leaving my fantasy world behind as I headed home.

7

Pains Growing

———

My father was not a bad person.

He was incredibly smart and well read, and he could be extraordinarily charming and funny. He just had an unpredictable temperament, primarily fueled by vodka martinis. The slightest thing a person might say could send him into a verbal rage, where he would rant expletives and storm out. For my sister and me, this was a frightening thing to experience: it would take me weeks to get over the shock of one of these vituperative rants. And they would happen way too often.

I loved my dad, but I panicked every time the vodka bottle came out, because there would inevitably be a battle brewing between him and my mom.

Despite their long estrangement during the Uncle Phil years, my parents decided to get back together during the summer of my junior year of high school. They wanted a fresh start, so my father accepted a new job opportunity and moved us rather abruptly to Baltimore, Maryland.

In their minds, a fresh start meant a new environment. For me, it meant a certifiable nightmare.

Everything I knew was in New York. I had lived in the same neighborhood and had the same friends for almost seventeen years, and now they wanted to uproot me? No. I was furious. I was about to enter my last year of high school, and I was determined to graduate with my friends.

Firstly, I was wildly uncomfortable with the fact that my parents were getting back together and were going to sleep in the same bed after ten years of them both being with other people.

Secondly, my sister was now living in her own apartment, while I was still transitioning and getting used to being the only kid in the house with my mom.

Thirdly, I still had disturbing memories permanently imprinted on my psyche of all of the yelling, screaming, drinking, and fighting of the past decade. What was going to be different now? All of a sudden they were planning on peace, love, and "Kumbaya"? I didn't think so, and I did not believe or trust that change was possible. They were forcing me to be a part of this great experiment in a new city where I didn't know a soul except for Mark Jerome, whose dad coincidentally had also taken a new job and moved his family to Baltimore just a year before. Yes, *that* Mark Jerome, who I guess you'd say was my first songwriting partner in the Four People. Crazy coincidence.

To me, however, the impending move was still akin to child abuse.

Technically, I was still a minor, so I did not have a choice. I packed up my stuff—mostly my beloved records—and begrudgingly moved to Baltimore. Saying goodbye to everyone I knew, including Herb Bernstein, was horrible, and I was petrified of entering a new high school where I had absolutely no friends. The only good news was that Mark might be in my class.

We left New York and moved to a split-level townhouse in the Baltimore suburbs. I had a little more than five weeks of summer to get adjusted to the new surroundings, make a few friends, and get ready for the torturous first day of school. Having Mark Jerome there to show me around, introduce me to some of his friends, and just hang out was the only thing keeping me relatively sane. The only problem was that Mark didn't live in my neighborhood. He lived fifteen miles away, in Pikesville, and went to a different school. My mother tried to get me into that school district, but there was strict zoning, and I was denied.

I tried to stay as positive as I could, but it was tough.

As luck would have it, I was at our community swimming pool one weekend, and there was a band playing a pool party. The band members were all my age, and the lead guitar player/lead singer was surprisingly good. This guy was the first person I ever saw that could play the guitar riff to the Beatles' "And Your Bird Can Sing." I later would learn that not even George Harrison himself could do that without an overdubbed second guitar.

I listened intently to the band for about forty minutes before they took a fifteen-minute break. I went over and introduced myself. The lead guitar player's name was Tony Sciuto, and he had formed the Ravens a year earlier with his little brother Mike—a crazy good bass player considering his bass was bigger than he was. I told Tony my story about writing songs and playing in bands myself, and he asked me if I'd like to play keyboards with them.

This was the beginning of a friendship that would take many turns over the course of our lives. I had graduated to a Farfisa organ that my parents had gotten me, in retrospect probably as a bribe for moving.

I spent the remainder of the summer playing gigs with the Ravens. I had a purpose again, but the summer was in the rearview mirror, and the first day of school was unavoidable.

To say that I felt like a fish out of water on that day would be the understatement of the century.

My entire life to this point was about me always trying to fight past the disappointment and make the best of every day. That's what I learned from my grandma, Gertie, who was the most positive female influence on my life. I tried desperately to hold on to that as I struggled through that first week as a senior at a new high school. I might as well have been thrown into a new universe.

The only tool I had to make new friends was music. Somehow, I needed to seek out those people at Woodlawn Senior High who would have common interests. At five-foot-five and one hundred and thirty pounds, I clearly wasn't going to make the football team.

Surely there had to be a few people there that wanted to either sing or write songs? My teachers had clearly spoken to my parents about my situation, because they went out of their way to introduce me to kids with whom they thought I'd have something in common. I was assigned a senior guidance counselor who also made my life there a lot better than I had anticipated.

Before long, I began to make some friends who I looked forward to seeing each day. Russ Margolis, Marc Bacon, and Bob Marvin were all talented music guys. Things were looking up.

I wasn't getting to see Mark very much except on weekends because of school commitments, and most of the Ravens lived in the inner city of Baltimore, so playing with them became more and more infrequent. About two months into the school year, I tried out for the drama/music club at the urging of Stuart Mason, a fellow student who would go on to be the senior-class president. He heard that I wrote songs, and as a senior-class project he wanted to write an original spring musical, instead of doing the usual high-school production of an existing Broadway show.

It was my first musical.

Stuart had an idea called *Protest Man*. Neither one of us really knew what we were doing, in terms of writing a musical from scratch, so he suggested I write a few songs and he would come up with a storyline that we could turn into a play script.

"Why not?" I thought. I certainly didn't have any better offers.

I wrote eight songs that had absolutely nothing to do with each other, but it was enough of a template for Stuart to craft a fun little story about a group of kids who were protesting something at school. I have no recollection whatsoever of what we were protesting about. Frankly, I'm not sure he did either, but it worked. The mid-year show was a big hit at the school, and it brought me quite a bit of peer notoriety.

The school year was rapidly coming to a close and I had managed to survive. With college options looming, the only thing I knew was that I needed to get as far away as possible. I loved my parents but I needed space to figure out *me*.

With the help of my guidance counselor at Woodlawn, we began to try to figure out where I might be able to attend college.

I had barely a C average when I graduated high school, so there weren't many good choices of schools I could get into. I had no formal training in music, and my dad wouldn't hear of me choosing music as a career choice. So, since my next favorite things in life were dogs, I decided I'd be a veterinarian.

I randomly pointed at a map of the United States, and based solely on which schools had the highest-ranked football team at the moment, I began to apply to colleges that had pre-vet programs. I also wanted to get as far away from home—and my father's endless, long-winded, alcohol-fueled speeches—as I could.

After being rejected by eight schools in a row, including Cornell University, I received an acceptance letter from Northern Arizona State University in Flagstaff. I was happy to have gotten into college but somewhat unimpressed with their football team. So, I waited to see if there were any more acceptances. Luckily, the University of Georgia somehow saw past my mediocre grades and accepted me. And their Top 10–ranked football team was amazing.

Kentucky and Arizona also accepted me late, but Georgia had the better upcoming football schedule. It was also an incredible party school, and as far away from my dysfunctional family life as I could get. They also happened to have a highly rated veterinary medical program.

My father had deeply ingrained in me that while music is a wonderful hobby, one can't make a living at it. One of my father's favorite things to do—usually lubed by his fifth vodka martini—would be to pontificate on how he didn't want his son playing for tips in a glass. So I was off to Athens, Georgia, to become a veterinarian.

During my tumultuous year in Baltimore, and due to the distance away from New York City, I was sadly forced to let Herb know that I would no longer be able to fulfill my songwriting obligations. He gave me a release.

The drinking, which was the chief cause of the bickering between my parents, never really stopped. I never fully accepted my dad coming back until maybe ten years before his death at the age of eighty-four. The scars of the four-year-old little boy whose father had left for another woman were etched deeply, and the truth is, it took me most of the rest of his life for me to fully come to terms with it.

8

KNOCKING ON DOORS 2

Bill Lowery

I WAS NOT REALLY HAPPY in college.

Sure, I made some new friends, and I loved going to football and basketball games, but that was about it. I wasn't following my dream. I wasn't being true to myself. I was trying to be a vet because that's what my parents wanted me to do, but it wasn't what I wanted to do. It only took me one trimester of chem 101 and advanced math to figure out veterinary medicine was not even a remote possibility in my future. I needed to switch majors, and my only criterion was that it did not require numbers.

I'm still somewhat perplexed why I am so allergic to math. My dad was a whiz at it, but I still can't do long division to save my life. Musicians are often good mathematicians because there is a mathematical correlation to rhythms and musical patterns. Perhaps, because I wasn't formally trained, I missed the connection. Perhaps the geometric plasmic bubbles took up so much space in my brain that there was no room left for equations and problem solving.

I switched majors to the journalism school's radio/TV/film program. It did not require math, and there were actual functioning film and recording studios on the premises.

Things were starting to look up.

I spent the majority of my first year as a Georgia Bulldog making friends and getting adjusted to the Southern lifestyle: fraternity parties, football games, and sneaking into the music school. The problem was, I wasn't a music major, so I technically did not have access to the practice rooms. I kept getting kicked out because music majors had set times for those rooms, and I was hijacking their spaces.

I feigned stupidity, but there were signs everywhere: *If you are not a music major, you are not allowed to be here.* I ignored the signs and practiced there a lot. I would look for a room that was empty and just act like I belonged in there. The biggest problem was that just as I would be getting into something really good, a student would barge in and say, "You're in the wrong room—I've got this one reserved."

"Shit, okay, sorry, I must've read the room number wrong."

I'd move a couple of rooms over and begin again. This went on for a while, but the interruptions were just a small part of the major problem; there would be trombones, timpani, violins, and singers all bleeding from the various rooms in close proximity, and it was fairly impossible for me to concentrate.

Eventually, I got kicked out so many times I became *persona non grata* there.

I did inquire about sitting in on an orchestration and music-theory class that was available to non-music majors. It was interesting, and I picked up a few tidbits of information that explained the mechanics of some of the things I somehow already knew innately. But I got bored quickly and dropped the class.

Truth be told, all I wanted to do was go to football games and date girls. With all of the excitement of my newfound college adventures, I can honestly say I put my songwriting on the back burner for the first three months in Athens, Georgia.

Until I found my destiny in the most unlikely of places.

One night I was picking up a date at Brumby Hall, the brand new all-girl dormitory on campus. My date was keeping me waiting, so I wandered around the lobby. It was massive, with couches, study parlors, a reception desk, and a glass-enclosed piano room with a baby grand Steinway in it.

I was like a moth drawn to a flame. I couldn't help myself as I immediately sat down and began to play. A huge rush came over me, and I wanted to call the girl and tell her I got sick, just so I could sit there and write songs for the next twelve hours. Of course, just as I was getting into it, the door opened and she said, with a big ol' Southern accent, "Sorry to keep you waitin' darlin'!"

She sat down next to me.

"Oh my, you play the piano? Play me something."

Thank God she didn't say "Sugar" at the end of that sentence.

You can guess the rest . . . I played her a few songs I wrote, and it was pretty much a done deal as to what would happen after the movie that night.

Brumby Hall became my new hotspot. I'd go there and kill two birds with one stone. I'd sit down at the baby grand and try my best to split my time between meeting girls and getting some song ideas down. Most of my fraternity brothers and the close friends I had made were also dating girls from Brumby, so on many occasions, Ronnie Hagen, Mark Fisher, and Jimmy Mischner would accompany me up there to sit in the piano room and scope out the Brumby coeds.

By the end of my freshman year, I had gotten back to writing some pretty good songs and was fully adjusted to college life. I was having a great time, the Bulldogs had a fantastic season, and I somehow managed to pass all of my classes.

After my freshman year, I headed to New York for the summer and met Nancy Masters, the first woman to have an indelible impact on my life. My sister had been promoted to producer of advertising commercials at Wells Rich Green, and she had arranged a summer job for me in the mailroom. It would get me back up to New York, where I could try and meet more music people, make a little money, and, at the very least, eat some great New York City food after a year of southern-fried everything.

My first day on the job, I met my sister's secretary. She had long brown hair, beautiful eyes, and a gorgeous smile. It was pretty much love at first sight. She was smart, beautiful, funny, and kind. I was hooked. Like an infatuated schoolboy, I found every reason to leave the mailroom and swing by Nancy's desk to see her and make small talk.

She had just recently broken up with her high-school boyfriend of three years, and she made it pretty clear to me she was not too interested in jumping into another "situation." But since the summer job was only going to last three months before I would have to go back to Georgia, I was pretty determined to make some headway in the romance department.

After ten days of working there, I got up the nerve to ask Nancy to have lunch with me. To my surprise, she said yes. We ate lunch together almost every day, which soon evolved into dinners, going to movies, and seeing the Bee Gees' first American concert at Forest Hills Tennis Stadium. We also went to a few Mets games at Shea Stadium, where her dad worked.

By the end of the summer, I was really torn about going back to Georgia. I was committed to Nancy, and I knew she was going to be the girl I would marry and spend the rest of my life with. Still, I had made a promise to my parents that I would graduate college, so I went back.

Nancy would come visit Athens often during my sophomore year. Having a long-distance relationship was challenging, to say the least, but somehow we survived being apart most of the time.

I dated Nancy all through college and continued to write music on my own. By the time my junior year had rolled around, Jimmy Mischner and I decided to leave the crazy frat house where we had roomed together during our sophomore year. We found a dilapidated apartment building above a pharmacy that had to have been built in the late 1800s.

It was sixty-five dollars per month apiece for this one-bedroom, one-bath flat, with a kitchen and living room, complete with one of those old Murphy beds that pulled down out of the wall. If you took a shower longer than three minutes, the clogged and rusted drain would have the water line almost to your knees. And there was usually a rat or three renting space in the kitchen pantry.

It was disgusting, but it was also cheap.

Both of us had cars, and different class schedules, so we hardly ever saw each other during the day. Jimmy was from the small town of Kingstree, South Carolina, and he would frequently head home for long weekends or holidays.

One day, I was shopping in downtown Athens when I passed an old piano/music store that I had never paid attention to before. I went in to browse around, dreaming of the day I could have my own piano, instead of having to steal hours here and there at Brumby Hall or the music school's practice rooms.

As I looked around the small store, I noticed what looked like a miniature upright piano in the corner. I walked over to it and played a few chords. Surprisingly, it sounded like a full piano. The brand name was Diapason. It was made in Hawaii by Kauai. The shop's owner came over and told me it was a pretty rare "practice piano" as it was an octave and a half short of keys. It had been sitting in his store for almost a year and no one had shown any interest. Because of its small size, I knew that it would be perfect for me . . . if I could get it up those three flights of rickety stairs and through the small door of the apartment.

"How much?"

"Eight hundred dollars, brand new."

I knew that there was no way my parents would ever go for that. I told him I was a student but was hoping to make a future in music and writing songs. He thought for a minute and asked, "Would you be willing to rent it from me, with an option to buy it?"

So, for $12.50 a month, I was the proud owner of my first piano. He delivered it, and with Jimmy's and my help the three of us got it up and in the apartment without a scratch. I finally had an instrument that was available to me 24/7 in the privacy of my own place.

During my junior year, I also started researching music publishers in Atlanta. Bill Lowery was the only game in town. The head of Lowery Music, he was an established music producer and publisher, and, from what I had heard, untouchable. I was undeterred. I cut class and drove to Atlanta, determined to see him.

The receptionist told me, in no uncertain terms, "No one sees the wizard." So I asked if I could play for her, in the hope she might at least pass along a good word to some higher up at the company. Minutes later, after listening to a few of my songs, she said, "Wait here," and ran out.

About twenty minutes later, she returned with Mary Tallent, the vice president of Lowery's company.

"Do exactly what you just did," the receptionist ordered. And I did.

Mary Tallent listened intently and asked if I could come back in a week to play for Bill, as he was out of town. I told her I'd be happy to cut more classes. The following week, when Bill heard me, he signed me on the spot.

"I want you to write for us," Bill said. "We don't have anyone who writes melody like you. We mostly have country and rock writers who are self-contained recording artists, and I can use someone here to write pop love songs for other outside artists to record."

Lowery likened me to a young Burt Bacharach, not knowing Bacharach was my idol. He also paid me one hundred dollars a week. And I didn't need my parents' signatures this time.

For the next two years, I worked for Lowery and continued my long distance relationship with Nancy. We spoke on the phone almost daily; she came to visit me in Georgia, and I would go to New York City to see her whenever I could.

In between writing songs, doing demos, and trying to get a few songs cut by the local Atlanta artists, I got my first job arranging a string session. This was a real milestone for me. There was an R&B vocal group called the Tams who were signed to Lowery's label. They had had a few regional radio hits in the South and were looking to record a few new songs for a new album. Mike Clark, their producer, had heard a song of mine called "How Long Love." The song was pretty lame, but Mike liked it and wanted to cut it with the Tams.

I was ecstatic! It was a breakthrough for me. I was getting a song cut. And the best part was that Mike asked me if I could do a string arrangement. Of course I said yes without any hesitation.

Always say yes.

I spent the next two days frantically trying to figure out how to translate what I was hearing in my head to paper. This was my first rodeo. I did manage to scribble out something, but the string players that we had hired couldn't really read what I had written, so I ended up humming what I wanted them to play. It was mostly unison lines, and fortunately, by the end of the session, I learned more about what not to do, than what to do. All in all, the song turned out just okay, but the Tams loved it, and that was good enough for me.

I spent the next two months going to the public library and studying everything I could about the instruments of the orchestra and their ranges, and revisited the basic fundamentals of scales and sharps and flats. I regretted so much not being a music major, but then again, I learned faster by experience and listening to my inner musical instincts.

One of my best experiences at Lowery's was in my early years there. One of my closest friends from school, Mark Yarbrough, had a band that he was still playing with on the weekends from his hometown of Albany, Georgia. One weekend, Mark asked me if I wanted to hear them play a gig that they had booked. I went with Mark and was pleasantly surprised at what I heard. I especially liked the raspy, bluesy sound of their lead singer, Stan Glass.

I asked Bill Lowery if he would let me go into the studio with Cotton (the name of the band) and produce a few songs. Bill gave me the green light.

Milton Brown and I had a really fun song called "Givin' It All I Got," so we went into the studio and recorded the band performing our song along with the old R&B standard "I Know." Everybody at Lowery's really loved the band's sound, and Bill said he thought he could probably get a record company interested. I was getting ready to head home to New York for a long holiday weekend, so we decided that when I got back, we would get into it.

It was good to be back in New York City in the late spring. Nancy and I spent most of my break together. Her dad—my future father-in-law, Nick Masters—worked in security at Shea Stadium. He invited us to see a Mets game that weekend. We had great seats three rows from the field, sitting next to a gentleman Nick was friendly with who attended every home game.

Nick introduced us. The man's name was Nat Tarnopol. He was the president and owner of Brunswick Records. The label was based out of Chicago, but Nat ran it from his New York offices. Nick had briefed Nat that I was a songwriter, and Nat asked me if I had any songs he might like for some of his artists. He invited me to get a tape together and gave me his card with where to send it.

When I got back to Georgia, I sent Nat a tape with three or four songs that I had written. A few days after he received them, I got a call from a man in Chicago named Eugene Record. At first I thought I was being fucked with . . . but his name was really Eugene Record! He had been in New York, where Nat had played him my tape. Eugene was head of A&R for Brunswick in Chicago, and he wanted to record two of my songs with the great Jackie Wilson.

"Are you kidding me?" was all I could say.

"No. Jackie and I really love the songs. We're cutting them tomorrow, and Nat wanted me to let you know."

I couldn't wait to let Lowery know that I was getting two songs on the next Jackie Wilson album. This was definitely a "pinch-myself" moment.

Some six weeks later, I was back in New York for summer break. I went up to the Brunswick offices to say hi to Nat and listen to the Jackie Wilson recordings of my songs. It was a thrill. I hardly recognized my songs, though, as Eugene's heavy R&B-influenced production took them to a different place. It was killer!

While I was meeting with Nat and some of his staff, he asked me if I had anything else I was working on. I said, "Yes, I'm producing a great Southern band out of Atlanta called Cotton. We've cut a few things and are looking for a label deal."

Nat said, "I want to hear it."

"I just happen to have a tape of our first two things we've cut, can I play it for you now?"

A verse and a chorus into the first song, we had a deal.

Nat asked me what else I wanted to do with the guys, and I said we had a few more songs we wanted to record. It took a few weeks to get the paperwork in order, but by September we were back in the studio in Atlanta, recording some additional tracks with the band.

Between juggling school, Nancy, holidays, and the other guys' schedules, it was difficult to find a good chunk of time to spend completing the project. God, I couldn't wait to graduate!

Nat told me he wanted me to do overdubs and have the songs mixed in Chicago by the Brunswick Studios engineer. Eugene Record was also there, and he wanted to be somewhat involved as well.

It was winter break by the time Mark and I went to Chicago. The studio was on Lake Michigan, and with the wind whipping off the lake, the cold was beyond any cold day I had ever experienced.

We had booked a three-girl group of background singers called Kitty and the Heywoods, whom Eugene had recommended I use. They were fabulous. But I still had not gotten to meet Eugene Record yet.

I wanted to put an additional piano part on one of the songs we were doing with the band. I went out into the studio and overdubbed the part. When I walked back into the control room, there was this guy with an enormous Afro standing there. He reached out his hand, smiled a big smile, and said, "Hi Steve, I'm Eugene Record; welcome to Chicago."

He apologized for not getting by sooner but said he had been next door, working on a record of his own with his group, the Chi-Lites. After a few minutes of catch-up and music talk, he said he would see me later, as he had to get back to his project in the next studio over. About an hour later, we were starting to mix the band's stuff when Eugene popped his head into our control room, asking me if I could swing by his studio when I had a minute.

I walked down the hall and into the studio where Eugene was working. He was overdubbing a melodica part on this cool song. He wanted a certain piano part put on his song that was similar to what he heard me playing on the Cotton record, and he asked if I wouldn't mind trying "something" for him.

I sat at the piano and started riffing to the track he was playing. It was a really simple part, but it was exactly what Eugene wanted. A few takes later, he hugged me, thanked me, and took us to dinner on the company.

Little did I know that I had just played the piano on one of the great R&B records of all time . . . "Oh Girl" by the Chi-Lites.

Cotton released two singles on the Brunswick label, one of which got some mid-chart play. "Oh Girl" was a monster hit for the Chi-Lites, and I later produced a Top 10 country version of the song with Con Hunley on Warner Bros. Records.

Eugene and I remained friends, and we would see each other occasionally until his death in 2005. He recorded a few more of my songs with several other artists signed to Brunswick. Nat Tarnopol passed away in 1987 at the age of fifty-six.

When I graduated, my future was clear. It was the mid-seventies, and in the South there was a specific protocol one followed: after you graduated college, you immediately got married to your girlfriend and started a family. All of my friends at school were following that formality, so I figured I would, too.

A month after graduating with an ABJ degree, which to this day hangs somewhere in a garage closet, I asked Nancy to marry me, and she said yes.

Our big dilemma was where to live. Nancy was the only one of us with a real job, but I was finally getting a foothold with some of the other writers and musicians in town. Nancy agreed that the best thing to do would be for her to quit her job at the ad agency and move to Atlanta. Fortunately, with her experience and good references, it didn't take her long to find a viable office job close to the cute two-bedroom duplex apartment that we rented on the rural north side of Atlanta.

Now all we needed was for me to get a few songs recorded, make some real money, and save up to start a family. To both of our delights, the family part came fairly quickly. About ten months into our marriage, Nancy informed me that we were going to have a baby.

Stephen Hartley Dorff Jr. was born on an exceedingly hot July day at Atlanta's Piedmont Hospital: July 29, 1973.

With a gorgeous newborn and a stunning wife, I felt like a million bucks . . . even though I was still only making a whopping $150 a week.

I worked at Lowery Music for four and a half years, and without question the single most wonderful thing that came out of my experience there had to be meeting one of my favorite collaborators and closest friends, Milton Brown.

Cotton Carrier was the general manager of the publishing side of Lowery's operation. As I wrote and demoed songs to turn in, I would play them for Cotton first. He would then put together a tape of all of the songs turned in by the various signed writers and play them for Bill at a weekly meeting.

Cotton was a sweet man and a big fan of my songs. He loved hearing my new songs, and together we would make a wish list of recording artists or producers he would try and get them to. Even though no one was recording them, just the thought of these artists possibly being exposed to my songs was encouraging, and this meeting was always the highlight of my week.

One day, I was in the office, meeting with Cotton, and he asked me if I had ever tried cowriting. Up to this point I was writing both the music and lyrics to my songs. Yes, I had cowritten a few things before at Herb Bernstein's request, when I was a teenager, but for the most part I considered myself to be a fully self-contained songwriter.

Cotton had been in touch with a songwriter from Mobile, Alabama, who was looking to affiliate with a publisher in the South. He was blunt:

"This guy Milton Brown is writing some pretty lousy, boring melodies, but his lyrics are fantastic! Your melodies are amazing, but your lyrics are the weak link in your songs. I think the two of you should try writing some songs together."

I told Cotton I would be happy to look at some of Milton's lyrics if he had a few that he hadn't done the music to already. Cotton called Milton, who replied that he would put some things in the mail that day. This was before the instant gratification of email, and I waited four days before Cotton called me in and handed me five printed pages.

It was the first time I set eyes on a Milton Brown lyric.

I was blown away.

The language, imagery, and sense of melodic fluidity—even without any music—was not something I was used to reading. I went home and I think I wrote all five songs that first day. One of them, written over forty years ago, remains to this day one of my most favorite songs we ever wrote together, "Tonight I Took Your Memory off the Wall." Con Hunley would do a beautiful version of the song, but he never released it as a single. I still believe this song will eventually find its way to another great artist to record.

I finished the simple piano/vocal demos of the songs and Cotton mailed them to Milton. Again, this was before the instant gratification of MP3s. It was old-school back then.

I will never forget that first phone conversation I had with Milton. The phone rang, and when I picked it up, a voice with a dramatic Southern drawl like I had never heard before said, "Hello Steve. I just heard what you did with my lyrics, and I couldn't be more amazed at the quality of these songs."

We talked for twenty minutes and agreed to meet in Atlanta for dinner to celebrate our newfound collaboration.

About a week later, Nancy and I got together with Milton and his wife, Margaret, and Cotton and his wife, Jane. It turns out that my obese farmer was tall and thin with a full head of dark hair, and he was wearing a nice sports coat and tie. Milton and I had turned on the faucet, and for the next three years we cranked out song after song (all lyrics first). The results would soon start to get us a lot of attention at the Lowery Group.

Needless to say, I don't think I wrote another lyric for twenty-five years.

A year before my contract came to an end, *IT* finally happened. A rockabilly/country artist from California, Dorsey Burnette, got a hold of one of Milton's and my songs, "It Happens Every Time." He recorded it, Steve Stone produced it, and Milton and I had our very first *Billboard* chart record.

This was a huge breakthrough for us. We were now considered legit writers within the Lowery Group stable.

With our sudden success as a songwriting duo, we were finally beginning to get some things going with some of the Lowery stable artists like Billy Joe Royal, the Classics IV, and some up and coming artists. Yet, I was feeling restless. The baby was now six months old, I wasn't making much money, and I felt like I was spinning my wheels and going nowhere fast. I knew what I wanted to do and it was time for me to take the leap and do it: I had always wanted to go to California, where I could write songs and scores for movies and TV.

That was always where I wanted to be.

I still own the little stand-up Diapason piano, some four and a half decades later. Just before graduation and my move to Atlanta, I was able to buy it with the money I was getting from Lowery. I paid $600 for the little piano that still sits in my bedroom, which saves me a lot of time running up and down stairs on the occasion I have a tune in my head in the middle of the night. I wrote several big hits, including "Every Which Way but Loose" and "Barroom Buddies," on that bad boy!

9

KNOCKING ON DOORS 3

Snuff Garrett

WITH MY CONTRACT with Bill due to come to an end in six months, I felt stymied.

I was still young, but I was impatient, and I felt like things weren't happening fast enough. I always had a burning desire to write music for television and film. I craved something visual. Bill had sent me out to Los Angeles on a writing trip in 1973, and I was hooked. I loved the vibe, the weather, the palm trees. I could never get it out of my mind, so Nancy and I saved some money so I could come back and try to make a dent. My sister helped out, too, loaning me $400.

I basically had enough money to last for one week.

My son Stephen was only six months old—the same age I was when I was knocking my head into the crib. I promised him I was going to make him proud.

Nancy, Stephen, and I drove to Mobile, Alabama, where they stayed with Milton and Margaret while I ventured out to L.A. on a weeklong trip that would change all of our lives.

I stayed at a fleabag Motel 6 on Sunset Boulevard in the heart of Hollywood, ready to make my mark. I had a backpack filled with demo tapes and a list of my favorite record producers. Every day, I would knock on doors and ask them if they needed songs. Every day, they said no. Mostly, a receptionist would say, "Leave your demo." I was so excited to be in the game, I had no idea they'd throw my demo in the trash the minute I walked out the door.

I had come to L.A. prepared with the knowledge of who the active and hot producers were in town, and the artists with whom they were working. If I could only land one song with any one of these guys, I would feel as if the trip was worth taking, and hopefully would open up the possibility of me getting to move to the West Coast.

One of the doors I knocked on was Garrett Music Enterprises. I was running out of demos and starting to catch on to the fact that everyone was most likely not listening to them. The guy behind the desk, Doc Babb, said in that bored voice I was getting far too used to, "You can leave the demos for Snuff. He doesn't see anyone, but we have a song plugger who will listen."

It was my last day in town: I was worn out, disillusioned, disappointed.

I left the demo and walked out the door, assuming that neither my demo nor I would get any traction. I felt like a failure. I felt like maybe my father was right and no one ever really made it as a pure songwriter unless they were a signed recording artist as well . . . which I was not, and was never going to be.

I bought a hamburger with my last couple of dollars and got back to the hotel at 6:30, just as it was starting to get dark. I needed to pack because I had an early flight out the next morning. I started feeling sorry for myself. What was I going to tell everyone? I was going back to Atlanta with my tail between my legs. Back to my wife and kid. Back to . . .

The hotel phone message light was blinking red.

I quickly picked up the message. It was from a MaryAnne Rowan: "Please call Snuff Garrett when you get this message."

Confused and a little bit panicked, I picked up the phone and dialed. MaryAnne answered on the first ring.

"Garrett Music Enterprises."

"Hi, uh, I got a message, this is Steve—"

"Yeah, hold on for Snuff."

Two seconds later, a thick Texas accent came on the line.

"How you doing, boy?"

"Um . . . I'm good."

"Where are you and what are you doin' right now?"

Now, I was a fairly sheltered Jewish kid from New York, so when he asked me, "What are you doin' right now?" I replied the way any sheltered Jewish kid from New York would.

"I'm in the hotel. I was going to watch TV and go to sleep."

Snuff didn't hesitate.

"How fast can you get over here? Come now, I'm in the office late."

I stopped packing and drove to 6255 Sunset, at the corner of Sunset and Vine. Snuff was waiting.

"Sit down and play me a couple of songs."

So I sat down and played him a couple of songs.

When I was finished, Snuff said, "So, what's your story?"

I told him that I was still under contract to Bill Lowery for six more months but I had always wanted to live and work in Hollywood. I told him I had a wife and a baby. I told him I was dead broke.

"I know Bill," he said. "Bill and I can work some arrangement out. I'll pay you $265 a week and move you out here. You'll work for me. You'll listen to unsolicited songs. You'll learn the ropes and write songs and we'll copublish with Lowery for your remaining six months. Sound good?"

Um . . . it sounded very good.

Snuff asked me to come back the next morning first thing to meet with the VP of the company, to go over details of my impending move west. I changed my flight by a day and went back to the office at 10 a.m. the next morning.

Don Blocker had worked with Snuff for years at Liberty Records, and when Snuff went independent with Garrett Music Enterprises, he brought Don over to be general manager of the company. Don was a down-to-earth Midwesterner from Nebraska who loved to talk college football. He asked me a million questions about my family, aspirations, and expectations.

"Are you sure you want to make this huge transition in your life?" he kept asking me. "Hollywood can be a tough place, and there are no sure things in this business."

My guess is that Don knew Snuff all too well, and maybe he was trying to warn me that if things didn't work out for me there, I would be stuck downstream without a paddle in a big, new, strange place, supporting a young family.

I finally asked Don, "Are you trying to advise me to stay in Atlanta?"

He said, "If you were my son, yes, I would say give yourself a few more years there before moving out here to a situation that is iffy at best."

I was scared, but I told him I was determined to make it out here one way or another, and this was a golden opportunity I could never pass up. With that, he shook my hand, and said, "Welcome."

Don was my point person for the move, and was helpful in every aspect of our adjustment that first year in L.A. I hopped on a flight, packed up my life, and moved my family to California.

Bill worked out a deal with Snuff where they would co-own anything

I wrote for the remaining six months. One of the first songs I wrote at Snuff's ended up being my first Top 10 record, "Hoppy, Gene, and Me" by Roy Rogers. It turned out that Snuff's boyhood hero had also been mine. What a trip.

After the first six months had gone by and I was clear from my Lowery agreement, I signed an exclusive three-year deal with Snuff, which I ended up extending for ten years. Snuff didn't want to let me go. Before me, he had worked with Leon Russell. Leon was also a piano player and Snuff's musical ears. When Leon left, Snuff needed new musical ears.

I happened to knock on the right door at the right time and unknowingly be exactly who and what Snuff was looking for.

Snuff Garrett was a song guy and a people person, but he was not a great musician. In actual fact, he wasn't a musician at all: he had needed Leon just as he now needed me. Frankly, it was smart of him to admit this, as one doesn't always need to be a musician to be a great producer. You just needed some luck, the ability to be a people person, and the uncanny ability to know a hit song when you heard one.

And, no matter what people said about Snuff Garrett's reputation of being a "tough horse-trader," he had a great ear for a great song.

Getting settled into my role at Garrett Music Enterprises, let alone living in Los Angeles, was exciting, scary, stressful, daunting, and rewarding, all rolled into one. Nancy's and my first priority was setting up an apartment in North Hollywood. Stephen Jr. was a toddler now, and we had absolutely no help. We hardly knew anyone in California, and our first order of business was to find a babysitter.

I was expected to be at work every day from 10 a.m. to 6 p.m., which was also a brand new experience for me. In Atlanta, I worked out of the house and would go into the Lowery studios to record demos. I had never had my own office before. Now, I was to have my own beautiful office on the tenth floor of 6255 Sunset, replete with a full-on view of the Hollywood sign, which reminded me every day that I had arrived.

In my mind, I was finally where I needed to be.

The first six months were pretty much a period of listening and learning the ropes. Snuff would have me listening to songs from outside sources for acts he was producing, and he occasionally let me do a few secondary arrangements on album cuts for some of the lesser-known acts he was working with. His primary arranger when I got there was Al Capps. Al was a great guy and a talented arranger who was in high demand with a lot of other producers, as well as Snuff.

What always impressed me about Al—and some of the other great arrangers in Hollywood, like Jimmy Haskell, Artie Butler, and Don Costa—was their ability to write such great arrangements so fast on demand. It would take me hours to work out what I wanted to do, where these seasoned skillful men would take forty-five minutes or less to churn out a brilliant chart.

One day, Snuff walked into my office and said, "Al is working on some other projects and I'm in a bit of a pinch . . . I need you to do an arrangement for a Roger Williams session that just came up."

I froze. He was throwing me my first major arranging gig. Roger Williams was a piano virtuoso who had done many successful instrumental albums, mostly covering the hits of the day. His record company, MCA, wanted to rush out a recording of Roger doing the theme to *Murder on the Orient Express*, which was a hit movie at the time.

This would be a far different chart to any that I had ever done before. There was no vocalist. I had to write an orchestral accompaniment to a solo piano playing the lead.

I spent the next day at Roger Williams's house in the Encino Hills, going over every aspect of what and when he was going to play during the session. I recorded him on a little handheld cassette recorder and went home to begin the process of what I would have the orchestra playing behind him. It was my first all-nighter.

I played the song over and over again, refining it until I felt it was right. Two days later, we were in United/Western Studio A with a thirty-piece orchestra and Roger playing a special nine-foot concert grand he had specially brought in. The session turned out really well, and I was thrilled. I had broken the ice with my first major recording session in L.A. When Roger was asked to do a recording of "Nadia's Theme" from *The Young and the Restless* for his next album, he asked me to do the arrangement for that as well.

The next arrangement I was asked to do was for a Jim Nabors inspirational album. I was thrilled, as I was a huge fan of *The Andy Griffith Show* growing up, and to actually get to meet and work with Gomer Pyle was going to be a lot of fun. Maybe he'd hear one of my charts and say, "Golllleeeeee."

We were at Larrabee Sound in Hollywood, and we were using both studios: the rhythm section in Studio A, a small orchestra in Studio B. Lenny Roberts was engineering and Snuff was producing. I, of course, was pretty much in awe of the band we had, which included a few members of the infamous Wrecking Crew: Hal Blaine on drums, Tommy Tedesco and Al Casey on guitars, Glen D. Hardin on piano, and Carol Kaye on bass.

In the back of the studio was a big church organ that had been brought in for the spiritual sound that Snuff wanted for some of the more inspirational songs like "Church in the Wildwood," "Onward Christian Soldiers," "Amazing Grace" . . . you get the idea.

Playing the organ would be the renowned Clare Fischer, a brilliant keyboardist and jazz composer in his own right. As I nervously went out in the studio, Hal Blaine came over and put his arm around me, making me feel like I belonged. He then introduced me to all of the guys in the band.

I saw Clare in the back of the room by himself, and now that I was feeling a bit more confident, I walked over to introduce myself to this jazz legend. As I approached, I stuck my hand out and began to introduce myself as the arranger and conductor of the upcoming session.

Before I could get a word out he looked up and said, "You're standing on my fucking wires!"

Okay, then . . . nice meeting you too, buddy!

Lenny Roberts, the engineer, was standing nearby, setting a microphone. He looked at me in shock before we both started laughing uncontrollably. We laughed for the next few hours during the session, and for the next fifteen years whenever it came up. Clare truly was a magnificent and tasteful player, and contributed greatly to the sound of any album he played on. I suppose he was just having a rough day with those wires.

It wasn't long before I was meeting some young writer/artists who heard through the grapevine that I was a "new guy" in town looking for great songs. I was also starting to get some recognition from the studio session players I was working with, and they started to refer some of their music relationships to me.

Snuff told me that if I could find a great act, he would encourage me to start producing on my own as well . . . under the Garrett umbrella, of course. Within the next year, I made a lot of good contacts with A&R people at most of the labels. I was primarily writing and pitching my own songs, but some of the label guys liked my demos and knew I was arranging for Snuff, so the door was opening for me to possibly produce acts that I found or who were already signed and looking for a producer.

My first experiences with mostly new acts were all fun, yet they came with a steep learning curve. Nathanson and Schoenholtz was a great duo I did for Capitol. I produced Richard Mainegra for Columbia, and Gail Davies and Arthur, and Hurley and Gottlieb, were two acts I did at A&M. I was getting acclimated to working with the great session players and feeling comfortable in different studios.

Snuff had recently produced an album for Tanya Tucker, so when Tanya was asked to perform on *The Merv Griffin Show* in Las Vegas, her manager asked if I would go to Vegas and conduct for her on the show, since I had done a few of the arrangements on the album. Nancy couldn't go because she was now pregnant with our second son, Andrew, so I invited my longtime best friend, Mark Jerome—yes, he of the famed Queens bar mitzvah band the Four People—to travel up there with me. He had recently moved to Los Angeles from Baltimore, partly to get a change of scenery, and possibly to contemplate a career change.

Neither one of us had ever been to Vegas before, so it was definitely an eye-opening spectacle. From being someone who was intimidated to play the piano in front of six people, I was now performing in front of an audience of 2,500 at Caesar's Palace. It was a rush.

Afterward, I was standing in the wings of the stage with Mark, watching another act, when I felt a hand tap me on the shoulder. It was none other than Merv Griffin himself. He told me what a nice job I had done out there and asked me what my story was.

I was starstruck. This was *the* Merv Griffin who starred in my mother's favorite show on television. Merv and I spoke for a few minutes. I told him I was just in town conducting for Tanya, that I was primarily a songwriter, and that I had recently moved to L.A. from

Atlanta. Merv told me he was looking for some original songs for himself, because he wanted to do a new album for MGM, where he had just made a deal.

"Maybe you have something you can play for me that I can sing?" he asked.

"I actually have a few songs that would be great for you," I quickly responded. I was not about to let this opportunity pass. He told me to call him in a few hours after he was done with his two shows, and he would arrange for me to come up and play for him as he had a piano in his suite at Caesar's.

At 10 p.m., Merv called.

"Come on up to the Crown Suite."

Mark and I went up to Merv's suite, which was as big as some hotels I had stayed at. I'd never seen anything like it in my life. It was a two-story, five-bedroom suite with a white grand piano sitting in the middle of a gigantic parlor. Merv had two young gentlemen working for him, and they offered us food, drinks, and pot. Merv was in a casual sweat suit. Suddenly, this was all starting to feel a bit strange, and I adjusted my wedding ring to make sure everyone could see it clearly.

Merv ushered me over to the piano and played a few things for me. I was surprised at what solid a musician he was. He played beautifully and had a terrific voice. I sat down and played him a new song that Milton and I had recently written called "Whoever You Are, I Love You."

When I finished, I looked up, and Merv was speechless. After a moment, he said, "My God, I absolutely love that song. Can you play it again?"

I played it again, and he began to sing the second chorus along with me. He sounded fantastic.

Merv smiled and said, "I want you to produce that song for me. I'll be back in L.A. next week. Call a man named Murray Schwartz who runs my company, and let him know whatever it is you need."

That was the beginning of a friendship that developed over the next several decades with Merv. When he returned to L.A., we met at his office, and he asked me how I would approach doing an entire album with him. I told him I thought it would be best to do some standards, some present-day covers, and maybe two or three original songs. He loved the idea and told me to prepare a budget and put together a song list. He wanted to move ahead with the project.

Over the next few days I put together a list of songs that ranged from "As Time Goes By" and "The Girl from Ipanema" to the Bee Gees' "How Can You Mend a Broken Heart" and my song "Whoever You Are, I Love You." Merv loved the song ideas and officially asked me to produce the entire album for him. I was beyond excited.

A week later, Merv invited me up to his house in Pebble Beach to get keys and go over the material. The house was spectacular. Overlooking the Pebble Beach golf course and the Pacific Ocean, it was a palace. I flew up from Burbank on his private plane, and he had one of his assistants meet me at the airport for the short drive to his home. Merv and I spent a day going over songs, getting keys, and discussing arrangement ideas and the schedule. Merv was an avid tennis player, and the next morning he asked if we could take a break from working on the songs to go play a doubles match with a couple of his tennis buddies. I told him I played a bit, and after breakfast we made our way over to one of his friends' nearby castles to play some tennis.

Merv and his friend and I were volleying for a while as we waited for our fourth to show up.

"Ahh, here he comes," said Merv.

I looked over, and here comes the tall, good-looking guy who ends up being my doubles partner, Clint Eastwood. How ironic that it was Clint who years later would give me the musical opportunity of a lifetime. But for that couple of hours, nothing was talked about except good and bad tennis shots.

Merv was excited to get started on the album immediately. MGM had approved the budget, and two weeks later we began to record the Merv Griffin *As Time Goes By* album. We cut the basic tracks over three days at Larrabee Sound in Santa Monica, with Lenny Roberts engineering. In spite of his incredibly hectic television-taping schedule, Merv showed up at every session to sing scratch vocals with the band. I was mostly using the musicians that Snuff had introduced me to at his sessions, as I hadn't really formed any of my own relationships to that point. But it was an amazing first experience to be sitting in the pilot's chair for a change, working with legends like Hal Blaine, Tommy Tedesco, Mike Melvoin, and Sid Sharp. I even had Al Capps do some of the charts for me.

I'm still incredibly proud of that project. It was, in its own way, a rite of passage.

Merv was the first major star artist I had ever produced, and he was extremely happy with the final product. As a gift, he rented a three-bedroom beach house in Carmel for my family and me for the entire month of August. Although I didn't see him too often, except for the occasional event in passing, Merv and I stayed friends until his death in 2007. He was a wonderful guy and a true talent.

Shortly after I had finished producing Merv's project at MGM, I got an interesting call from Loren Saifer, the senior VP head of A&R for the Portrait label, a division, then, of Columbia Records. They had just signed an artist from Baltimore whom they were excited about, a singer/songwriter named Tony Sciuto.

Loren asked if I would come over and take a meeting to discuss the possibility of me producing his debut album. I knew the name sounded familiar . . . but I didn't think there was a chance in hell it could be the same person. Sure enough, though, it was the same Tony Sciuto who I had played with in the Ravens back in Baltimore.

I hadn't seen Tony in over a decade. It was crazy, but it was no coincidence. It turns out that Tony had mentioned me to Loren; since he was familiar with my work and songs, he wanted to work with me . . . and he thought it would make quite a "meta" story.

It was so great to get to see Tony all grown up, still playing and singing his butt off, with great new songs that he had written with his writing partner, Sammy Egorin. Tony came to L.A. and we agreed to do the album together. It was the most ambitious production I had done up to this point. The songs were laced with elements of rock, jazz, and blues, and all tied together thematically. It was an opportunity for me to write bits of underscore to go between the songs, to tie them seamlessly together. This was something I had always wanted to try.

The album project would be called *Island Nights*. We worked for the better part of a month tracking and doing vocals at Britannia Studios. Lenny Roberts was the engineer.

Tony was a perfectionist, but in a good way. His demos were impeccable, and I had to figure out a way to make the record sound better than the demos, which wasn't easy to do. Together, we handpicked great musicians, which started the important transition for me away from the players that Snuff had always insisted on using. New, fresh, and upcoming session superstars like Ed Green, Ronnie Tutt, Bill

Cuomo, Steve Lukather, Mike Porcaro, and Tom Scott were just some of the fabulous guys who played on the project.

After months of mixing and remixing with several different engineers, the album was released to great reviews but not so great chart success. It was disappointing because the album was so good.

Japan, however, was a different story. The album was extremely popular over there and is still considered a cult classic. When I was working in Japan last year, all people wanted to ask me were questions about Karen Carpenter and Tony Sciuto's *Island Nights*.

Back at Snuff's, I continued to work around the clock. Snuff had me composing, recording, arranging, and writing. It was mostly drama-free. However, Snuff's secret claim to fame was that he liked to create drama and suck the wind out of your sails, so at the eleventh hour he could ride in and save the day. Control was something Snuff relished and often used to his advantage in key situations.

One night, Snuff called me at eleven o'clock.

"I need a song and I need it quick."

Nancy had just given birth to our second son, Andrew, and neither one of us was sleeping well.

"How quick?" I stuttered, trying to wake up.

"Yesterday."

Snuff had gotten a call from a music supervisor from Warner Bros. The song that had been written for Clint Eastwood's new movie had fallen through. Clint didn't like it and needed another song ASAP, due to postproduction deadlines, in order to make the scheduled release date. The movie was a comedy, *Every Which Way but Loose*. Snuff didn't know much about the film other than it was about Clint Eastwood bareknuckle fighting for cash and driving around with an orangutan. He told me I should call Milton Brown and whip something up.

I called Milt, who still lived in Mobile, Alabama. It was two in the morning, and Milt picked up on the eighth ring. "Somebody better be dying," he barked into the phone.

"Have you ever heard the phrase, 'Every which way but loose'?" I asked. "It's a Southern phrase, right?"

"Yeah, it means I'm gonna kick your ass or love you. Listen, I'll call you later, I've gotta go back to sleep."

"No . . . get a cup of coffee. We have to write it."

"When?"

"Yesterday."

Milt and I wrote the song over the phone in thirty minutes. We had to. We both needed sleep.

The next day, I went into the office and played it for Snuff. Snuff had me play it for Steve Wax, Eastwood's record-company executive at Elektra Records, which was going to release the soundtrack album. There was a flurry of phone calls back and forth.

At three in the afternoon, I went to Warners to meet Clint for the first time—well, the second time, if you count the tennis court. I was sufficiently starstruck. Again. Clint was a laid-back icon, wearing a tight T-shirt and grinning at me out of the side of his mouth.

"Let me hear your song, Steve."

I played him the song.

"Play it again," he said.

And that was it.

Thanks to Steve Wax, we were able to get Eddie Rabbitt, who was on fire as a country artist at the time, to agree to record it.

A funny thing happened on the way to this becoming my first #1 record. There wasn't a whole lot of time to do a proper demo with a band. Snuff asked me to run over to Criterion and do a quick piano/

vocal demo so we could play it for Eddie, who would be in town over the weekend, playing with his band at the Orange County Fair in Irvine. The idea was to record the song with Eddie while he was in L.A., before he headed back to Nashville, where he lived. I did the demo—which admittedly wasn't very good—myself, but Snuff and Clint loved the song, approved the demo, and asked me to drive down to Irvine to hand-deliver it to and play it for Eddie.

I was told that Eddie would be expecting me, and would make time to meet with me to discuss the session. Except Rabbitt, never got the memo.

I drove for two hours, trying to find the private tour-bus parking lot, all the while excited for a productive friendly meeting with one of the brightest stars in country music. Finally, after making a few wrong turns, I found the correct parking lot and walked over to a large fancy tour bus. I knocked on the door several times before a man opened the door and said, "Yeah?"

"Um, I'm here to see Eddie Rabbitt."

"What fer?"

"Uh, I have a demo that I'm supposed to play for him."

"He's not lookin' for any outside songs, he writes all his own."

I was getting a bit anxious at this point, stammering a bit, and finally I mentioned that it was a song for a movie that Eddie was going to sing in two days, and that I was told to deliver it to him in person.

The guy grabbed the package out of my hand and said, "I'll give it to Eddie when I see him."

"Well, I'm supposed to play it for him, we had a meeting scheduled."

At this point, a member of his band came over from the kitchen area of the bus and said, "Yeah, Eddie will listen to the song when he gets here later." He then turned to the other guy and said, "Eddie really wanted to write his own song for this movie, and is not happy at all about singing some other guy's song."

At this point, I figured they thought I was just a messenger service delivering the package, and it was obvious that Eddie had not been informed about our meeting.

So, I slithered away.

Three days later, I was at RCA Studios in Hollywood, standing on the podium rehearsing with a sixty-piece orchestra, when Eddie Rabbitt walked in with Steve Wax and a few of his bandmates. Snuff and Clint were there too, of course, and everybody was happy and excited about the song we were about to record.

Eddie couldn't have been nicer to me. He told me how much the song had grown on him over the past couple days, and I never mentioned that I was the delivery guy who dropped the tape off for him.

To say that this was an unconventional session would be a monumental understatement. I think we had four guitars, two pianos, and two drummers in the rhythm section, surrounded by strings, French horns, and a host of woodwinds. I thought either Snuff was trying to impress the shit out of Clint and company, or he had lost his mind completely. I had pleaded with him to let me cut the rhythm track first, so we could have no leakage into the orchestra. This would have made Grover, the engineer, very happy when he started mixing. But no . . . Snuff wanted it to be "different"—and different it would be for sure.

Magically, the track turned out to be incredible and "different" indeed. Eddie was singing his heart out in a vocal booth. When we went in to the control room to listen to the playback, everyone was excited.

Then Snuff came over to me and said, "Let's double it."

"What? Double what?"

"Double the whole damn orchestra," he said.

I looked at Grover and thought he was going to have a stroke.

"You mean the strings, right?" I said. "You can't really double all of those guitars and keyboards and drums . . . it will sound like a train wreck."

"I said double the whole damn bunch of 'em."

And we did . . . and, to his credit, somehow Snuff was right.

Milton Brown, who had flown out for the session, said he knew it was a #1 record, as did I. I was walking on air during the playback, I was so happy.

I took a bathroom break and Snuff Garrett sidled up next to me at the urinal. He smiled and said, "Great arrangement."

"Man, I'm so excited," I said. "This is a monster track, can you feel it?"

He quickly deflated me.

"We're not out of the woods yet."

"What do you mean?"

"We have to give up 25 percent of the publishing to Warners and 25 percent to Eastwood to make it work . . . and I'm not gonna do it."

In one second, my heart broke.

This was my big break. This was Milton's big break. We were going to be denied a hit song because of corporate greed?

Snuff sensed my worry and rode in on his primed white horse.

"Here's what we can do. You and Milton can give me a percentage of the writing that I'm going to be giving up on the publishing end." It was kind of a masterful shell game.

"Of course," I said, without a second of hesitation, "Whatever you need."

"Great. So, you give me 25 percent of the writer's share and we can make this work."

I had a six-month-old baby; this was my first rodeo. Milton agreed, too, and we gave Snuff 25 percent of the writer's share. We didn't have any of the publishing.

Snuff saw the opportunity. He'd been around the block and probably had it done to him. In hindsight, we were lucky we didn't give up half or a third.

"Every Which Way but Loose" became the highest-debuting record in the history of the *Billboard* country singles chart, coming in at #18 with a bullet the first week. It also set a dangerous precedent to where Snuff could come up with a line or change a word and ask for 25 or 30 percent of a song that Milton and I wrote. He would do that a lot in the years to come.

True, he was the catalyst for getting the projects made, and he relied on Milton and me to deliver hits for him, but he wasn't doing the actual writing. Still, it opened doors for me, including to Clint, who then asked me if I'd ever scored a movie. I told him it's all I'd ever wanted to do. It was the reason I came to Hollywood.

"Okay," he said. And that was it. He hired me not only to write the song but also to score the film.

Clint was serious but likable. He was about as big as they came and everyone around him had the greatest respect for him. He was a regular guy. He played a lot of ping-pong and lifted weights at the dubbing stage, but he kept his private life private. The one subject he loved to talk about was music. He knew every aspect of the making of his films. He and I spoke on a musical level that had to irk Snuff, because Snuff was a businessman, not a musical guy. Clint and I had a shorthand that Snuff didn't understand, which became a problem, because Snuff liked to be the center of the action, the "music guy."

In 1980, Clint Eastwood released *Any Which Way You Can*, the sequel to the huge hit *Every Which Way but Loose*. Milton and I were once again asked to write the title song. It wasn't an easy song to write. We were conscious of trying not to write anything that remotely sounded like "Loose," yet the five-word titles of both films were similar, and it was a challenge for us to stay away from similar chord changes, tempo, and lyric content. After all, these were the same characters as in the first movie, and basically the same storyline.

After a few bad starts of song ideas, we were finally happy with the one we came up with. Snuff, of course, had to approve it, and threw in his two cents and took a third of the song. The great Glen Campbell agreed to sing it, though, and the session was fabulous. I remember Snuff wanting a classical-sounding piano to be featured, so I asked David Foster to play on it, which he did. It was perfect.

Ironically, Clint decided that he wanted the song to be played over the closing credits, instead of at the beginning of the picture. I hinted at and threaded the melody of the song within the underscore, so when the Glen Campbell version played over the end credits, it sounded somewhat familiar to the ear.

Snuff thought the opening song should be another fun duet like the one we had written for Clint and Merle Haggard in *Bronco Billy*, "Barroom Buddies." He had a perfectly corny title idea, "Beers to You," and asked me to write with two of his other writers, John Durrill and Sandy Pinkard. I hated the idea, but we did manage to come up with a song. And Snuff was able to get Ray Charles to sing the duet with Clint.

Now, I absolutely worshipped the genius of Ray Charles, but this particular session was anything but fun. In the first place, I felt like the song was mediocre at best. The track was kind of a train wreck. Ray and his manager, Joe Adams, were, in a word, kind of difficult. Okay, three words.

My sister Sherry and me, 1950.

Mom and me, 1957,
Fresh Meadows, New York.

The Four People at the World's Fair Singer Bowl, 1965.

Signing writer's contract with Bill Lowery
in Atlanta, Georgia, 1972.

Nancy Masters Dorff.

My Diapason.

With Dusty Springfield at A&M Studios.

Roy Rogers, King of the Cowboys.

Burt Reynolds session at
Universal Scoring Stage.

Kenny, Marty, and Lionel at
"Through the Years" playback.

The one and only Sir George Martin recording "Honky Tonk Freeway."

Larry Herbstritt recording "Spenser: For Hire" at the Warner Bros. Soundstage.

Ray Charles in the studio recording "Beers to You."

Marty Panzer.

Milton Brown.

Songwriting heroes Jimmy Webb and Gerry Goffin.

Glen Campbell, "Any Which Way You Can" session.

Ray was fidgety, most likely coming down from something, and he was having a rough time getting his parts down. I think he probably hated the song almost as much as I did, but he was being paid a nice fee to sing it. He did the best he could under the circumstances.

Joe Adams was arguing about something with Snuff, so the atmosphere in the control room was anything but copacetic. Eventually, the song did play over the opening sequence, but it was not a successful record by any means. It's a shame that when I got to work with the great Ray Charles, it had to be on a song I never truly believed in.

The movie turned out to be another huge success at the box office, and while Glen's single of the title song went Top 10, the big surprise hit from the soundtrack turned out to be the breakout single for David Frizzell and Shelly West, "You're the Reason God Made Oklahoma," which Snuff and I coproduced. David and Shelley went on to have an amazing recording career with many hits, all produced by Snuff and me.

I went on to do several more films with Clint. We'd spot the movies together, watching them and deciding where to score the music. Snuff was always around but didn't contribute creatively. I could always tell that Snuff felt a bit uncomfortable with me communicating directly with Clint, or, later, with Burt Reynolds, because, after all, he was the boss. Clint knew that I was the one to talk to creatively, but he also understood the protocol. We both did. And with Snuff Garrett, I always followed protocol and made sure not to overstep my boundaries.

Bronco Billy was probably my favorite of the films I worked on with Clint. I liked the story. It was a fun film, and we had a big #1 hit with Ronnie Milsap's "Cowboys and Clowns." It also enabled me to work with Merle Haggard.

Now, other than "Okie from Muskogee," which Milton Brown had once blasted over an intercom in order to wake me up at 6 a.m., I was not familiar with the beautiful tone of Merle Haggard's unmistakable voice.

Merle had agreed to do a song in *Bronco Billy*: a great song written by John Durrill (with Snuff Garrett) called "Misery and Gin." I was asked to do the arrangement, and I must say, as we were recording the track live with some sixty pieces, it was one of those times when it was quite apparent to me that it was not only going to be a big hit but a country standard. Everything about the track and Merle's vocal performance was in total sync. Just a great record that kind of produced itself.

When Merle first came into the studio, saw the live orchestra sitting there, and realized we were going to record this in one big take, he said, "Geez, them's a lotta fiddles out there for sure."

He sang live with the orchestra at RCA Studio A—the old Wally Heider's on Sunset—and said afterward how much he loved doing it that way.

That same day, we went on to also record a song that Milton and I wrote called "Barroom Buddies," which ended up being a Merle Haggard/Clint Eastwood duet.

It went to #1.

"Misery and Gin," astonishingly, stopped at #2.

Go figure.

In filmmaking, music can sometimes be the long-lost stepchild. It is often the last creative element that happens in postproduction. I've been involved in some projects where the caterer gets more forethought than the music, and, frankly, indie films sometimes spend more time and money on craft services than they do on the music.

Clint was different; he understood the power of music and its intrinsic value both in the score and in the songs.

Eddie Rabbitt and I hadn't seen each other for many years, other than maybe the occasional quick hello at the BMI Awards dinner in Nashville every year. I was on a flight from Dallas to Nashville one day, and Eddie and his longtime road manager Bill were sitting behind me.

Eddie didn't look very well. He was thin and seemed tired, but he was genuinely happy to see me. He got up and gave me a hug before we took off. He had enjoyed an incredible career of hit songs that he had written with the talented Even Stevens, and he certainly didn't have to say this to me . . . but he told me how much "Every Which Way but Loose" had come to mean to him, and that he was so glad that he was the one who got to sing it and make it a hit.

I told him that it was his voice that made it magical, and how much I appreciated him saying that. Eddie passed away from cancer about ten months later.

After doing two movies with Clint, I finally felt comfortable enough to ask him if he remembered playing tennis with Merv and me in Pebble Beach. He took a long pause, looked at me, and said, "That was YOU?"

10

BURT AND BURT

SNUFF HAD TWO CAMPS: the Clint Eastwood camp and the Burt Reynolds camp. Both were huge stars, and he liked there to be a clear delineation between the two galaxies. I was part of the Clint army, so I never got to interact with Burt. The problem was that all of the hits were coming out of the Eastwood camp. Clint was having hit song after hit song from his films, and Burt, despite the fact that he seemed to already be up to filming *Cannonball Run 47*, was getting bupkus in the hit song department.

So, when Burt Reynolds wanted to have Anne Murray sing the end-title song for his new film, *Stick*, Snuff had to break his own rule and bring me over to Burt's side. He knew he couldn't get Anne Murray without me. I'd written six songs for her, including "I Just Fall in Love Again," which won a Juno Award (the Canadian equivalent of a Grammy) for Song of the Year.

So, I got the call to go to Burt Reynolds's home in Malibu.

Loni Anderson answered the door in a green, skintight terrycloth jumpsuit. She was smiley and sweet, and told me, "Oh, Burt's upstairs, go on up."

I would have preferred to stay downstairs with Loni. She looked spectacular. Instead, I went upstairs to Burt's bedroom, where he was lying in bed, watching TV without his toupee on.

"I love your song with Anne Murray," he said. "Can you get her to do a song for our film?" He was engrossed in a college football game and didn't really look at me, which was fine because I was having a bit of a hard time wrapping my head around the fact that Burt even wore a wig in the first place.

"Sure, but we've gotta write a great song. Anne and her producer, Jim Ed, are both incredibly tough when it comes to choosing material for her to sing."

I waited for his response, but he continued to watch the game.

"Any ideas?"

He still wasn't looking at me.

I had read the script. It was based on an Elmore Leonard novel—good, not great—but I did have a pretty good idea.

"In the film, there is a line which Candice Bergen says at the beginning and you say at the end of the movie."

"What's that?"

He still wasn't looking at me.

"'I don't think I'm ready for you.' I think it would make a great song idea."

Burt finally looked over.

"Yeah, great idea. Great. Send it to me when you have it."

I sent the script to Milton, and Milton wrote a brilliant lyric. After finishing the song I then went to Nashville and played a demo for Anne's producer, Jim Ed Norman. He loved it, and so did Anne. Milton flew up to Nashville, and the next day we were all on a plane to Toronto to record the song.

The plane ride to Canada was not one of my favorites. We had to connect to another flight in Detroit, and as we approached the landing, the horizontal blizzard conditions were frightening. Detroit shut down

the airport right after we landed, and we spent about eight hours playing poker until the next morning, when we were finally able to get a
short flight over the border. Exhausted, we managed to get to our hotel
long enough to rest a bit before the session.

Recording Anne Murray is about as effortless as it gets. The chemistry between her and Jim Ed in the studio was so much fun to watch
and be a part of. I remember thinking what a blast it was to be doing
a song for one of Burt's movies without Snuff actually being in the
driver's seat for a change. The record Jim Ed made was beautiful. It
worked perfectly at the end of the film over the closing credits.

Burt loved the song, and it was a Top 5 hit, but it wasn't only written
by me and Milton . . . as we would later find out. Both Snuff Garrett
and Burt Reynolds were listed as cowriters on the song as well. No
doubt this was Snuff skimming a little extra for finally letting Milt and
me get into the Burt Reynolds camp. It's what I call bending over and
grabbing your ankles . . . or paying your dues.

I had worked for Burt once before, although I was kept at an arm's
distance. Snuff came into my office one afternoon and said, "I need you
and Milton to write a song for *Cannonball Run.*"

I was excited to write a love song for Burt, but Snuff informed me
he needed an up-tempo, Jackson 5 kinda song, for a young Puerto
Rican boy band called Menudo.

"Yep, right up our wheelhouse," I thought sarcastically.

It turned out that Menudo was one of the biggest acts in the world,
and unquestionably the most successful Latin boy band in history.

I would have to say that Milton Brown and I have worked on some
crazy assignments throughout our careers, and that's putting it lightly,
but getting asked to write a song for Menudo is right up there with
the best of them. With all of the really classic and great opportunities

Snuff would offer to Milton and me over the years, he would also occasionally come to us with some cheesy idea and ask us to write it. I still shake my head and have to laugh to keep from crying over such beauties as "Who Dat," "Cajun Invitation," "Beers to You," "Bad Wind," and "Como Cannonball."

"Bad Wind" . . . really?

Milton wrote a nice lyric called "Like a Cannonball" with the message, "Your love hits me like a cannonball" (we had to get love in there somehow). Three days later, we were in the studio tracking the song with John Hobbs, Joe Chemay, Paul Leim, and Billy Joe Walker.

After years of making me use musicians from a past era, Snuff was finally listening to me and letting me choose the appropriate players for sessions we were doing together. Don't get me wrong, it's not that the those players were not fantastic for their time, but the sound of radio was changing, and we had to sound relevant to what was happening now. Snuff was having a tough time making that transition.

The track was fun, and the vocal session the next day was a circus. The boys from Menudo had to be twelve to fourteen years old. Ricky Martin (yes, *that* Ricky Martin) was one of the kids in the band. They were great kids, but along with them came an entourage of some twenty people, including Jose Menendez, (yes, *that* Jose Menendez, who was heading up RCA International Division at the time and was personally taking charge of this project), and his two young sons. Years later, Eric and Lyle Menendez would murder their parents in cold blood in their Beverly Hills home. I vividly remember shaking all of their hands. Freaky.

The boys in the band did a nice job vocally on the song, and they would later also record it in Portuguese for their huge Brazilian fan base. Milton and I were told we were going to have a huge, worldwide hit with this one. It's a miracle that Snuff didn't move in and claim part of the writing on the song, but in all fairness, it was Milton's title.

The movie came out, and it was a typical Burt Reynolds hit, but the record was not. They tell me it was a hit in South America, but if I remember correctly, I think Milton and I made about sixteen dollars apiece on that one. Like I said, it's not always about the big paydays. It's always a crapshoot.

I ran into Ricky Martin some fifteen years later at an awards show, after he had his monster hit with "Livin' La Vida Loca," and reintroduced myself to him. He vaguely remembered me, but we had a nice brief laugh when I mentioned the song.

Years later, after leaving Garrett Music, I was glad to get the opportunity to work solo with Burt again on several projects he was directing at Universal. Fortunately, he remembered me. He was always very appreciative and a great guy to be around.

Burt Reynolds was one of the biggest celebrities in the world, but it was the *other* Burt who was one of my true heroes.

One day, I was on one of my many trips back and forth between Nashville and Los Angeles. I had just been bumped up to first class and the seat next to me was empty. Perfect, I thought. I wouldn't have to make inane small talk with anyone. This was pre-9/11, so airport security was minimal, and you could get to your plane only five minutes before takeoff.

Shortly before the plane door closed, there was some brief commotion and a gentleman who was a bit out of breath got onboard and slipped into the unoccupied seat next to me. I looked up from the magazine I was flipping through and my eyes widened. I took a deep breath of panic with the realization that I was sitting next to the man

I had idolized for years before I even had a career of my own . . . Burt Bacharach.

I owned every Burt Bacharach record ever released, and even the unreleased demo recordings from his musical, *Promises, Promises.* I could play any of his songs on the piano, and I learned more about arranging from studying his records than I ever could have by reading books about orchestration.

I may have known his discography as well as he did.

I was busy giving myself a pep talk of what to say to my idol when he interrupted my internal dialogue.

"Have we met?"

Now, we had in fact met. Briefly, several years earlier, when I first came to Los Angeles. I had about a year's worth of sessions under my belt at the time, and I had been working with Jimmy Getzoff on a string date I was arranging for Snuff. Jimmy was a wonderful man and my longtime concertmaster for just about every string date I had ever done in L.A. before he retired at the age of eighty-something.

At the end of the session, Jimmy and I were talking, and he told me he was heading over to the A&M Studios soundstage to rehearse with Burt Bacharach for a television special he was hosting. I told Jimmy what a huge influence Burt was on my music, and Jimmy invited me to come over as his guest, sit in on some of the rehearsal, and he would introduce me to Burt.

The soundstage was packed with people, Burt was conducting while playing, the music was incredible, and I was like a kid in a candy store, trying to soak up every second of what was happening in there. Finally, somebody called for the band to "take a ten," and Jimmy motioned for me to come over and say hi to Burt.

Burt was speaking with several people at the same time, obviously multitasking in many directions, so it wasn't much of an introduction. Jimmy told Burt who I was, and basically Burt looked at me, shook my hand quickly, said, "Nice meeting you, kid," and walked off talking to someone else.

I wasn't about to tell Burt that story, so I simply said, "Not really."

I did tell him that I was a huge fan, and what a huge influence he had been to my career. When I told him my name, I was shocked that he not only knew of me but also loved some of my songs, which he knew by name. I was truly blown away. I felt honored that Burt Bacharach actually knew who I was.

We went on to talk about all kinds of music stuff: players and demo singers we liked and had in common, lyricists we had both worked with. He asked me almost as many questions about my processes of writing and working in the studio as I asked him.

He told me he was thinking about adding a guy or two to his concert shows. He had always used three girls and asked me if I knew anybody who he might audition. I did. I had been working with a great, soulful singer named John Pagano. I told Burt about him, and he asked me to have John get in touch with him the following week.

I hated for that flight to end, as we talked nonstop for nearly four hours.

I'm happy to say that John Pagano has been working with Burt for some twenty years, and I'm glad that I had something to do with putting them together.

11

WHITNEY HOUSTON

―――――

JERMAINE JACKSON AND I met through a music contractor named Ben Barrett.

Ben was an all-powerful studio contractor who controlled most of the major recording sessions in Los Angeles. If you were a studio musician, you definitely wanted to be on Ben's good side—and on his "call list."

Ben had heard a song of mine on a Julio Iglesias session that he was contracting, and he called me one day out of the blue to see if I had any more songs like the one he loved on Julio's session. I happily put together a few songs on a tape and sent them over to his office.

He called me after receiving the tape and went on and on about how great he thought the songs were, and . . . did I have a publisher? I imagine he looked to get a piece of the publishing pie whenever he could from new writers. He would do this in exchange for promoting those songs to the artists for whom he was contracting sessions.

No harm. No foul. Many people were doing that.

I told him that I was signed exclusively to Snuff Garrett as a writer, but that I was flattered. I heard the slight disappointment in his voice, but he said he'd still love to introduce me to Jermaine Jackson, and that he'd send along one of the songs I had sent him for Jermaine's consideration.

―――――

A week or two went by, and then I got a call from Jermaine himself. He loved one of the songs Ben had sent called "Why Can't I Believe You Love Me," a song I had written with Marty Panzer. He asked me who was playing piano on the demo, and I told him it was me. He asked me if I would record it with him, and a few days later we were in the studio doing a piano/vocal version of the song. He was making his last album for Motown, and I was thrilled to be a part of it.

To this day, I'm not quite sure whatever happened to that track, as it never was commercially released, but Jermaine thankfully never forgot the song, or me.

It was several years later when I heard from him again. After catching up for a few minutes, he asked me if I had a song that could work as a great duet. He was recording his first solo album for Clive Davis and Arista Records, and he was calling some of his favorite writers in hopes of finding that magic song. He wanted something with a similar tone to the song we had worked on together before, but for a duet. I asked him when he needed it by.

"Today. I'm tracking this afternoon."

I hung up the phone and immediately panicked. I started ransacking my office, looking for a song that could be a good duet. I didn't have a duet version of any of my songs, so he would have to imagine how the female part might go. I stuck four cassettes into my jacket pockets and headed over to the studio in Silverlake where he was recording.

Yes. Cassettes. My kids don't even know what cassettes are.

I arrived at the gate where the guard told me Jermaine would be right out, and to just park. After a few minutes, Jermaine jumped into the passenger front seat of my car and said, "Whataya got?"

The first song I indiscriminately pulled out of my pocket and shoved into the cassette player was one I wrote with Pete McCann called "Take Good Care of My Heart."

Jermaine listened intently, and after the second chorus, before the song was over, he started singing along with the demo and yelled, "This is it!"

For a second, I was wishing I was at a craps table in Vegas—my luck had never been this good.

"Great," I said. "When are you planning on cutting it?"

"We're going to cut the track tonight, because my duet partner is in town."

I was over the moon. I knew both Dionne Warwick and Aretha were both signed to Arista, and I was starting to get very excited by the possibilities. I would have been thrilled to have either one of them.

"Is it Dionne or Aretha?" I blurted out in excitement.

"Neither . . . I'm doing it with this new artist from New Jersey. She's done some modeling, she's beautiful, and she sings good, too."

"Great," I said, forcing a smile to mask a bit of disappointment. "What's her name?"

"Whitney Houston."

I had never heard of this model, but as I drove home I figured, hey, I'm getting a Jermaine Jackson cut, how bad can that be? The great Michael Omartian, Paul Jackson Jr., and Nathan East are on the session. It's gotta be a monster track, and hopefully the "beautiful model" from New Jersey could really sing. Well, the world soon found out just how incredible that girl could sing!

After Jermaine sold two million copies of his album, Clive put our track on Whitney's debut album, too, which sold close to twenty-five million more copies.

Every once in a while you get a song that gets recorded by several artists at the same time. This was true of "Take Good Care of My Heart." Within six weeks of each other, Anne Murray, Roy Head, and Whitney had all recorded it. Fun when that happens!

Lesson learned: within reason, let anyone cut your song. You never know who the next Whitney Houston is going to be.

About a year after Whitney's debut album came out, and maybe five years since I had heard from Ben Barrett, I received a call out of the blue from Ben's wife, asking me when they could expect the 10 percent fee that was due them on all records sold for introducing me to Jermaine.

Um . . . nice try.

While Whitney Houston surprised me more than any other artist, Tony Newley inspired me more than any other artist. I distinctly remember the day Snuff came into my office and told me he wanted me to write an arrangement for a session he was going to produce on Anthony Newley. I froze and could not believe what I was hearing. In the 1960s, when most of my friends were standing in front of the mirror pretending to be Paul McCartney, I was standing in front of the mirror pretending to be Tony Newley singing "What Kind of Fool Am I," "Who Can I Turn To," or "Once in a Lifetime."

He was a profound influence on my love for theatricality in songs and melody.

Snuff asked me to arrange a meeting with Mr. Newley so that I could hear a song that he wanted to record but hadn't really found the right arrangement for. We met at his home in Beverly Hills, and I was immediately and completely awestruck in his presence. After a few minutes he played me a version of a song he wrote and performed called "The Man Who Makes You Laugh." Needless to say, I was blown away. We chatted about what his ideas were for the arrangement, and he couldn't have been nicer or more open to listening to several ideas I wanted to try to incorporate into the arrangement.

We recorded the song the following week. I had begged Snuff to let me record the rhythm section first and then overdub the orchestra, but Snuff was old school and wanted to record everything live, including Tony's vocal. Sad to say, I was not happy with the way it turned out. The mix was not good, the clarity of the individual instruments was all over the place, and it was pretty much a disappointment that could have been so much better.

Snuff was stuck in his obstinate ways, and this was the first clear signal that I needed to start branching out on my own. Regardless, getting to know Tony personally for that brief time, and being so honored to have the chance to actually work with him, was a "Once in a Lifetime" experience for me that I will always cherish.

12

DUSTY SPRINGFIELD

I HAD JUST FINISHED doing some arrangements for several artists on UA Records when I got a call to have a meeting with the head of the label, Artie Mogull.

Artie and I had known each other for quite a while, as he was close friends with Snuff. I had also coincidentally dated his daughter, Andrea, once in college, long before I knew who Artie Mogull was. He would kid me about that almost every time I saw him.

Artie asked if I would be interested in possibly writing and producing a legacy artist they had just signed, in the hope of resurrecting her career . . . Dusty Springfield.

I nearly jumped out of my pants.

Dusty was my favorite female artist. Like most people, I wore out three copies of *Dusty in Memphis*, one of the greatest albums ever made, as far as I was concerned. Dusty had been through some pretty rough patches. She was gay before it was socially accepted, often suffered from bouts of severe depression, and had attempted suicide. I knew that it would be a challenge for me, but I worshipped her as an artist, and I told Artie I would kill for the opportunity to work with her.

Artie scheduled a meeting for the three of us the following day. I brought along some songs that I thought would be great for her.

Dusty was hungry for a comeback. She had recently moved to L.A. and was surrounding herself with good, supportive people who were on her team. In the meeting, I played two songs that I had written with Molly-Ann Leikin. Dusty loved them both and had some creative ideas as to how they should be recorded. I really wanted this to be a special session, and I was able to get some of the guys from Toto (before there was a Toto) to do the tracking date: David Paich on piano, Jeff Porcaro on drums, Steve Lukather on guitar, and Colin Cameron on bass. We recorded at Kendun Recorders in Burbank. It was a great tracking room, with Lenny Roberts engineering.

Everything was perfect . . . until it wasn't.

We were going for a traditional, almost "British Motown" kind of sound with the arrangements. We recorded two songs that first day, "Let Me Love You Once Before You Go" and "You Set My Dreams to Music." Both tracks were epic. Dusty sang and sang, and sang some more, doing both leads and stellar background parts that she came up with. She was a master at that. I then brought in the legendary Waters family to beef up the backing vocals and copy Dusty's parts. Maxine, Julia, and Oren Waters are arguably the greatest background vocalists of all time, having sung on countless thousands of recordings in their illustrious careers.

Dusty then wanted to resing all of her tracking vocals, but she would only sing at night . . . late at night. I had two young boys at home, and always liked to be finished working by 6 or 7 p.m. so I could be home with them.

I wasn't used to *starting* at 10 p.m.

It was only the three of us at A&M Studio C in Hollywood: Lenny, Dusty, and myself. She didn't want anyone else around while she was singing. That was not unusual, and fine by me. She sang the first song over and over for at least an hour with every take being better than the previous one. It was mind-blowing how soulful and great she was. After about an hour, I pushed the talkback button down and said enthusiastically, "Dusty, we've really got this! Plenty here to comp from."

"We're not even close," she snapped back.

Lenny and I shared a look: this was going to be a long night. Somewhere around 3 a.m., Dusty got upset with some kind of distortion in her headphones. She was frustrated. This was after she absolutely killed the song. It was really perfect, in my opinion. But my opinion was clearly not the one that mattered. I told Dusty that we had it. I really thought we were done. She disagreed, and as actions sometimes speak louder than words, she proceeded to throw a nearby chair at the control-room glass.

Her vocals would be "done" when she said they were "done."

Other than that, we loved each other.

Some four or five hours later, she completed the two songs. I was anxiety-ridden, Lenny was shaking from being so tired, and my ears were completely fried. I couldn't hear anything with any clarity. I remember driving home from Hollywood as the sun was eerily coming up, feeling like I was half-dead. It had been one of the longest nights of my life.

After that harrowing evening, things did get better. We put a string section and some French horns on both songs, and Dusty was delighted with the final mixes. "Let Me Love You Once Before You Go" charted nicely in the UK, but it didn't make a big dent on the *Billboard* charts here in the States, which was disappointing.

Dusty and I got to work together years later when she did a duet with B. J. Thomas on the *Growing Pains* theme song, which was a Top 10 Adult Contemporary hit. She would also go on to record a beautiful version of "I Just Fall in Love Again" that later would be used as a duet with Anne Murray after Dusty had passed away.

Dusty Springfield is one of the great female artists of all time. I always say that Adele is this generation's Dusty Springfield and Sam Smith is this generation's male version of Dusty Springfield. Still, as far as I'm concerned, there will never be anyone quite like the woman who was a leading inventor of blue-eyed soul.

Looking back on my career, one of the most exciting things for me has been the diversity of all of the many different artists who have recorded my songs. Soulful in an entirely different way was the unmistakable voice of Kenny Rogers.

13

KENNY ROGERS THROUGH THE YEARS

———

EVERY ONCE IN A WHILE you finish a song and just have that undeniable feeling that you've written something important or special.

It is one of the world's best feelings and, unfortunately, it doesn't happen often enough. It has happened to me on a few memorable occasions, including one night in mid-November, when Marty Panzer and I had what would be a life-changing pasta dinner together.

I first met Marty through Ron Anton, then the vice president of writer relations at BMI. Ron was a great friend who cared about songwriters, and there wasn't a more perfect person to be both representing and waving the flag for the songwriters at BMI.

One afternoon, Ron called me and asked me if I would be interested in meeting and hopefully writing with one of their New York–based writers who was relocating to Los Angeles.

Up to that point, Marty Panzer had been exclusively writing the lyrics to songs by Barry Manilow. "Even Now," "It's a Miracle," "All the Time," and "Just Another New Year's Eve" were just some of the great songs they had written together. Marty was looking for a change of scenery and a chance to expand his writing by branching out a bit and working with different composers. He had asked BMI for help in contacting some West Coast–based writers who might be a good fit for his style of writing.

———

From the outset, Marty and I had a terrific chemistry.

I could tell from our first meeting that we would write some wonderful songs together. Our first three were so much fun for me to write. If it took me an hour to finish a melody, that was backbreaking work for me. His lyrics were so perfectly crafted that the melodies usually just fell out of the sky and wrote themselves. In some cases, I would literally hear the song in my head before my hands ever touched the piano.

Soon we were three for three as collaborators, as we had recordings by Julio Iglesias, Bettye LaVette, and Bruce Murray as fast as I could get the songs demoed.

After writing three love ballads, it was time for us to try something a bit more up-tempo. We were enthusiastic, but artists often mistake exuberance for talent. And we fell way below the bar we had set for ourselves. The only thing I remember about our fourth song together was that it wasn't good. Afterward, we looked at each other and decided to stick with what we do best.

One night, Nancy and I invited Marty over for dinner. He arrived at seven, said hello to Nancy in the kitchen, and we sat down in the living room to chat while waiting for Nancy to let us know when dinner was ready. She was making stuffed shells.

As I took his coat, I noticed he had one of his brown envelopes with him, so I asked him my favorite Marty Panzer question: "You've got something for me?"

He said he had been working on this one for a while and wanted to make sure it was right before he showed it to me. I was curious. I yelled in to Nancy, "How long before dinner's ready?"

"About fifteen minutes."

At my impatient urging, Marty pulled out the lyric and began to recite it:

I can't remember when you weren't there,
When I ever cared for anyone but you.

When he finished his dramatic recital of "Through the Years," I had tears streaming down my face, and I think I ripped the lyric out of his hands and immediately went to the piano to *finish* the song. Most of the melody was magically being written in my head as I was listening to him read it for the first time. By the time I had the sheet of paper in my hands and on my piano, it was just a matter of adjusting a couple of chord substitutions and wrestling with a few phrases of the three different choruses.

Marty didn't make it easy for me to remember the words to this song. Each of the three choruses is completely different, lyrically, which of course is one of the reasons why the song is so great. I've been singing this song now for thirty years and I still have to look at a cheat sheet when I perform it. God only knows how Kenny Rogers has remembered it, night after night. Maybe he has a teleprompter? I'll have to ask him.

Nancy's Italian stuffed shells were fabulous. In the fifteen minutes it took to get dinner on the table, Marty and I had already baked "Through the Years."

Now that we had this big ballad written that we felt could be a huge hit for someone, the work of finding it a home was about to begin. We decided to do a simple piano/vocal demo of the song. I couldn't get the vocalist I wanted because he was out of town, so I ended up singing the guide vocal, thinking it would be only temporary until I could get someone really good on it.

The demo was okay. It was just one of those songs that we felt didn't need elaborate production because it was truly about the story and what was said between two people that were committed to loving each other through any challenge they might face.

I asked Marty if he would consider sending it to Barry Manilow, knowing that it might be a bit of an awkward situation, since Barry only recorded songs of Marty's that he had written the music for. Marty didn't think it was a good idea. But I knew this was a hit song.

Take one.

I sent it to Clive Davis. Clive had recorded several of my songs with Dionne Warwick, Melissa Manchester, and a few other acts. He was a great song man who had always been receptive to anything I sent him, so I thought I'd take a shot.

As Clive would often do, he wrote a brief critique about why he was "passing" on a song. Usually he would do this in the margin of the lyric sheet that accompanied the demo. I still have the "Through the Years" rejection note from Clive somewhere in my file cabinet. He passed because he didn't think it met his criteria for it "to be a hit." Fair enough. I have the utmost respect for Clive, and he certainly knows what he likes and what he doesn't.

Take two.

I got a call from Stan Schneider, who in addition to being my business manager at the time was also the longtime business manager for Glen Campbell. Stan told me that Glen was looking for a special song he could sing for a *Bob Hope Tribute Special: The 50th Anniversary of Bob Hope on NBC.*

I thought "Through the Years" would be the perfect song for that kind of anniversary event. Stan arranged for me to go to Glen's house and play him the song live. I had recently worked with Glen, having had a Top 10 record with him singing "Any Which Way You Can," a song I cowrote with Milton so I felt relatively comfortable going to see him.

Feeling confident that he was going to love the song, I drove up to the top of Kings Road in the Hollywood Hills, trying to find Glen's house. It was a pretty massive place, tucked away in the canyons. I was simultaneously nervous and excited as I reached the front door and rang the bell. As I was getting myself together, I heard screaming coming from the house. The shouts were loud but indecipherable and I wasn't sure what to do.

After ringing the doorbell three or four more times, I was about to turn and just get the hell out of there when the door opened and there was Glen Campbell, looking quite flustered and disheveled.

"Is this not a good time?"

Just as I asked, a hairdryer came flying across the doorway. I dodged it just in time to not get brained. Apparently, my arrival had coincided with the ending of a lover's quarrel between Glen and Tanya Tucker.

As I entered the house, I realized that it probably wasn't the best time to be playing a quintessential love song about long-lasting commitment. It also wasn't a great time for me to say hi to Tanya and ask her how she was doing.

Glen quickly ushered me to a beautiful white grand piano sitting in the living room. Despite the enormous tension in the room, I sat down to play. Almost as quickly as he had ushered me in, he stopped me in the middle of the first chorus. He apologized and told me he didn't think the song was right for him, and escorted me out, thanking me for coming by.

It was the epitome of "bad timing." Finding a home for this song was looking pretty challenging at this point.

Take three.

Now, I'm not really quite sure of the true story, as I've heard several different versions from the principal players involved, but somehow

Lionel Richie had heard my demo version of "Through the Years" and was thinking about recording it. How he got it is still a mystery to me. Jim Mazza, the president of EMI Records, claimed that he got it to both Lionel and Kenny. I also heard a version that MaryAnn Rogers, Kenny's wife at the time, had heard Kenny playing the song and told him, "You've got to cut that song."

Whatever story is the factual one, both Kenny and Lionel wanted to cut the song. Maybe they arm-wrestled for it. Kenny must have won! They compromised and Lionel produced it.

Gene Page, the fabulous arranger who did the string arrangements on Kenny's record, once told me that it was he who found the song and played it for Lionel and Kenny. Whatever and whoever steered that song into Lionel's and Kenny's life, they did Marty and me the favor of a lifetime.

Lionel had just produced "Lady" for Kenny, who at that time was one of the biggest-selling artists in the world. They were in the middle of recording the *Share Your Love* album and were still looking for songs.

Every songwriter on the planet wanted Kenny Rogers to record a song because he was a great artist who loved singing other people's songs. Whenever he was doing a new record, every publisher in town would send him material. It was almost impossible to get to him. So I was stunned when I got a call from EMI:

"Kenny wants to put your song on hold."

"Kenny who?" I asked in all seriousness.

"Rogers."

"Which song?"

"'Through the Years.'"

"Seriously?"

"Yeah. He's intending to record it, but no guarantee."

It was no secret that Kenny would take a lot of songs that he liked into a session to see what worked for him and what didn't.

I had no idea when this was actually happening; I just knew my song was on hold, no guarantee. So I was pleasantly surprised when I got a call from my friend Joe Chemay, who happened to have played bass on the session.

"Kenny just cut your song."

Two minutes later, the great Gene Page, who arranged it, called me as well.

"Beautiful song, Steve. Just wait until you hear it."

I hung up, ecstatic. I rushed to the office and danced around.

"We got a Kenny Rogers cut!"

Snuff—never one to disappoint with his ability to suck the air from any balloon of joy which didn't involve him 100 percent—said, "I guess I'll just sit by the phone and wait for them to ask me for half the publishing, and I'm telling you right now, I'm going to tell them to go fuck themselves when they do."

I looked at him in shock. My stomach turned.

He rolled his eyes.

"Don't be naive, Steve. It's like Elvis. They'll cut your song and say, 'We want half the publishing or we won't put it on the album.'"

Days later, before I had time to fall down the rabbit hole of Snuff's paranoia, I got a call from Don Grierson, the head of A&R for Liberty Records, Kenny's label.

"You wanna hear your song?" he asked. "Kenny said you guys can go over to the studio."

I called Marty and we raced over to Lion Share Recording Studios in the heart of Hollywood.

At this point, Don Grierson decided to share his opinion.

"This song still sounds like a Barry Manilow reject to me."

"Thanks, Don."

"Gotta be honest. Hey, it's lucky you're even on the album—doubtful you'll ever get a single."

Marty and I arrived at the studio and listened to the song. It sounded good—great, even. I was pleased, but when I looked over at Marty, his face turned red. He was sputtering.

"What's wrong?" I asked. "It sounds pretty great?"

Marty's face was so twisted I thought he was going to have an aneurysm.

"Kenny is missing five lines of the lyric . . . maybe more . . . and the opening line makes no fucking sense."

"Wait? What?"

I listened again. It still sounded great.

Marty was now apoplectic.

"Listen, Steve. It's a double negative. He's singing a double negative. Plus, he's ruined the best line of the song. It should be, 'I've learned what love's about by loving you.' He sang 'I've learned what *life's* about by loving you.' No. No. Absolutely not. It's cliché, trite."

I reminded Marty that Kenny Rogers is the biggest star in the world, and our song's going to sell eight bazillion records, but Marty didn't care.

"We've got to tell him. He has to fix it," Marty insisted.

So we walked down the hall to the big studio where Lionel and Kenny were working. Lionel asked us what we thought.

Marty took a deep breath and said, "The opening line is wrong."

This perked Kenny up. He quietly asked Marty to explain.

Marty tried to be calm. He spelled it out.

"You sang 'when I didn't care.' It's a double negative. The line should be, 'I can't remember when you weren't there, when I *EVER* cared for anyone but you.' But, instead of singing 'when I ever cared,' you sang 'when I didn't care.' It doesn't work. It's a double negative." Marty was on a roll. "You also sang, 'I've learned what life's about by loving you.' It should be, 'I've learned what love's about.' Not 'life.' 'Love.'"

Satisfied, Marty finally stopped talking and waited for Kenny's response.

Kenny closed his eyes for what seemed like twenty minutes, reviewing the song in his head. Finally, he opened his eyes.

"Let me give it some thought."

The tension was thick. Kenny was steadfast and Marty was still sputtering.

Lionel tried to break the friction.

"How about them Dodgers?"

No one spoke.

Finally, Lionel Richie realized what had happened.

"Guys, it's my fault. Blame me. My wife took down the lyrics off the demo. She must have taken them down wrong."

Only I knew what was going on in Marty's head. Later, after we had left the studio, he would insult Brenda Richie, but in that moment, he was just cursing under his breath. Kenny then smiled and said that he would consider resinging those few lines.

I could see Marty start to bristle at the word "consider," so I grabbed him by the back of his neck and snarled, "My kids need new shoes. Do. Not. Fuck. This. Up."

We left, and Marty just said, over and over, "I learned what life's about by loving you."

"Maybe he'll change it," I said.

Marty then dragged me to Greenblatt's Deli, where we bought the biggest magnum of champagne they had, a $450 Dom Pérignon, and wrote the following card:

> *Dear Kenny and Lionel,*
> *We've never been so proud.*
> *Love, Steve and Marty.*

We drove back to the studio and Marty hand-delivered it. It's probably why we still made the album.

Liberty put "Through the Years" on the B-side of Kenny's fourth single from the *Share Your Love* album, "Blaze of Glory." "Blaze of Glory" was not getting any traction at radio. It's rare for an album to have four hit singles from it. But then something happened.

Two radio stations in Charlottesville, West Virginia, and Buffalo, New York, started playing "Through the Years," and phones started to light up.

Within a few weeks, "Through the Years" finally got a shot at radio as the fifth single released from the album. Since then, it has become a modern standard, thanks to Kenny and Lionel and all of the people behind the scenes that made it possible. Along with "The Gambler," it became one of Kenny's all-time greatest hits. It's had over five million broadcast performances with BMI, and is considered one of the top wedding and anniversary songs of modern times.

When the sheet music was printed, I said to Marty, "At least we can get the lyric printed correctly in the sheet music." But we couldn't. According to our contract with the record companies and publishers, they had to print it exactly as it had been recorded. Perhaps Kenny considered redoing it; in the end, however, he did not resing any of the lines.

To this day, the only person who sings the song the way it was originally written is me. Kenny's record was magical, and the truth is, he could have sung a few other lines differently and it still would have been the standard that it's become.

Thank you, Kenny, for your masterful performance, and for the other six songs of mine you've recorded—forgive the pun—through the years.

Marty and I have written a total of only thirteen songs together to date. I have to say, percentage-wise, we've almost batted a thousand. Nine of them have been recorded by the likes of Jermaine Jackson, Michael Crawford, Kenny Rogers, Davis Gaines, Bettye LaVette, and Dolly Parton, among others.

Marty, you're as good as it gets!

As much as I loved having big-time recording stars starting to record my songs and help me start to carve out my own identity, I still had to go to the office every day at 6255 Sunset Boulevard and work for someone else, which was beginning to get progressively difficult to do.

14

FROM SNUFF TO WARNERS

———

6255 SUNSET BOULEVARD was one of the central hubs to most of the record business: Motown, Polygram, Warner/Chappell, the Welk Group, Michael Jackson, Jim Ed Norman, and many other prominent producers and entertainment attorneys were all located in the building. Columbia, Capitol, and RCA Records were just down the street, as well as some of the hottest smaller studios at the time. Not a day went by when you wouldn't have some kind of interaction with a person who might be looking for a hit song for someone they were working with.

Sometimes, it happened in the elevator.

Being at the right place at the right time can definitely be the catalyst for good things to happen in the music business. I had just finished a morning demo session at Criterion of a new song I had written with Milton Brown. It had a kind of light R&B feel to it, and I was happy with the way it had turned out. Robbie Nevil had sung the demo for me, and he sounded a lot like Michael Jackson. I was going back up to the office and got into one of the six elevators in the lobby, when my friend Eddie Lambert jumped in behind me just before the doors closed.

Eddie was a VP of A&R for Motown, and his office was two floors above mine. We made a little chit chat, and he asked me if I had anything that might be good for DeBarge.

———

"Wow, that's crazy, I just finished a song that could be great for them," I said. "The demo is thirty minutes old."

Eddie said to get it to him right away as they were having a song meeting that afternoon for their new album. I got to the office and immediately had a tape made and delivered upstairs to him.

At about 5 p.m. the phone rang. It was Eddie.

"How'd we do?" I asked.

"DeBarge passed. It just wasn't right for them. Great song though!"

"Yeah, thanks," I said, rather disappointedly.

Eddie went on to tell me that it wasn't all bad news. After DeBarge had left the meeting, Eddie was playing our song again when there was a knock on his door. The guy at the door asked, "What's that song you're playing? I want a copy of it. That demo is cool."

It was Smokey Robinson.

Smokey's office was right down the hall from Eddie's, and Eddie told me that Smokey was in the middle of doing his new album and was still looking for a few songs.

"Let's keep our fingers crossed," I said.

The next morning, Eddie called me and asked if I owned the demo track. I did.

"Smokey took the song home and wore the demo out. Rather than recut it, he'd like you to produce him on your track for his album."

"Reeeaaally?"

This was a bit too good to be true . . . but a guy's gotta do what a guy's gotta do.

I met with Smokey that afternoon. He was amazing! We decided that since the track was perfect for him, we'd go in the next day, put his vocal on, and mix it. Not only did the song end up on Smokey's *Essar* album, Snuff also played it for Burt Reynolds, and Burt ended up using it in his movie *Stick*.

All because Eddie and I happened to get in an elevator at the same time.

When I wasn't working in my office or making connections in elevators, lunch was the best place to work, connect, and schmooze. Lunch was also the prime meeting time for me and several of my friends in the business who were close by. Jim David, who was Hal David's son and ran Hal's publishing company, and Bo Goldson, who ran Criterion Music with his dad Mickey Goldson, were two of my closest friends. Jim, Bo, and I would have lunch together at least twice a week.

Sometimes, Jim would talk about his father's older brother, Mack David, a legendary lyricist himself with eight Academy Award nominations, including "Bibbidi-Bobbidi-Boo" from *Cinderella* and the title songs from *It's a Mad, Mad, Mad, Mad World* and *Walk on the Wild Side*. Mack also had several hit songs, including the Shirelles' "Baby It's You" and Duke Ellington's "I'm Just a Lucky So-and-So." I had heard the stories of how Hal and Mack had not spoken for years, and the fairly complicated history of them both being award-winning lyricists sometimes working with the same composers, and the conflicts that arose from those certain situations.

I had met Mack a few times when he came up to see Snuff at the office to play him some songs. Mack hadn't really had too much going on for a while. He was living in Palm Springs and was pretty much retired, but he still loved writing songs and couldn't really sit still—he got the itch to come to Hollywood every few weeks or so to pitch some new ideas to the newest crop of relevant songwriters.

I suppose I was one of those relevant songwriters.

I was already five minutes late for a lunch meeting at Martoni's with Jim and Bo, and was scrambling to get out the door, when Rhonda, the front desk receptionist, buzzed me and asked if I could take a moment to meet with Mack David, who had dropped by without an appointment. I came out of my office, shook hands with Mack, and politely told him I was running late and really didn't have time to chat. He told me he just happened to be in the building and was heading back to Palm Springs that afternoon, and had a "hit" lyric he wanted to show me.

Ugh. I knew this would probably take five minutes, but looking at Mack, who was an extremely large man with visible health issues, I agreed, and we walked back to my office.

Mack plopped his 250-plus-pound self on my couch, leaned forward, and excitedly proceeded to recite one of the worst song ideas I had ever heard. He thought it would be a great idea for David Frizzell and Shelly West, a hit duet act I was producing with Snuff. "A-Hup Two Three Four Five Six Seven Eight Nine Tennessee." Yes, Tennessee, like the state. Sigh.

As politely as I could, I told Mack it was a terrible idea, and it just wasn't for me. I started to get up, but he said, "One more, I have one more."

I was halfway out the door, and I was starting to sweat almost as much as he was . . . and I didn't have emphysema, like Mack did.

The second idea he had was worse than the first one. It was something about "Polyester Love."

At this point, I was standing at the door and imploring my unwanted guest to leave.

"Mack, I've got to go. I'm running late."

I was starving and already planning what I was going to eat for lunch.

It took him about a minute to get off of the couch and upright. As I shook his hand, he pulled a crumpled piece of yellow pad paper out of his jacket pocket, and said, "Can I just read you a verse and chorus of something I started this morning?"

Before I could say no, he started to recite a few lines that stopped me in my tracks. I listened to the first verse and chorus, and I asked him to recite it again. I immediately called Rhonda and asked her to call and apologize to Bo and Jim for having to cancel my lunch. Something came up . . . in the way of a great song that Mack and I would write that afternoon called "Hate the Lies, Love the Liar."

I was stunned that the same guy who just read me "Polyester Love" and "A-Hup" could write such a brilliant lyric as "Hate the Lies." For that brief moment when Mack obviously got struck with lyrical lightening, he was on the top of his game again.

I think it took all of fifteen minutes for me to write the melody to Mack's verse and chorus. The challenge was now going to be getting a great second verse out of him before he left the building. With Mack, you never knew when you might see him again.

We sat for a while and brainstormed, but he was empty. He said a lot of things but nothing was profound. It was all so staid and old-fashioned. Nothing worthwhile was coming out. It was completely off point to what he had said so beautifully in the first verse.

"It's only four lines Mack. Dig deep," I urged.

Finally, after throwing out hundreds of clichéd lines, causing me to nearly having an anxiety attack, he hooked it. We had a great song, well worth the lunch I ended up missing, and respite from the hour and a half of anxiety.

A few really nice versions of "Hate the Lies" were cut, but it was Ronnie Milsap who recorded the signature version.

Mack and I never wrote another song together, but on that one crazy lunch hour way back when, I lived a fun story that I would tell affectionately for the rest of my life. And I proudly have my name on a great song with the legendary Mack David.

After working for Snuff for a decade, I knew it was time for me to move on. When I thought about my real motivating reason to come to California in the first place, it was to work in the entertainment business. I absolutely loved writing songs, but I felt like there was so much more music in my head than just the three-and-a-half-minute format of a pop, R&B, or country song. I wanted to do professionally what I had been doing in my head my entire life: writing music to visual events.

Thanks to some incredibly talented directors and producers who I would get to meet in some of the oddest ways imaginable, I would get that chance.

Snuff Garrett had certainly been the catalyst for me getting to meet and work with Clint Eastwood and Burt Reynolds. These were opportunities that I probably never would have had if I hadn't been signed exclusively to Snuff. I owe him a great debt of gratitude and thanks. But I also knew not to sell myself short, as my involvement in all of these projects helped make them musically successful, and kept the flow of new projects coming in Snuff's door. It was an equitable partnership that worked very well for six or seven years.

When I decided to leave Snuff after ten years, it opened up the possibility of me getting representation for the first time. While I was working for him, Snuff would not hear of me having an agent to represent me for film and TV projects. That would have totally usurped his control of how, where, and when I would be able to do anything.

I had many good years with Snuff, but I knew it was time for me to move on. When Warners made me an offer, I wanted to give Snuff right of first refusal to match that offer. Loyalty is a big deal for me, and Garrett Music, for all of its plusses and minuses, had become family to me. After all, Snuff developed me. He gave me my first shot at arranging big orchestras' greatest musicians. As I unofficially became Leon Russell's replacement, Snuff's dependency on me grew.

Now, it is common knowledge that Snuff was not an easy guy to work for. He was extremely demanding and stubborn. There were two ways to do things: Snuff's way and Snuff's way.

One has to have a certain kind of personality to work under those conditions. And because Snuff gave me a shot and opened the doors that enabled me to show what I could do, I developed that certain kind of personality. Snuff trusted me with everything and spent less and less time in the studio and more time on his ranch, developing western art businesses, while allowing me to handle the daily mechanics of the music company. . . but only at arm's length. Every major decision still had to be run by and approved by him.

Eventually, after ten years, I was ready to move on. I called Snuff. He knew exactly why I was calling and had his guard up. He spoke preemptively.

"Steve. I understand Warners offered you a deal. What do you want?"

I took a deep breath. Even after ten years, the man still slightly intimidated me.

"Snuff, I want three things: copublishing; I want to have auspices to write and make deals with whomever I want to without you riding herd; and I want $125k a year." (I was getting $65,000 a year, and Warners had offered me $125,000.)

Snuff then said, without preamble, "Copublishing is not a problem, and you've always written with who you've wanted to. But for one hundred and twenty-five thousand dollars, I think I'll find the next Steve Dorff."

BOOM! And that was it: the end of a ten-year relationship.

I was devastated. I felt betrayed and unappreciated. But that's show-biz, and I sucked up my pride and moved on. On the upside, for the first time in my career I was finally in control of my own creative destiny. And I was excited about the possibilities.

I got representation immediately.

Michael Gorfaine and Sam Schwartz were, without question, the premier agents for film and TV composers. Michael and I had known each other from when he was working at ASCAP, before he and Sam started the Gorfaine/Schwartz Agency. I met with Michael and Sam, and we agreed that it would be a great place for me to be. I was honored to be represented by them. All of a sudden I was being submitted and exposed to a whole world of film and television projects. I knew then that I had made the right decision for my family and me, and while I appreciated every door that Snuff had opened for me, I never looked back with regret at having left.

Having already scored four films of Clint's, as well as having worked with Burt Reynolds on several of his projects, I already had a nice list of credits for Mike and Sam to build upon. And build they did. I had been gone from Garrett Music for about a year when I got hired to compose the score for Hugh Wilson's *Rustler's Rhapsody* at Paramount.

Sometimes you get a job in the quirkiest roundabout way.

The director and screenwriter, Hugh Wilson, was looking for a great costume design for the fictitious cowboy star Rex O'Herlihan, who would be played by Tom Berenger in the movie. Rex would change outfits five or six times a day for whatever the activity he was doing at that particular moment. Wayne Finkelman, the costume designer for the film, had gone to Tower Records on Sunset Boulevard to thumb through all of the western-themed albums to get some ideas to show Hugh. One of the albums he found was a Rex Allen Jr. album, with a fabulous picture of Rex on the cover in a stylish full cowboy getup from the sequined pleated shirt, right down to the silver spurs on his boots. The name of the album was *The Last of the Silver Screen Cowboy*, the title song of which Milton Brown and I had written for Rex in honor of his dad, Rex Allen Sr., as well as Roy Rogers, Gene Autry, and Hopalong Cassidy.

Wayne showed Hugh the album cover back at his office on the Paramount lot, and Hugh screamed, "That's my Rex's outfit right there!"

He was excited, and toward the end of the day, with the album cover sitting on his desk, Hugh had a little downtime and started looking at the album more closely. He wanted his Rex to sing in the movie like all singing cowboys did in the B-movie westerns. I suppose he was just a bit curious about the sound of the album, so he played Milton's and my song and quickly called Steve Bedell, who was head of Paramount's music department, and told him to track down whoever wrote that song, because he wanted it to be the end title song of his movie.

I had known Steve Bedell from way back when I was with Herb Bernstein in New York City. Steve called me and told me the entire, crazy, unbelievable story that had been unfolding, and asked me to come over to the studio and meet Hugh Wilson.

Hugh and I met and talked about his musical vision for the film, and he asked me to write a few more songs for his lead character to sing in the movie. This was going to be a big project: we would have to do all of the prerecords before shooting and thread the song melodies throughout the orchestral score. Steve suggested to Hugh that they hire me to do the entire project. And to think I got this amazing job simply because a costume designer happened to like a picture on an album cover. Talk about kismet!

I wrote most of the songs for this movie with Milton. One in particular, "Lasso the Moon," became a hit for Gary Morris, who recorded it for the end titles. I demoed all of the songs that Tom Berenger would be lip-syncing to in Los Angeles. Jon Joyce, a fabulous studio singer with whom I often worked, did all of the prerecords for me. It was then off to London to record the orchestral underscore.

While we were still in London finishing up recording *Rustler's*, Mike Gorfaine called me and asked if I would be interested in doing a backdoor pilot movie for Warners' television division. If they liked the two-hour movie, it would likely turn into a series. It was *Spenser: For Hire*, starring my close friend Robert Urich.

Sometimes it helps to be friends with big stars.

I had known Robert for several years. When my son Andrew was a baby and we were busting out of the small house we were living in on Kraft Avenue, Nancy was looking for a new home. She was always looking around the neighborhood for a bigger place where we could have more room. She loved a particular street not far from where we were, called Carpenter Avenue. It was a beautiful, tree-lined street with much bigger and nicer and far more expensive houses. One weekend she announced to me that she had found the perfect house on Carpenter that we just had to buy. The fact that it was twice the cost of the house we were in was secondary.

Being a typical artist, and assuming that the job I had just finished was probably going to be my last, and that I would never work again, didn't help. Luckily, we sold our house for twice what we had paid for it and went out on the proverbial limb and bought the Carpenter Avenue house.

The house directly across the street from us was the killer house in the neighborhood. It was the one house everyone coveted—it was truly gorgeous. The owners had done loads of custom work on it: bay windows, stained-glass doors, converting the garage into a beautiful study and office, huge stone fireplace.

One day I was out on the front lawn, playing ball with my boys, and the ball rolled into the street. I went to get it and was met halfway by actor Robert Urich. He was getting into his car, saw me, and thought he'd say hello to the new across-the-street neighbor. He was a really nice guy, down-to-earth; he loved living in a non-pretentious, homey neighborhood. He invited me over to see his house sometime, after I told him how much I had admired the aesthetic work he had put into it.

We would see each other on the street almost every day, and it wasn't long before we became friends. We would have each other over for a drink, and even went out for dinner with our wives. Bob loved music and had a really nice singing voice. We would sometimes sit at the piano, and he would ask me to play songs that he could sing.

Bob was a popular actor who went from one hit show to another. When we met, he was just coming off the big hit *Vega$*, where he starred as Dan Tanna. One afternoon he knocked on my door and asked me what I was doing this coming weekend. I told him I had no particular plans.

"We're going to Venezuela," he said. "I'm doing this crazy show down there where they want me to sing. I want you to play for me and I'll sing one of your songs."

Two days later, Bob, his wife Heather, his agent Merritt Blake, and I were headed to Caracas. It was an absolutely bizarre weekend. We got off the long plane ride at two in the morning to a crowd of screaming fans throwing their underwear at Bob.

You would have thought the Beatles had landed. Apparently, *Vega$* was a huge hit in South America.

The hotel we stayed at was supposedly meant to be a five-star resort. It was more like an old Ramada Inn on the outskirts of Des Moines. We did the *Sabado Sensational* TV special the next day. It was the equivalent of a six-hour *Ed Sullivan* show on steroids: singers, dancers, jugglers, magicians, and us. The piano was out of tune but no one seemed to care. Bob had learned a song of mine and Marty Panzer's called "From Now On." The crowd went nuts.

I was afraid to drink the water for three days, so I was brushing my teeth with Polar Beer—the Venezuelan beer that was in all of the hotel rooms. I think I stayed tipsy the entire weekend.

I almost got into a fight with some guy I was talking to about the Falkland Island crisis, which was currently ongoing. Venezuela was the only country that was supporting Argentina. I didn't realize that as I was spouting off about how Great Britain was going to kick Argentina's ass if they didn't back off of the Falklands, and some Venezuelan guy at the hotel bar told me he was going to kick my American ass if I didn't shut my mouth.

So much for a political dialogue in a foreign country.

All in all, it was a fun experience that I was so happy to see come to an end. When we landed in Miami, I got down and kissed the ground, grateful to be back in America. One has no appreciation of how great we have it in the United States until you've spent time in an impoverished country.

When Bob was offered the series *Spenser: For Hire*, he talked to the producer, John Wilder, and recommended me for the show. When I had gotten the call from Michael Gorfaine while working on *Rustler's* in London, it was about setting up a meeting for the same project when I returned. It felt like I had this gig surrounded.

I was already doing the music for *Growing Pains* and *My Sister Sam* at Warners, and I was getting ready to do *Major Dad* over at Universal, as well as a new pilot. I knew I needed help if I was to take on an hour show every week. Larry Herbstritt had been orchestrating for me almost exclusively for years, and he was the logical choice to help me do *Spenser: For Hire* on a week-to-week basis. This was a big action/adventure, private-eye show with a good twenty-five to thirty-five minutes of fully orchestrated score every week. We would customarily use a thirty-five-piece orchestra for every episode. We would spot music for a coming episode, write all week, record, and then start the process all over again every week for twenty-two episodes.

Bob told me he had to relocate to Boston, where they would be shooting for three years if the show went well. Before he put his house on the market, he asked me if I wanted to buy it. Did I? Absolutely. We moved across the street into our dream house.

It was the easiest move I ever made.

Spenser ran for three seasons and it was a great run. Bob and I remained close and played golf occasionally when he moved back from Boston to a beautiful custom mansion on the Lake Sherwood golf course. It was there, while playing golf one afternoon, that Bob shared with me that he was about to undergo treatment for some cancer that they had found during a routine physical. Tragically, at the age of only fifty-seven, Bob lost his battle with a rare form of sarcoma. He was definitely one of the good guys, and I think of him with a smile often.

I assumed that because I had such a successful collaboration on *Spenser:*

For Hire it would be a no-brainer that I would be hired to work on the spinoff show, *Hawk.*

I assumed wrong.

Larry Herbstritt and I were writing between thirty-five and forty minutes of music each week for every episode of *Spenser: For Hire.* The treadmill was definitely going full throttle. The fun thing about *Spenser* for me was the great relationship I had with both Robert Urich and Steve Hattman, who became the executive producer for the show's second season. Steve was a great writer and a big supporter of the music for the show . . . and there was a lot of it.

The character of Hawk, played by Avery Brooks, was a fan favorite. Musically, Larry and I would always try to thematically make something of his scene entrances and exits. We would usually play a somewhat dark, jazzy, heavy bass line–type cue in order to punctuate Hawk's onscreen presence.

I remember Hattman specifically telling me how much he loved the way we played Hawk musically.

Shortly after *Spenser* went off the air, after three seasons on ABC, Doug Frank, the president of television music at Warner Bros. Studios, called me and told me of plans to do a spinoff series starring Avery Brooks: *A Man Called Hawk.*

Steve Hattman was the creator and would be the executive producer of the series for ABC. Again, I guess I just assumed that Larry and I would be asked to do the music. Whoops—not so fast. Although Steve wanted me to do it, Avery Brooks was adamant about having everything to say about the music for *his* show.

Doug asked if I would take a meeting with Avery for a discussion about the music. I was a huge fan of the character Avery had brought to life. He *was* Hawk as far as I was concerned. In fact, when we had our meeting at the scoring stage on the Warners lot, I felt as if I was sitting there with the big bad dude with the long silver gun in his vest, not Avery Brooks the actor.

Avery was quiet, and deliberate with his speech, much like the character I had lived with onscreen, a good six hours a day, for the past three years of my life. It was just a little bit intimidating. I told Avery how much I enjoyed doing *Spenser: For Hire*, and how I would love to continue on doing the music for *Hawk*.

There was a long pause before he slowly said, in his eloquent, serious, Shakespearean baritone, "There is a universe in which Hawk lives musically, of which I am not sure you understand."

Hmmmm, I thought. This was getting a bit deep. He went on to explain the jazz fusion and ethereal, unpredictable, sounds he would be wanting to hear every time he, or Hawk, would be on camera.

He couldn't have been nicer to me, and he complimented me for my work on *Spenser: For Hire*, but it was pretty clear that he wanted me to "audition" for this show, with a type of music that was definitely not in my comfort zone. Plus, I really wasn't sure at all what the "Universe of Hawk" that he kept referring to was all about.

To his credit, Avery did invite me to submit some music for him to listen to, but I knew I was not the right person for this project. I told Doug and Steve Hattman that the meeting had gone okay, but I felt like, under the circumstances, I was not the right composer for this show. At lunch with Doug a few months later, he recalled how he went to one of the initial scoring sessions, and how totally differently it was conducted compared to the sessions we always did for *Spenser*.

Apparently, the sessions were done with a rather small jazz ensemble of some five or six pieces. Very little was written out or scored, and the music was often an extemporaneous jam session. Scoring to picture is as mathematical a process as it is musical, especially when you are trying to hit, or musically punctuate, dramatic sequences or specific events within a scene, because frames of film go by in a millisecond.

Well, each to each his own . . . let's leave it at that. To be honest, I never got to see the show. The network canceled it rather quickly. I guess I wasn't the only person who couldn't understand the "Universe of Hawk."

From there, the floodgates really opened up for me at nearly every studio. Over the next ten years I would write music for over sixty motion-picture and television projects, including films like *Back to the Beach*, *Pink Cadillac*, *Babe Ruth*, *Love Story*, and *Pure Country*; the TV series *My Sister Sam*; *Murphy Brown*; *Tremors*; *Alien Nation*; *Reba*; *Uncle Buck*; *Murder, She Wrote*; the made-for-TV movies *Columbo*, *Sam McCloud*, *Kiss Shot*, *B. L. Stryker*; and a slew of others. It was like being on a treadmill that wouldn't turn off. And I must admit, although crazy busy as it had become, I loved it. It was an entirely new career for me, and it presented all kinds of new challenges as well.

And a great deal of it was about being in the right place at the right time.

That same year, I was hired to do the pilot and theme song for *Growing Pains*, and Burt Reynolds called me to score an episode of *Alfred Hitchcock Presents* and an episode of *Amazing Stories* that he directed for Universal. I was thrilled that he called me without being attached to Snuff. Clint would also call me to work with him on another movie without Snuff attached.

Those calls mean so much more to me now because they represented me being my own guy in their eyes. Maybe I always had been . . . . I guess Snuff just didn't want to me to know it.

15

RINGO STARR

I'VE BEEN ASKED so many times: What are the greatest experiences I've had, and who are the greatest artists I've gotten to work with? That's kind of like asking a parent to name their favorite child. I have four remarkable children who are each exceedingly different and extraordinarily wonderful in their own way.

But I do have a favorite . . . experience, not child.

As a teenager at the beginning of the mid-sixties British Invasion, I used to glue myself to the TV and watch the pop music shows *Hullabaloo, Shindig!,* and *Where the Action Is.* I could only dream about the chance of meeting, let alone writing songs for, some of my favorite stars. I look back now and really can't believe I was so fortunate to get to work with so many of my musical heroes—musicians who inspired me, and whose albums I would rush out to buy as soon as they were released.

Bill Medley of the Righteous Brothers, Petula Clark, Dusty Springfield, Tom Jones, Engelbert Humperdinck, and Paul Revere of the Raiders were just some of the many people I used to admire and subsequently got to write songs for. As a young writer, hearing these artists' interpretations of what was in my head when I wrote those songs was absolutely mind-blowing for me. Here were the very performers whom I idolized, singing songs that I wrote.

It never ceases to be an absolute thrill.

The truth is, all of the amazing artists who have recorded my songs—including Barbra Streisand, Céline Dion, Dusty Springfield, Dolly Parton, Whitney Houston, Dionne Warwick, Michael Crawford, Anthony Newley, and so many others—each brings his or her unique style and voice to every project. They are all my favorites. But . . . if I had to pick . . .

I have always been a Beatles freak.

I clearly remember watching the Beatles make their history appearance on *The Ed Sullivan Show* on February 9, 1964. It influenced thousands of garage bands across the country including, the Four People. I was obsessed with them, so the idea of one day producing one of them was basically inconceivable.

Until it happened.

Getting the chance to produce Ringo Starr has to be right up there with the most surreal experiences of my career. It was spectacular, even though it was not the easiest of sessions. One day, I received a call from Gary Lemel, the president of the music department at Warner Bros. Pictures, asking me if I could come to his office for a quick meeting about a project Warners was doing. Famed director John Hughes had just finished what would be his last film, a sweet movie called *Curly Sue*. He needed a song for the end credits ASAP, and Gary had suggested to him that John Bettis and I would be a good choice to write the song. Gary gave us a copy of the shooting script, and after reading it, John had a great title idea.

We got together the next day and wrote "You Never Know," a breezy, soft-shoe kind of swing-feel tune, with a great lyric that perfectly fit the message of the film, *"You never know which way a day is gonna take you."*

I did a quick piano/vocal demo to show Gary the song, and a day later John Hughes gave us the thumbs-up. Hughes was briefly in town from his home base in Chicago doing postproduction on the movie, and he wanted to meet with Gary and me to determine who should sing the song.

We met the next day in Gary's office on the lot. I was such a fan of John Hughes's staggering list of blockbuster films, such as *Ferris Bueller's Day Off*, *Home Alone*, *The Breakfast Club*, *Uncle Buck*, and *16 Candles*, just to name a few. He was a genius, and I felt so honored to be a small part of his legacy as a filmmaker.

We talked about the song, listened to it a few times together, and then, since I had Harry Nilsson in mind as I was writing it, I threw out his name as who I thought would sound amazing singing it. John and Gary both liked that idea, but John suggested someone even . . . bigger.

John told us he'd envisioned Ringo Starr singing it the entire time he was listening to the demo. He wanted to approach Ringo first. I gulped, and I think my heart skipped several beats. It was highly doubtful that one of the greatest musical stars in history would sing my song. He was untouchable. Except there was nobody that Gary Lemel couldn't get to, or at least get an answer back from.

Sure enough, Gary called me a day later to tell me that Ringo liked the song and had agreed to sing it for the movie. I was to produce the track that week, as Ringo was only in town for a few days before heading over to Europe.

I truly thought I was dreaming and, this time, my heart almost stopped. Intimidation took on a whole new meaning for me. Scrambling to put this session together so quickly was not easy. Obviously, it was the most important session I had ever done up to this point. My God, this was one of the Beatles!

Miraculously, the band came together perfectly: JR (John Robinson) on drums, Randy Kerber on keys, Dean Parks on guitar, and Joe Chemay on bass. I had Doug Rider engineering the tracking session, which we did in Hollywood at Conway Recording Studios.

We cut the track on a morning session so we could break before lunch. Ringo was not available to be at the tracking session but would arrive at 3 p.m. to meet and start doing vocals. The track came out flawlessly, and we all broke for an hour for lunch.

My excitement level was truly off the charts. I couldn't even eat lunch, I was so nervous, so I went back to the office for thirty minutes just to clear my head. I wanted to get back to the studio early to plan out how I was going to approach the vocal session and calm my nerves before Ringo arrived.

As I walked up the tree-lined pathway up to Studio A, I saw a guy leaning against the front of the studio. He had a shock of dark hair and an unassuming stance, and was focused on the cigarette that was dangling from his mouth. As I got closer, I thought, "Shit that looks like Ringo." As I got even closer, I thought, "Shit, that *is* Ringo."

My mind was racing and I had to give myself a pep talk to calm down.

"Relax Dorff, calm down, be cool, act like a pro, don't say anything stupid."

I got within a few feet of him and started babbling like a seven-year-old fanboy. I shook his hand and said, "I'm sure you hear this all the time, but you're the reason I got into this business."

With that unmistakable voice, he smiled and said, "First time today."

We walked into the studio and I played him the track, which he was extremely happy with. He had a few ideas about how I could fix a couple of things, one of which was the hi-hat. We then went out to the piano, where he asked to go over the song several times. It was pretty clear that he hadn't really practiced the song much, if at all.

By now, John Hughes, Gary Lemel, and a few other Warner execs had come over to the studio to say hello to Ringo and see how things were going. We were all a bit awed as I sat at the piano and we heard that distinctive voice. The guy who sang "With a Little Help from My Friends," "Yellow Submarine," and "Act Naturally," as well as so many other classic hits, was singing a song that I wrote.

Eventually we would clear everybody out so we could get to the task at hand of recording Ringo's vocal, but before that a funny thing happened. John Hughes, who proclaimed himself the #1 Beatles fan of all time, had a burning question for Ringo. We were all standing around chatting in a circle as John asked, "Is it true that you put a towel over your hi-hat in 'Taxman'?"

I thought to myself, "What an odd question. Maybe John is a drummer."

Ringo must have thought it quite odd as well, as he thought for a moment and then replied, "I can't remember what I did last Thursday, let alone remember what I played in those days." He laughed and alluded to the era of the Beatles' well documented, chemically enhanced sessions.

When it was time to finally go into the studio to sing, Ringo asked me to go out first and put a guide vocal on the track so he could sing to me line by line. "That's how I always did it with Paul," he said.

The teenage boy inside of me was dying with excitement as I said, without missing a beat, "If it was good enough for Paul, it's good enough for me."

For the next two hours we did take after take. I don't think I've ever enjoyed saying a sentence more than when I pushed down the yellow talkback button to ask him to resing a line or punch in a few words.

"Can we do that again, Ringo?"

Ringo did a great job singing the song. I had gotten everything I needed to do a terrific comp, but before he left, he told me he wanted to overdub the hi-hat to make the track "swing a bit more."

Watching Ringo play the hat, cigarette dangling out of his mouth, brought back all of the memories I had of watching him play throughout the years as that teenager who was one of the biggest Beatles fans imaginable.

We did an overdubbed orchestra session two days later. Bill Watrous, the fabulous trombone player, was also a world-class whistler, so I asked him to do the whistling on the record that many people still think Ringo actually did.

Curly Sue still runs quite often on cable, and whenever I see it, I am reminded of the experience of a lifetime, having worked with the iconic John Hughes and the even more iconic Ringo Starr.

It definitely dates me, but my fanboy infatuation with Ringo Starr and the Beatles was somewhat akin to 1980s kids across America and their collective infatuation with burgeoning teen heartthrob Kirk Cameron.

16

Growing Pains

The eighties were ripe with Reaganomics and burgeoning yuppies. It was the decade of greed.

I was enjoying the pinnacle of my personal and professional career. I had been Snuff Garrett's right-hand man, I had scored films for Clint Eastwood and Burt Reynolds, and now I was scoring a string of television shows. I hadn't fucked up my marriage yet, and I was enjoying enormous personal and professional success. Of course, this would all soon come crashing down, but for the moment, I was living the high life.

Because I had access to the stars who had sung pop hits for me, TV networks turned to me when they wanted to marry recording artists and theme songs. Essentially, this was the precursor for Barenaked Ladies singing the theme song for *The Big Bang Theory* or the Rembrandts singing the theme song for *Friends*.

The first song I wrote and then married with a celebrity singer was the theme song from *Growing Pains*. Of course, most people think that Alan Thicke wrote the song . . . and understandably so, because he was the star of the show. But it was me.

I got a call from my agent to go see a pilot the network was interested in me doing the music for. I went to Warners and met with the three producers: Neil Marlens, Marlens's wife Carole Black, and Mike

Sullivan. The four of us went into a room and watched twenty-two minutes of what I thought was pretty mundane television. Of course, I didn't watch too many sitcoms, so I wasn't exactly an expert.

It was a family show starring Alan Thicke, Joanna Kerns, and three cute, engaging kids, one of whom would go on to be a teenage heart-throb for girls all around the world . . . Kirk Cameron.

After viewing the pilot episode, the producers and I went to their conference room to discuss the music for the show. What happened next is pretty much classic television by committee. There were several cooks in the kitchen, and everyone had their way of baking the proverbial musical cake. Each of the three producers gave me their musical take, from John Sebastian to Pat Metheny to Latin percussion. Everyone had a personal favorite style.

I listened to it all and was baffled, wondering how they were going to settle on a united decision. So I just kept politely listening and nodding as each producer waxed on lyrically about their chosen type of music. Finally, I said, "These are all good ideas; let me give it a shot."

To be perfectly honest, I remember leaving the meeting thinking, "This show is probably not going to go anywhere, so it really doesn't matter what I write." I went home to meet John Bettis, with whom I had a previously set up writing session that afternoon.

"Change of plans," I told him. "I got this thing I gotta write called *Growing Pains*."

I gave John the thirty-word CliffsNotes version of the sitcom.

There was silence, and finally John said, "'Growing Pains' ain't gonna fly as a song title . . . sounds more like, 'As Long as We Got Each Other.'"

He nailed it.

We wrote the song in roughly thirty minutes. We only had to write a verse and a chorus. John wrote it like he was writing The Pledge of Allegiance. We cranked it out so we could work on another far more pressing project, an already-started song that we were excited about (as I remember, that song went nowhere).

I called the producers the next morning.

"I spent all night working on this thing," I told them.

"How soon can we hear it?"

I hadn't had a chance to make a demo yet. Again, I figured it was most likely not going to fly. It didn't even come close to Latin percussion, and it sounded nothing like John Sebastian or Pat Metheny.

"Come over when you can and I'll play it for you."

An hour or so later, they arrived at my house in Studio City, which was a fairly short ride from the Warners lot. I watched them park and approach my door: the Holy Trinity. Suddenly, a wave of panic came over me. This was really happening. I actually wrote a song that sounded nothing remotely like what they asked for. They were going to hate it.

After a minute or two of niceties, and me explaining John's and my process, I took a deep breath and played the song. It was the longest thirty seconds of my life. When I finished and looked up, all three producers were smiling.

"That's exactly what we wanted."

We started to talk about who could sing it. All sorts of names were thrown about before we settled on B. J. Thomas, a terrific legacy artist and a friend of mine who had recorded several of my songs. B. J. put his signature vocal on the track, and it was the perfect fit. The show aired and it was a monster breakout hit, which clearly demonstrated how little I knew about network TV.

As the second season approached, the producers asked if we could do the theme as a duet. We hired Jennifer Warnes, who had an absolutely amazing voice and was coming off a big hit single of her own.

From the moment the vocal session started, I had a feeling we were in for some trouble. Although Jennifer ultimately did a great job singing the song, she seemed to have an issue with it being too "commercial-sounding." Jennifer had been gravitating in her own career toward more Leonard Cohen–sounding songs. She told me after we were finished recording the sixty-second version that she was worried that it sounded like it could be a radio hit.

I was concerned.

"Jennifer, why is that going to be a problem? Isn't that what we're after here?"

She looked at me matter-of-factly.

"I don't know if I want to deal with having a hit record, Steve."

I thought that to be a bit odd, but hey, whatever floats your boat. Her duet version with B. J. kicked off the second season, and the show was as hot as ever, soon becoming the #1 sitcom on television. By now, everybody was asking me to record a record-length version for a possible commercial release to radio. Jennifer had made it pointedly clear that she did not want to be a part of that, so we replaced her with Dusty Springfield, who happily had no problem with having a hit record.

John and I added a second verse, made the record version with B. J. and Dusty, and we had a Top 10 single.

Growing Pains was my first half-hour, and when you have one hit, everyone comes a-calling. I next did the theme song for *My Sister Sam* and had Kim Carnes sing "Room Enough for Two." Then I did the theme song for *Just the 10 of Us*, "Doin' It the Best I Can" with Bill Medley of the Righteous Brothers.

I suppose because of my background in doing records I brought something new to TV theme music. Producers wanted their theme songs to sound like hits on the radio, and John and I were able to deliver. We were among the first to really cash in on the pop music connection, using pop icons to do television themes, as opposed to anonymous studio singers. A lot of the artists I'd worked with—Kim, B. J., Dusty, Jennifer Warnes, Bill Medley—came from relationships I had from the record business that John and I were able to bring to television.

I did a lot of television theme songs over the years. *Murphy Brown* was probably my favorite, *Spenser: For Hire* was the most challenging, and *Growing Pains* was the most well known.

Bettis and I were asked to write a song that would be featured in a special one-hour episode of *Growing Pains* where the intrepid Seaver family goes to Hawaii on vacation. While they are there, Kirk Cameron's character, Mike Seaver, falls madly in love with a Hawaiian native girl. The producers wanted a beautiful flowing ballad that they could thread through the entire two episodes. John had a fabulous title, "Swept Away," which perfectly captured the mood of the piece.

As we sometimes would, John and I got together and wrote what would be the chorus refrain first. It just fell out. I kept hearing a high, pretty, Art Garfunkel–type voice for the song.

John had been working with Christopher Cross on his last album, and he said, "How about we get Christopher to come in and write this with us?"

It was a fabulous idea.

A few traded phone calls later, I made a plan to get with Christopher and show him what I had started musically on the song.

I first met with Chris at his place in Pacific Palisades. He had a great little studio in his basement. What struck me most about him, other than his unmistakable voice, was how great a guitar player he was. I had no idea he was that skilled or that he had such a unique style of playing, with which he ultimately put his musical signature on our song. It didn't take long at all before he had a great verse melody that seamlessly flowed into the chorus. It was a painless writing session.

Later, John and Chris would get together to finish the lyric and write a short bridge. We had the song.

The show's producers were ecstatic. Christopher liked it so much that he went in and also recorded it for his new album. The ratings for the Hawaii episodes were through the roof, the song was charting, and we got nominated for a primetime Emmy Award.

This would be my fifth nomination without a win.

Clearly, we had a great chance. We were the only song nominated that was an actual "hit song," and Christopher had already won an Oscar and five Grammys, so this would nicely round out his award mantle at home.

Emmy night is always exciting, especially when you're nominated. We were feeling pretty optimistic about our chances as we took our seats at a great table along with the producers of the TV show, Mike Sullivan, Dan Guntzelman, and Steve Marshall.

Wouldn't you know, the first award to be announced was our category, Outstanding Achievement in Music and Lyrics.

Here we go . . . who was I going to thank first?

As they opened the envelope, I could see Christopher start to push his chair back a little to get up.

"The award goes to: *The NBC Kids Search for Santa!*"

Our collective eyes rolled. The guys who wrote that had only won about forty Emmys between them, and I guess their old friends in the voting academy felt like they needed another one.

After a few minutes, the shock of not winning began to wear off, and we decided to go have a great dinner at Chasen's in Beverly Hills rather than eat the rubber chicken they were serving at the awards dinner. Sour grapes? Not at all. We knew the politics, accepted it, and celebrated the nomination and the Top 10 record we were going to have. Nope, never got to hear the Santa song that won.

I'm pretty sure 99 percent of the world's population never heard it, either.

Christopher and I have remained good friends over the years. We wrote a great song together for another one of his albums with Cynthia Weil called "Is There Something," and Chris also recorded a Christmas song I wrote with George Green called "The Best Christmas," which I still hear every holiday season.

Growing Pains ran for eight seasons, which again shows how much I knew about network television. All of the actors, producers, and production staff became a family. Mike, Dan, and Steve couldn't have been more supportive of the music for the show, and they were always open to hearing any creative ideas I had. It was truly one of the more fun experiences I've ever had in television. I wish all the television shows I worked on could have been that enjoyable.

Alan and I remained friends for many years. When he first came to L.A. from Toronto, he hired me to do some record arrangements for him. We became social friends as well, because our kids went to school together. Andrew and Robin were in the same class.

In addition to being a TV star, Alan was also successful as a song-writer, penning several theme songs including "Different Strokes" and "The Facts of Life," which he wrote with his then wife, Gloria Loring. Because he was a star, he was often asked to go on talk shows and give personal appearances, where he would play a medley of his themes.

The host would invariably say, "Alan, you're not only a star, you write theme songs. Play us some." And Alan would play the same medley every time: "Different Strokes," "The Facts of Life," and "As Long as We Got Each Other."

In fairness, he didn't say he wrote them all, but he also never said he didn't. I can't tell you how many times people have come up to me and said, "I thought Alan Thicke wrote the theme song to *Growing Pains*."

It was with great sadness that I learned of Alan Thicke's sudden passing this year. His personality was a bright light in any room, and he had that rare gift of always making everybody smile who was around him. He was fun, intelligent, good-looking, super-talented, and a great father to his three sons. I was lucky to call him my friend. The other legacy he left us all was the character of Jason Seaver, an iconic "father knows best" for future generations who watch Growing Pains.

17

REBA

SOMETIMES, one bad apple spoils the whole barrel. Especially if he is a producer who mistakenly believes he is a musical guru.

I first got to work with Reba when my friend Keith Stegall asked me to do a few string arrangements for an album he was producing. Reba wasn't there when I overdubbed the string session in Los Angeles with Keith, so it wasn't until later that I would actually get to meet her.

Keith and I pretty much started in the business at the same time, and we had known each other for many years. I really like the records Keith makes, and I'm thankful he often thought of me to do the strings for him on projects ranging from Alan Jackson to Sammy Kershaw, Billy Ray Cyrus, and, of course, Reba.

I would see Reba and her husband, Narvel Blackstock, from time to time at awards shows in Nashville, and they were always kind, although we didn't really know one another until I officially introduced myself one night at the BMI Awards and told her how much I enjoyed working on her album. Narvel always kept the door open for me to send Reba songs when I thought I had a good one for her, and I've always appreciated that. I came close a few times, but unfortunately never made one of her albums with a song that I had written.

One day, I was driving home from Hollywood over Coldwater Canyon when my phone rang. It was Narvel, calling from Vegas. Reba had just finished taping a television pilot for Fox, and he asked me if I would be interested in doing the music for the show. Now, I hadn't done a half-hour show in quite a while, and I was trying to move away from that format to concentrate more on films and theater. But how could I possibly say no to Reba?

She and Narvel thought I was the right guy because they knew that I was familiar with both country music and the rigors of weekly television music. Narvel set up a meeting for me with the creator and executive producer of the show, Alison Gibson.

It was a fairly typical meeting—I had to pretty much audition for the gig by submitting cues from other projects I had done, and then explain how I would make this show sound totally unique in flavor. That process never ceases to amaze me, as most of the people making music decisions don't know much about music. Alison, however, did know music, and I liked her from the start. We had a great meeting, and the next day my agent, Cheryl Tiano, called to say she had made the deal for me to do the series.

Reba's show was really fun for me to do . . . at first. The cast was awesome and the writing was funny and fresh. The only issue I had was a bit of annoying meddling from one of the other exec producers, who I assure you, did not know a C-sharp from an X. Let's call him "Mr. Musical Genius."

On almost every TV show I have ever done, the postproduction staff have been wonderful and extraordinarily helpful, and for the most part have given me the creative freedom to do what I do best . . . write music.

This show was different.

I had a few people working in postproduction who knew their jobs very well, and one who seemed to know my job better than I did. It would be one thing if Mr. Musical Genius remotely knew what he was talking about . . . but he didn't. It would be like me stepping into a script meeting and giving notes to the writers, or suggesting editing trims to the film editor, or telling a cardiac surgeon how to operate on a heart.

Other than my infrequent bumping in to Narvel or Reba on the set, they weren't at all involved in the postproduction of the episodes. Besides, it was not my style to complain or do an end around with the star of the show. Post was all under the supervision of Mr. Musical Genius.

Reba was the star, and she was involved in every detail of the show, from scripts to set design to production and, oh yes, headlining the series and acting every day. By the time I was given an episode to score, they were already two shows ahead of me.

I loved doing the music. George Doering and I were having a great time recording keys and guitars at my house every week, and, at Mr. Musical Genius's request, I would attend the dubbing sessions whenever I could. Inevitably, he always had an issue with one or two of the music cues or transitions.

"Could I make it a bit more happier . . . sadder . . . more purple?"

Seriously? I wasn't exactly sure of how to make a cue a color. Did he want violet? Mauve? Aubergine? Was he looking for a peppy lavender sound, or more of a poignant plum cue?

Geez, this wasn't *Gone with the Wind*. It was a twenty-two-minute television sitcom with maybe a dozen or so six-to-ten-second music cues or transitions. I would usually have to go back and rescore a few things just to satisfy this color-obsessed control freak.

By the end of the first season, I was drained. I never wanted to bother Narvel with this, so during the hiatus I asked my agent to find a way to creatively get me out of doing the show. I'm quite sure Mr. Musical Genius was thrilled.

From a strictly musical standpoint, it was not one of my better television experiences, I'm afraid. I had been totally spoiled by Mike and Dan of *Growing Pains*, Diane English of *Murphy Brown*, Rick Hawkins of *Major Dad*, Tim O'Donnell of *Uncle Buck*, and all of the other great producers who thoroughly supported me in all of my creative choices for their shows.

For the very last episode of season one, however, there was a very beautiful moment where Reba holds her newborn baby granddaughter and sings a lullaby to her at the end of the show.

I'm proud to say I wrote "My Angel's Lullaby."

I had finally gotten Reba to sing one of my songs after all.

18

THE EIGHTIES WERE A GOOD DECADE

The eighties were a good decade for me professionally.

I was one of the networks' go-to guys, and they were using me for everything from sitcoms to movies of the week. The heart of this business is the marriage of talent and relationships. I was fortunate to have built up a lot of strong relationships, thanks to my agents, Mike, Sam, and Cheryl.

Hal Needham, who directed all of Burt Reynolds's *Smokey and the Bandit* movies, was one of them.

I was in the studio recording the score to a movie of the week called *Bandit*, based on the Burt Reynolds movie, which Hal had also directed. I was recording a rather lengthy action cue with the orchestra. The bandit was being chased by the bumbling sheriff, on road, off road, through water, and back on road, where he finally escapes.

For whatever reason, the cue I had written was just not working. It was falling flat, and not elevating the excitement of the chase, even though I was hitting all of the desired moments. After about forty-five minutes of trying to fix the piece of music, I was frustrated. I needed some distance in order to have better clarity, so I moved on to a different scene.

A few hours later, at the end of the session, Hal came in and wanted to hear some of the cues put to picture. He was delighted with everything until I played him the big chase scene. I had pre-warned him that I wasn't totally happy with this important sequence. We watched it together, and I kept sneaking a peek at Hal to see his reaction.

When the scene ended, Hal looked at me and said, "This isn't working for me. You've got all the right excitement in the band, but it's missing the most important element."

I looked at him, stumped. I had tried everything. I was certainly open to his suggestions, but I hadn't anticipated his excitement and certainty when he confidently said, "There's only ONE WAY to move a car on down the road . . . with a banjo!"

Spoken like the great stuntman that Hal Needham was.

Somewhat dubious, I called George Doering and asked him if he could come back in and overdub a banjo on the cue. George had already been doing the guitars on the entire project that day, so he knew exactly what I wanted. He came back in and played it perfectly. We all listened back in the control room, and I thought, "Damn, if Hal didn't call that one on the nose."

Sometimes the director does know best.

And sometimes the star knows best.

Peter Falk was one of the legends with whom I had the great fortune of working. Who didn't love *Columbo*? The character that Peter Falk created so brilliantly was certainly one of my favorites. I could be in the middle of almost anything, and if a rerun came on I would immediately get sucked in watching it. Peter was doing a series of two-hour *Columbo* mystery movies for Universal. I got a call to meet with the man over at his offices on the Universal lot. He was looking for a specific score for a film he was currently shooting called *Death of a Rock Star*. The plot was set in the pop music world, and he needed the score to have elements of rock and the traditional *Columbo* orchestral flavor.

I was excited to meet him. When I first saw him sitting in his office, feet up, puffing on a cigar and looking a bit disheveled, I smiled. Peter Falk and Columbo were one and the same. I sat down opposite him at his desk, and before he got into the conversation about music, he talked about his beloved basketball team, the New York Knicks, and showed me his collection of Knicks memorabilia. We jumped around various subjects, and the more we talked, the more I was completely surprised that I couldn't distinguish between Peter Falk the actor and his alter ego, Columbo. It was fascinating.

Eventually, Peter told me all about the project, was happy to have me onboard, and thanked me for coming in. As I was leaving, just as I was almost out the door, I heard that voice say, in typical Columbo fashion, "Oh, Steve, one more thing."

I turned around and he motioned me to come back. "I think it would be good for us to have a song over the main titles, sung by the female rock star who gets murdered."

"Great idea. Anything in particular you want the song to say?"

"No. Just something . . . peppy." He winked.

I smiled all the way back home. John Bettis and I wrote a song called "Closer, Closer." Peter loved the demo I did with Susie Benson singing and said it was just what he was hoping for. I didn't see him for the next two weeks as they were still in production and editing, but eventually I was asked to come over and musically spot the film with him and his staff.

The movie was great fun, and, as usual, Peter was amazing in the role of Columbo, methodically figuring out who the killer was. My music editor and I took all the spotting notes, and Peter said he'd hopefully see me at the recording session in ten days. By now I seriously couldn't tell the difference between Peter and Columbo. They just seemed to be the same person to me.

I felt to some degree like I was in a *Columbo* movie myself.

The recording session at Universal's scoring stage was really going well. I had a fantastic rhythm section complemented by a thirty-five-piece orchestra. Peter was not able to be at the session after all, due to a conflicting meeting, but he was hoping to come down toward the end and catch a little bit of it.

We were pretty much cruising through the score without any hitches, recording a slow, dramatic piece, when I heard through the talkback in my headphones a familiar voice.

"Steve, can I have a word with you?"

It was Peter. He had made it over to the session with about an hour to go. I called for a quick ten-minute break and went to the control room to see what was up. Peter told me he had been there for a few minutes and absolutely loved what he was hearing, but he had a question about the last cue we were rehearsing.

"I'm not sure I like that French horn line in the middle of the piece. Can we do something about that?"

I was a bit surprised, but I told him I would happily look at it. When the band came back from their break, we began to rehearse the cue again. I couldn't find the French horn line Peter was referring to. I asked the control room if Peter wouldn't mind coming into the studio and identify the part he had issue with, so I could fix it.

As Peter walked into the studio, the entire orchestra started to applaud. He waved to everybody, offered a brief hello, and said how honored he was to have such a great group of musicians playing on the project.

We rehearsed the cue again, and I asked him to point out where it was exactly that he was having the issue. Standing next to me on the conducting podium, he tapped me and said, "Right here."

I stopped the band and looked at the score. There was no French horn playing. At this point you had to either be there, or be a dedicated *Columbo* expert. Peter cocked his head slightly to the side, squinted a bit, and took the cigar stub out of his mouth.

"Are you sure there's not a French horn playing right there?"

Was this a trick question? All that was missing at this point was the tattered raincoat.

I took a deep breath.

"No, Peter. The horn is not playing that line. There are a couple of cellos playing there though. Let me isolate them for you."

I had the cellos play solo and, sure enough, that was what Columbo was hearing. He asked me to play the cue without that cello line. We did, and with a smile and a wink, he said, "Ahh, that's much, much better."

In spite of the fact that he didn't know the audible difference between a French horn and a cello, for that moment, Peter Falk was the Maestro!

As he stepped down from the podium, he waved a salute goodbye to the band.

I went on to score another *Columbo* movie later that year for Peter. He was just great to be around, and to this day, as far as I'm concerned, Peter Falk and Columbo were one and the same person.

Around that time, Milton Brown came out for a visit and a writing trip. We'd try to organize several of those each year so we could work together in person. Milton was good friends with a British gentleman named Bob Mercer, who happened to be an A&R executive with EMI. Bob was also married to Margie Buffett, who had been divorced for some time from Jimmy Buffett. Milton and Jimmy were lifelong friends from their hometown of Mobile, Alabama, and Milton had always stayed friendly with Margie after their breakup. So, when she married Bob, Milton became friends with him as well.

While Milton was out on this trip he got a fairly urgent call from Bob, asking if they could meet while they were both coincidentally in L.A. Milton asked Bob if I could come along as well, and Bob said, "Please—in fact, I'd love to speak with you both about a project I have that you might be interested in writing a song for."

We met at the Polo Lounge at the Beverly Hills Hotel the next day. Bob was putting the music together for a new film by the Academy Award–winning director John Schlesinger. It was called *Honky Tonk Freeway*. It was kind of a zany comedic road picture, a forerunner to the successful *Cannonball Run* movies that Burt Reynolds would star in years later. Bob wanted us to write the title song for the movie. He needed the song very quickly, and he didn't have a big budget for us to write it.

What else was new?

Not having an agent at the table, I skirted around, trying to feel out what he wanted to pay us.

"Well, what do you guys need, money-wise, to make this work?" Bob asked.

Thinking I had him where I wanted him, I blurted out, "How about twelve thousand dollars as a creative fee?"

"Really?" He seemed kind of taken aback, and I was sure I had just priced us out of the gig.

There was a moment of uncomfortable silence before he shot back,

"Okay. Twelve thousand it is." He grinned. "Honestly, I was prepared to offer you fifteen thousand, but yes, twelve thousand is better," he added, in his most polished British accent.

As I was silently cursing myself out, Bob continued. "Oh, and George Martin will be producing the soundtrack, with the Little River Band singing your song. Are you in?"

"Is the pope catholic?" Milton replied.

"Does a bear shit in the woods?" I added.

We were thrilled. Now, as far as I am concerned, there are record producers, great record producers, elite record producers, and there is George Martin. And it was going to be impossible for me to not ask him four billion questions about the Beatles recordings that he had probably already been asked five billion times.

Milton and I finished the song in the next few days, did a quick work-tape demo with me singing, and played it for Bob, who was still in L.A. Bob loved it and played it for Mr. Schlesinger, who also "liked it very much." We were a go.

George was also writing the score for the movie and was coming to Los Angeles to do the recording, in addition to producing our track for the Little River Band to sing in Australia. Upon arriving in L.A., he asked to have a meeting to discuss possible studios and musicians. He liked the song so much that he invited me to coproduce the track with him, as he was handling so many other recording chores at the same time.

I suggested a studio I really liked in the Valley owned by Gordon Mills and Tom Jones, Britannia Studios. I had been working there quite a bit, and I was familiar with it. George seemed to like it as well. I also suggested a great rhythm section of Ed Green on drums, Joe Chemay on bass, John Hobbs on keys, and Billy Joe Walker on guitars.

It was an incredible session.

George was a master. He was filled with fluid creative ideas that made a fairly simple song sound somewhat complicated. He and I spent a lot of time talking about film music, and I actually ended up doing a few rescore cues for the film after George returned to England. A couple of film sequences were re-edited after George's scoring sessions, and since I knew the music well, I was asked to write a few new cues.

The end result for Milton's and my song was a little surprising, as the Little River Band ended up not finishing the record. Russell Smith, the talented lead vocalist for the Amazing Rhythm Aces, came in at the last minute to sing the title song. Neither the film nor the song did much box-office business, but in the end the experience of getting to know Sir George was all that really mattered. We kept in touch over the years, and on two different occasions while I was in London, I stopped by Air Studios to have tea with him.

He was a lovely man, and an unparalleled giant in the world of recorded music.

And, yes, over tea one rare quiet afternoon in his office, he showed me the quartet sketch of "Eleanor Rigby," and I asked him just a few of those four billion questions.

19

Céline Dion's Miracle

Next to Sir George Martin, I'd have to say that, in my opinion, David Foster is the greatest record producer of our time. His versatility, musicianship, and arranging skills, as well as his remarkable piano playing, puts him in a class of his own.

David and I got to Los Angeles at roughly the same time. We met on many recording sessions, our kids went to school together for a time, and over the years we have remained friendly and even got to work together on a very special Céline Dion project.

We both did a BMI-sponsored concert event in the early eighties, and after the show, at a cocktail reception, David introduced me to his wife, Linda Thompson, and suggested that the two of us get together and write. I remember it taking a while before we could get our schedules to jibe with each other, but finally we set a day to meet and possibly collaborate.

Linda had several lyrical ideas that she read to me from a notebook, but there was one in particular that I just loved. It was called "A Little Thing Called Life." Linda's lyric was like this beautifully laid-out poem, its form perfectly symmetrical to write a melody to. On our first writing session together, we wrote a really amazing song.

Linda played a little work tape for David, and he suggested we use a singer named Warren Wiebe to do the demo. David discovered Warren, and I often tell people he was the most brilliant singer I have ever worked with, bar none.

I did a piano track the day before our vocal session. We were to meet at David's studio in Malibu at 7 p.m., and I arrived early. As I got out of my car, I saw a rather large person pacing and muttering to himself. I was immediately on guard. He was a pretty large dude with a handlebar mustache and a ponytail, and he didn't seem like he had it all together. I thought maybe he was an assistant, an engineer, or maybe the janitor.

He finally stopped muttering, acknowledged me, and asked if I was Steve Dorff. I said yes, and he introduced himself as Warren Wiebe. Admittedly, I was a bit taken aback, as I wasn't quite expecting him to look or act like he did.

As we waited, I was sure that there had been some kind of mistake, or that David was pulling a prank on me. This guy definitely did not look or act like a professional singer. Warren was kind of hyper; he repeated himself often and spoke in a childlike, high-pitched tone. It was terribly disconcerting, and I was just a tad worried.

Linda got there shortly after, and we went out to the studio piano, where I played the song for Warren and was prepared to go over it until he was ready to try and sing it. After listening to it twice, he told us that he was ready. Now I was really concerned. Who learns a brand new song after only hearing it twice?

Warren Wiebe, that's who.

What happened next is something I will remember for the rest of my life. In one take, Warren sang the song as if he had sung it his entire life. His singing voice magically transformed into the richest, most beautiful angelic tone I had ever heard. With tears streaming down my face as a result of his performance, I just shrugged and said, "We're done."

For the next six years, until his tragic and untimely death, I wouldn't do a demo of a new song without Warren Wiebe. We had lots of laughs in the studio. It took a while, but once you got to really know him, he was a funny, charming musical genius. He could sing the phone book and make it sound romantic. At Warren's beautiful funeral service, David honored Linda and me as they played Warren's version of "A Little Thing Called Life" to close the service and put him to rest.

Aaron Neville recorded a beautiful version of the song, as did several other artists, but it is Warren's recording that made the song what it is.

Linda and I went on to have quite a bit of success together with the theme to Kevin Costner's movie *Tin Cup*, "This Could Take All Night," and "Miracle (Who Could Ever Love You More)," the title song of Céline Dion's *Miracle* project.

I really enjoy working with Linda because she's always got a great idea coming in the door as a jumping-off place. We don't have to spend a whole lot of time wondering what we're going to write about, because there's usually a really good verse or chorus lyric already started.

One afternoon, Linda came over to the house to work on a song. As was usual, we spent the first thirty minutes catching up, talking about the kids, our relationships, gossip, and dirt until we finally got around to business. Linda told me that Céline Dion was looking to do a lullaby album to celebrate the birth of her first child, René-Charles. David Foster was the masterful producer of most of Céline's giant hits, and he and Linda were close, lifelong friends of Céline and her husband, René. Céline had gone through a much-publicized struggle to get pregnant, and having this beautiful child was the most important moment of their lives.

"Let's write a lullaby for Céline's baby," she said. "I have a nice title idea, 'Who Could Ever Love You More.'"

I can always tell when I love a great title, because instantly I start to hear a melody, or the feeling of what the shape of the music should be. In this case, that is exactly what happened. Linda threw out a few opening lines:

> *You know, you're the reason I was born,*
> *There is nothing you could ever do to make me stop loving you.*

Linda then said to me, "All we have to do is think about what our children mean to us." Those words immediately struck home. It was universal. With four kids of my own, including baby Kaitlyn, who was less than a year old, I totally related.

Linda excused herself to go to the bathroom and left me sitting at the piano by myself. By the time she got back a few minutes later, I had something to play her. The melody for this one simply fell out of the sky. Thankfully it was my hands that were hitting the keys.

Linda just loved the melody, and the lyric came just as fast. We had the song written in less than an hour.

We both had chills.

We wanted get this demoed ASAP for Céline to hear. Linda had a great idea: we would put a CD of the demo in a baby basket filled with baby clothes, bibs, teething rings, and a few crib toys, and send it to her in Florida, where she was living. I did a nice, simple piano/vocal demo, with Kellie Coffey singing. Linda put together a beautiful basket with a touching note and sent it to Céline and René.

Within a few days of receiving it, Céline got in touch with Linda and told her she was completely in love with the song. She had only one request: she wanted to call our song "Miracle (Who Could Ever Love You More)," because she considered little René-Charles their miracle, and she wanted to name the album after our song.

We were absolutely thrilled. What made it even better was that David then called me to tell me how much he loved the song.

He then asked me who was playing the piano on the demo.

"Me," I said. "Why?"

"Do you have the MIDI files?"

"I think so, but surely you're going to recut the piano yourself?"

He really liked the magic of the demo, and the key was perfect for Céline, so he offered to have me coproduce the track with him. I was beyond honored. I went out to his studio a few days later, and David laid down a bass part, a Rhodes overdub, and a pad. Dean Parks came in and, as always, put a beautiful gut-string guitar part on the track.

Céline was now in Montreal, and we did the vocal by synching up Pro Tools over the phone lines. We monitored Céline on a TV screen. Every vocal take was impeccable. Céline's voice is simply a magnificent instrument.

After about eight or nine takes, David said, "That's a keeper."

In reality, each one was a keeper: he had plenty of amazing lines to comp from.

It would be a few weeks until we put an orchestra on the track, as David wanted to have a few more songs finished before the orchestra session. The fabulous Bill Ross would be doing the orchestral arrangement, and I was so happy about that. I thought the possibilities for this project were limitless.

The session was set for September 12, 2001.

And then we all woke up to the horrific event of September 11.

I, like most Americans, was numb and glued to the television most of that day. It was late in the afternoon when I got a call saying that the session on the 12th would go ahead as scheduled. The financial penalty for canceling would have been prohibitive, and we figured if the world was going to end, we might as well go out with beautiful music and finish the project.

The session the next day was eerie. The players were all assembled, and it was hard for anyone to concentrate or talk about anything other than what the past twenty-four hours had been like for our country. And we were all justifiably scared of what might happen next.

When Bill finally went to the podium and began to rehearse the orchestra, something quite beautiful happened. For those next few hours, we were all enveloped by the sound and joy of the music we were hearing played by this incredible sixty-five-piece orchestra. There were tears everywhere, and it was unlike any session I had ever experienced or will ever experience again. The entire session was fueled by a collective emotion of love and compassion. We all felt that way, including the players. In the control room, we were all hugging and telling each other that we would be okay. Everyone crammed into the control room listening to the playback of our song.

It was, indeed, a miracle.

When the album was released, accompanied by a beautiful full-color coffee-table book featuring Anne Geddes's photographs, it was as proud a moment as any I have ever had in this business. It represented much more than just having a song recorded by a world-class artist and one of the greatest voices of all time. The album itself is a timeless masterpiece of David Foster's making, and what we all had to endure that terrible, tragic day in September.

Linda and I have remained good friends over the years and have written some beautiful songs together. Just recently, she published her memoir, and I was thrilled that she called it A Little Thing Called Life.

20

LUNCH

———

EVERYTHING WAS GOING GREAT . . . until I ran into a dancer in Michigan.

During the big writers' strike in 1988, I was juggling six successful TV shows and I had to take a break. No one could work. I was definitely not one to cross the picket lines, so I decided to use my time productively: I collaborated on a musical with Rick Hawkins, a successful showrunner (*Mama's Family*, *Major Dad*, *The Carol Burnett Show*), and my longtime collaborator John Bettis.

Rick came up with the idea for *Lunch*, five stories that take place during the same lunch hour in New York City. We wrote the musical and got backing for a soft opening at the Cherry County Playhouse in Muskegan, Michigan. We got a terrific cast, including Brian Stokes Mitchell in his first stage musical gig, and Barney Martin, Jerry's dad on *Seinfeld*.

During dance auditions, something happened for which I was not prepared. Amid the countless dancers, one particularly leggy dancer auditioned, and my world stopped. I had seen those legs before. They were in the George Michael video "Faith." Being a leg man, I remember watching that video and thinking, "Boy, I would love to see what is attached to that."

Two years later, the woman walked into my audition room.

———

"The one in the back with the curly hair," I said to John. "What's her name?"

He thumbed through the pile of headshots.

"Lori."

"Okay, we gotta hire Lori."

"She's trouble."

"Great. Let's hire her."

In addition to having legs that ran forever, Lori was an exotic beauty who I definitely wanted to get to know better. Part Lebanese, part Irish, she was a tall gymnast who was extremely flexible. We went to Michigan, and I had a crazy affair with her. I had been married twenty-three years, and my boys were seventeen and fifteen. Meanwhile, Rick had also been married twenty-three years with four kids, and John had been married fifteen years.

A total of sixty-one years of marriage and six kids.

We did a regional run.

I fell in love with a chorus girl.

Rick fell in love with the male director.

John came home from being on the road, and his wife had emptied the house and left.

Nancy moved out of the house, but first she smashed every gold record I had.

Our collective worlds were turned upside down both professionally and personally.

When Nancy and I went through our divorce in 1995, it was the beginning of an extremely difficult time for me. I have always thought of my career as this rollercoaster ride, with its unexpected highs, lows, and sharp careening turns. With the divorce, the wheels had definitely come off the track emotionally, and, as a result, my career got stuck in some serious lows and sharp turns. I felt as if everything I was trying to do creatively was just a fraction out of sync.

After just about every pilot I had scored for television got picked up for a series run, I now did six or seven in a row that weren't even getting past the pilot phase. Songs that were on hold for artists with whom I had previous successes were either not making the albums or not getting cut at all.

The pain, sadness, and confusion caused by our breakup took a terrible toll on our family. My son Stephen was justifiably furious with me. My younger son, Andrew, was scared and confused, as well he should have been, because, to be honest, I was scared and confused, too.

After twenty-three years, I totally felt like a small boat lost in a turbulent ocean. The security of my home and family had been shattered, and although there were many extenuating circumstances and reasons behind our split, it was I who had taken the selfish turn in the road that brought our marriage to an end.

For almost two years, I was fairly consumed by the upside-down nature of the divorce proceedings, therapy, repairing my frayed relationships with friends and family, and, most importantly, trying to stay close to my sons. Whether or not I was truly cognizant of it at the time, my career suffered as a result of the upheaval my life was going through.

Shortly after the divorce was final, I got engaged to Lori. We were married seven months later, and we began what I had hoped would be the healing process we all needed. After having an early term miscarriage four months into the marriage, Lori became pregnant again, and this time everything was looking good. On a visit to her doctor at about six months, we were asked if we wanted to know the sex of the baby. I held my breath and said yes. When she told us it was a little girl, I cried tears of joy. In addition to being so thankful for the chance to experience being a dad to a little girl, I had hoped that bringing Callie Dorff into the world might just be the event that would also bring acceptance, forgiveness, and healing to my entire family.

If there was one thing in this world Nancy loved more than anything, it was children. Nancy was one of the first people to come visit Callie when we brought her home from the hospital, and it was an emotional and beautiful moment for all of us. Two and a half years later, my second daughter, Kaitlyn Hannah, was born. Once again, Nancy was there to help and love both of our girls. From then on, we were invited to every Thanksgiving, every Christmas, as one extended family. Nancy truly loved Callie and Kaitlyn as if they were her own. The gift of healing had touched us all.

Things began to get better on all fronts after Kaitlyn was born. Shortly after we brought Kaitlyn home from the hospital, it became apparent that we needed some help with the baby. Lori was battling a bout of postpartum depression, which she hadn't experienced with Callie, and was struggling to keep everything together with the house as well as an infant and a toddler. We found a wonderful woman named Martha who would become like a second mom to all of us for the next fourteen years. Martha was the platinum standard of a nanny to our girls, and is one of the most selfless, decent people I have ever known.

We moved to a beautiful house in Hidden Hills, California, which would prove a wonderful place to raise the girls. Although she was still suffering from the depression, Lori was excited for a fresh start in a new home, and we were both looking forward to making new friends in new surroundings. Little did I know that some of her "new friends" would be the beginning of the end for us.

The Hidden Hills community was nicknamed "Horses and Divorces," and for a good reason. Sometime during our sixth year of living there, Lori was befriended by several women, whom I will refer to as the Misery Loves Company bunch. They will remain nameless to protect the guilty. If they are indeed reading this book, and I hope they are, they are well aware of who they are.

All of these women were walking clichés . . . Stepford wives who were fairly miserable with their own lives, often cheating on their husbands, possessing a universal jealousy of any woman prettier and happier than they were.

And, trust me, Lori was a lot prettier and happier.

They derived their desperate relevancy and self-importance from bringing other women into their club in order to have someone new to jump off the cliff with. The women were snakes who slid out of their houses at 8 a.m. in full makeup, with their coffee klatches, to go on trail walks while spreading rumors and giving bad advice. They were filled with toxicity and anger that spread like a biohazard of which even the CDC would have been wary.

Unfortunately, Lori fell prey to their shenanigans—innocently at first, but nonetheless it was deadly for our relationship. I knew exactly what was happening, and although I tried to communicate to Lori what was so obvious to me and everyone else around us, it landed on deaf ears. I was all of a sudden the bad guy, trying to get between her and her new "soul mates."

I watched and lived that movie, and it was apparent that our marriage was quickly heading south.

I suppose, in retrospect, I wasn't really blindsided, as I saw and felt it coming for a period of six months with these devious twits she called her friends. Yet I was shocked and bitterly disappointed that after all the sacrifice I had gone through with Nancy and my boys, that now the poison spewed by these ignorant women was the reason for another divorce. It was unfathomable.

My daughters were barely six and four, and I knew how devastating this would be for them. Lori began to go to therapy with a woman that was recommended to her by one of "the club." It was time for me to make a last-ditch effort to try to salvage this mess. I agreed to attend a joint therapy session with one of the biggest charlatans I have ever met in my life.

How she ever got a degree as a therapist will forever be a mystery to me. After the second therapy session with Dr. Disaster, I knew the situation was hopeless.

Later, after Lori and I had one of the most inane conversations of my entire lifetime, the writing was clearly on the wall. I tried one more time for my girls' sake to convince her that these women were toxic, had no other motive than to derive self-importance from invading her life, and, most importantly, would probably vanish from the scene within a year after they had accomplished their mission. Once again ... deaf ears.

As I predicted, the misery bunch vanished from Lori's life, having undoubtedly found some new victims or eaten themselves into oblivion. Probably both. They can go to hell for all I care—not for what they put me personally through, but for what they put my innocent daughters through at such young ages.

I had no other choice than to file for divorce.

The hardest part for me this time around was making sure that my girls' best interests came first. Fortunately, the proceedings went quickly and, under the circumstances, as well as possible. I didn't much care for Lori's attorney, but in the mood I was in I suppose I would have hated any attorney opposing me.

The adjustment to being a single dad to two young daughters would be one of the toughest yet most rewarding things I've ever done. We agreed to joint custody, and I stayed in my house in Hidden Hills, while the girls and Lori moved to a condo nearby. Helping them move out was the saddest day of my life, and yet somehow, during that sleepless first night alone, I wrote one of the most meaningful songs of my career, which I knew would never get recorded because it was too personal.

After about a year, at my son Stephen's urging, I sold the house and moved to Malibu. I found a great three-level condo on the beach. My studio was on the lowest level, a sliding glass door from the sand. My daughters loved it there, and they would spend as much time as possible with me. After being married for my entire adult life, some thirty-one years, I was single, living in paradise with four beautiful kids. I was starting a brand new chapter of the journey, and although I was still hurting from not having my girls with me 24/7, I felt like we were all going to be okay.

The next two years flew by. I loved being in Malibu, eating regularly at Nobu, staying busy with new projects, and meeting a lot of women who were either going through or had been through what I had. It was an interesting time, to say the least.

On one beautiful July 3 afternoon, I was in the ocean with Callie and Kaitlyn. We were playing in the waves and having fun. The undertow was a bit stronger than usual, so I was keeping the girls fairly close to the shore. I was in water up to my waist when I heard someone yell out, "Look out for this one!"

I turned and saw a humongous rogue wave approaching. In a split second I determined that I was not going to negotiate trying to dive under this one. Instead, I would run for my life to the shore. I took two steps against the unusually strong pull of the undertow and felt like I had either been shot, hit by a rock, or bitten by a shark in my right calf muscle. I went down immediately, got totally smashed by the seven-foot wave, and felt like I was in a washing machine for about twenty seconds, until being beached like a dead whale.

My terrified daughters ran over to me and asked, "Daddy, are you okay?"

I slowly got up, took a step, and collapsed on the beach. I couldn't put any weight on my right leg. A friend saw me and ran over to see if he could help. With his aid, I slowly hopped to my house, and he offered to take me over to urgent care, as it was apparent that something was very wrong.

We dropped the girls off at Stephen's house down the beach and then went directly to Malibu Urgent Care. The doctor checked me out and determined, without an MRI, that I had torn either my calf muscle or my Achilles tendon. Because it was the July 4th weekend, the specialist she wanted me to see in Santa Monica had gone on holiday, and short of going to a hospital and sitting in emergency for six hours, she put me in a cast as if it was the Achilles that would require surgery. She then gave me a shot of something for the pain that was so potent it temporarily sent me to another planet.

I remember little of the next few hours, how I got home, or what had happened. When I finally "woke up," I was on my living room couch with my leg elevated. The front door was wide open, the refrigerator was open, and chicken bones and cheese were littered all over the kitchen floor. The whole day had become something out of a surreal Fellini film. I have no idea how the news spread, but I started receiving calls from friends to see if I needed help or food.

My friend Laurie Seigman, who is in the party events and catering business, thought it would be fun to send over two cute twenty-something girls with wine, cheese, pizza, and sandwiches for me. They brought enough food for fifty people, and I was still out of my mind, buzzed from whatever that shot was that the doctor gave me. One of the girls, Amy Handelman, was a delightful, intelligent, and sweet person who was interested in show business. A few days later, when I was a bit more coherent, I called Laurie to thank her, and asked if Amy might be interested in working for me as my personal assistant.

Amy had moved to Los Angeles from the suburbs of Detroit, Michigan, to become an actress, and was working as a hostess at a Hollywood restaurant. Luckily for me, she agreed to my offer, and for the next seven years she became a part of our family. Her contributions to my career, and to helping me with my girls, were invaluable. I still often say, "Geez, where's Amy when I need her?" when I get frustrated trying to multitask at things that I'm not very good at in the first place. I'm happy to say that Amy has gone on to a successful casting and acting career.

I finally got to the orthopedic doctor on July 5. I had the MRI and spent the next six weeks with a cast and boot on my torn calf. I didn't need surgery. It was a crazy ordeal, but I never would have met Amy if I had successfully dived under that wave. Funny how the slightest of decisions affects our destiny.

With the girls getting older and more involved in school and activities, and having less time to go back and forth to Malibu, I decided to buy a house closer to them, so I could be in their lives much more frequently. Lori had become engaged and was going to get married and be based in Orange County, so she was selling her house. I saw the inevitable coming. Rather than do the back-and-forth thing, we decided that the girls would have more stability, and be happier living in one place: they would live with me full time. It worked out to be the best decision I ever made for the girls and me. Lori and I have a good, friendly relationship, which I think, in the big picture, has benefitted all of us.

A year before I met Lori, she was doing a dance gig for Adidas at the Trump Hotel in Atlantic City. Donald Trump had seen her and told one of his wingmen to invite her up to his suite after the show. Being fairly naive, Lori thought Trump would possibly invest in her singing career, accepted . . . but brought along six of her dancer friends. He offered to help her with her career by introducing her to high-end people he knew. She said no because she had a boyfriend.

She didn't leave her boyfriend for Trump . . . but later she left her boyfriend for me.

Looking at today's politics, I'm not quite sure she made the right decision—or then again, maybe she did!

21

The Assistants

I have always considered myself to be adept at multitasking.

I had never really had a personal assistant of my own. When things started to get busy for me on the television/film front, it became pretty evident that I needed some extra help to get me through the daily grind.

When I first got to Warner/Chappell, I was given an office on the executive floor. There was a receptionist working at the front reception desk named Debbie Datz who had recently made the move to L.A. from New York. Mostly manning phones and distributing messages, Debbie felt like she needed to do more.

I was starting to get unbelievably busy in the studio, with both recording and TV/film projects. Often, I had to be in three places at one time, and I was in desperate need of someone to point me in the right direction, take accurate messages, and, in general, help assist me in getting a daily laundry list of stuff handled.

Debbie quit her job as receptionist and started to work for me full-time.

At first, Debbie would work out of my office at Warners, but since she lived near me in Studio City, it became easier for her to just be based out of the house. Basically, she would follow me to sessions, do a lot of the necessary paperwork, help Nancy and me driving the boys to various after-school activities, make calls, return calls, and run all kinds of errands. Debbie became a member of our family. She was single, didn't know too many people in L.A., and was eager to learn the music business.

Eventually, since Debbie was familiar with all of the musicians and studios that I used, I began to have her help do my session contracting for me. I had been using Patti Fidelibus Zimitti to do all of my television and film dates, and Debbie and Patti had become friends. I was averaging about five sessions per week, and together they would coordinate who was playing on which session at what studio.

As time passed, I sensed that Debbie didn't want to do all of the other "stuff" that I needed her to do. Her passion had become music contracting, and she wanted to do it full-time. After four years of working for me, we parted ways, and she and Patti went into business together. They were successful for many years as maybe the busiest contractors in town.

I had gotten to know Debbie's family well over the years, and her brother Glen is still a great friend to our family. After Debbie left to go to work with Patti, I went without an assistant for a while. It was a difficult transition for me to make. I'd been spoiled by having someone there to help me deal with unexpected things as they came up.

John Bettis had an assistant, Steve Cassling, whom Debbie and I had become close with through our working relationship with John. Steve had recently left John to pursue his acting career, and in talking with him one day, he said he wouldn't mind having a part-time job as my assistant if I was interested.

Boy, was I ever.

There was a natural camaraderie between Steve and me that made my life a lot easier. Steve was also amazingly smart, talented, and incredibly thorough. We had a shorthand: he was one step ahead of me in knowing what needed to be done, and, much like me, he was a stickler for detail.

What started as a part-time "let's see where this goes" job became a valued four years together. Steve helped me get through the tough period of my divorce to Nancy. He was a good friend to all of us.

After Steve left, first to pursue his acting and then to move to Big Bear with his family, I went through several male assistants in the hope that I could find another Steve. I was totally spoiled. Nobody worked out. I was now remarried and had my two daughters and was living out in Hidden Hills, balancing home life and career pretty evenhandedly. But you eventually miss what you don't have, and when Amy Handelman serendipitously came into my life, I was thrilled to have an assistant again.

The great thing about Amy was that she possessed all of the best qualities of Debbie and Steve rolled into one. I could talk to her about anything, anytime . . . except maybe politics: girl stuff, guy stuff, kid stuff. It was all on the table.

Amy did everything for me, from making trip reservations to banking, taking my clothes to the cleaners, phone calls, girl advice, dog care, even making me hard-boiled eggs in the morning when she got to the house. It was a different time in my life as I was single for the first time in thirty years, and my schedule and lifestyle had adjusted to that.

Amy was a godsend . . . but we had some pretty crazy episodes along the way.

We had just recently moved back from Malibu and into my new house in Bell Canyon. One morning I was showing Amy around the house, explaining a few things that she would need to get done for me that day. I had to leave for an appointment. I gave her the list of things to do and went out to get into my car, which was parked right by the front door. As I shut the door to the house, I noticed something move behind my car. It freaked me out a little as I thought it might have been a coyote. I approached the car slowly, and then all of a sudden a giant peacock with full colored feathers was standing by my car door.

"What the fuck?" was all I could say. I had only seen one of these before at the zoo. I ran back into the house and screamed, "Amy, you've gotta see this, come quick!"

Amy came running down the stairs, alarmed that something bad had happened.

"There's a peacock standing next to my car!"

She looked at me, unsure how to respond. I certainly hadn't put "peacock wrangler" in the job description. Still, she followed me outside as I gingerly walked back toward my car . . . where there was no peacock.

Amy looked at me like I was either insane or hallucinating.

"Trust me, I'm not crazy, there was a fucking peacock the size of my Golden Retriever Maggie, right here!"

"I'm sure there was," she said, rolling her eyes, and then added, "I'm going to get started now, okay?" She went back into the house.

Now I was wondering if I was indeed crazy and hallucinating. I looked all around and there, up on the driveway hill about thirty feet away, I saw the peacock behind a tree.

I barged back into the house, screaming, "There he is."

Amy came outside again and looked to where I had been pointing. No peacock.

"Shit, he must've gone over that hill, get in the car."

Now, even writing this, I realize how deranged I must have sounded. Frankly, I'm surprised she even got into the car with me. But she did.

"I'm going to find that damn thing!" I said, speeding down my driveway. I was acting like a madman, and Amy just buckled her seatbelt and hung on.

We drove around the neighborhood until he finally decided to show himself to Amy.

She saw him first and screamed, "Holy shit, there it is."

We watched the peacock walk around for a minute and then it disappeared over a hill and out of sight.

I wondered if we should call someone or get my dog to try to catch it.

"It's gone, Steve," Amy said dryly. "Now take me back to the house and go on your appointment, which you are now late for, by the way."

I heard somewhere that the usual burnout time for a personal assistant job in this town is between two and four years. Amy was my indispensable right arm for seven years.

Most artists don't give their assistants enough credit, but it would be nearly impossible to do our work without them. Whether they are full-time or part-time, assistants are indispensable. Usually they are on their own journeys toward fulfilling their personal goals, but while they work in an assistant capacity, they are confidantes, soundboards, girl Fridays, wizards, helpers, and gatekeepers. Because sometimes it is hard to suss out the crazies from the legitimate artists . . . and they all come a-calling.

22

Damn Near Righteous

———

Every few months, I get a cold call from a writer I'm not familiar with who is interested in writing a song with me.

Usually, I can tell in a few minutes whether this is a person I might want to work with or not. I know how important chemistry is for me, and getting in a room with someone I don't know, just to try and churn out a song, usually has not worked for me. However, there was something different about this caller. This guy had a deep baritone voice that drew me in immediately.

"Steve Dorff? My name's Bobby Tomberlin, and I'm a songwriter with Curb Publishing company in Nashville. I've been a longtime admirer of your work and I'm coming to L.A. and thought what have I got to lose, I'm gonna call Steve Dorff and possibly see if I could write a song with you . . . or at least meet you."

He spoke without stopping and then paused, waiting for my response.

Normally, I'd make excuses. My standard line is "I tend to write with the same people." But there was something about this guy I liked that I couldn't quite put my finger on. I suppose I appreciated his sincerity, so we made a plan for when he got out here.

My instinct was right. Bobby was a joy to work with. We initially wrote two songs and enjoyed the whole experience. Since then, we've gone on to write many songs together, including the Barbra Streisand/ Blake Shelton duet "I'd Want It to Be You" on her *Partners* duets album and "Dream Big" for *Pure Country II.*

Bobby's become one of my best and most trusted friends over the years. To my sons and daughters, he's a member of the family. Even though our backgrounds and upbringings were vastly different, we have always had this commonality to the way we look at life, love, and music. We've both shared sorrow and disappointment, and have always been there to support each other during those times.

Bobby was also the key catalyst for me getting back behind the piano and doing shows again.

"Steve, man, you play so great and sing so well, why don't you perform?"

With a little bit of encouragement, I did, and he's often joined me in my shows, doing duets, kibitzing, and singing his own songs. When I was the music director of *The Singing Bee*, Bobby helped me to get to the point where I could own that and not be self-conscious. I made him one of the singers on the show, and he did all fifty episodes with me.

From time to time, Bobby would do a live radio broadcast with guest writers and performers. On one occasion, he invited me to Muscle Shoals, Alabama, to go on his *Writers in the Round* show along with Bill LaBounty. Bill and I had known each other from years before in Los Angeles, and after he moved to Nashville, we had an opportunity to write a few songs together.

I hadn't done a whole lot of these *Writers in the Round* events, and it was somewhere in the middle of the show when Bill played one of his newer unrecorded songs called "Sit Down and Hurt." The song absolutely blew me away. After the show, I asked Bill if I could have a copy of it. I told him I would love to send it to an artist I had been working with.

I knew the song would be absolutely perfect for Bill Medley.

Bill Medley and I had first worked together in 1988 on a TV theme song John Bettis and I wrote for *Just the 10 Of Us*, a spinoff comedy from the hit series *Growing Pains*. The show starred standup comedian Bill Kirchenbauer, who played Coach Lubbock, a regular on *Growing Pains*, as the father of eight kids.

Medley sang the theme song, "Doin' It the Best I Can." I was always such a fan of the Righteous Brothers, going back to when I first saw them on *Shindig!*, so when we were thinking of someone great to sing the theme, Bill was our first choice.

A few years later, we would work together again on the main title song for the Bruce Willis film *The Last Boy Scout*. Bill did such a great job singing our song "Friday Night's a Great Night for Football" that the director, Tony Scott, decided to film Bill doing the song and use it over the opening credits as well as the closing credits.

Bill and I kept in touch here and there after that. Although he had done some solo work, he and Bobby Hatfield continued to tour as the famed Righteous Brothers. Tragically, Bobby passed away while out on the road.

It had been a good while since I had been in touch with Bill, but he was always accessible to me, and because we had had such a friendly and successful working relationship in the past, he was always open to hearing anything I might send him.

An opportunity came up when a close friend of mine since college, Shayne Fair, sent some lyrics for me to look at called "The California Goodbye." I fell in love with the words and knew I just had to write the music, and that it was a song that I just had to get Bill Medley to sing.

The underlying theme of the song was that it was a tribute to Bobby, and Bill agreed to record it. It was an absolutely stunning and emotional vocal that Bill did. I was hoping that we could find more songs and record an entire Bill Medley album, but the timing just didn't feel right—and, besides, we didn't have the material that would define him as the great solo artist that he is in his own right. Yet as soon as I heard Bill LaBounty's "Sit Down and Hurt," I felt like that song could be the catalyst for getting Bill Medley back in the studio.

I called Bill Medley and asked him to listen to the song. He listened, and he flipped over it as I'd hoped he would. LaBounty had some other great songs that helped create the direction we took with a new studio album that I arranged and produced along with Shayne. Bill Medley was very enthused about the project, and we began recording a bluesy, R&B, rootsy album of some great songs that he wanted to do. One of the songs was the Beach Boys classic "In My Room," for which Bill was able to get Brian Wilson and Phil Everly to come in and do background vocals.

A Beach Boy, an Everly Brother, and a Righteous Brother, all singing together. It was epic.

We tracked the album at Capitol Studios in Hollywood with a sensational rhythm section of Vinnie Colaiuta on drums, Jimmy Nichols on keys, Dean Parks and George Doering on guitars, and Joe Chemay on bass, plus a full orchestra and the Waters doing backing vocals. The only thing left to do was to think of a title. Bill was pretty adamant that he did not want to reference the Righteous Brothers on this project.

Over lunch one day, we were discussing the album and throwing out various title ideas. Somebody said, "Bill, it's your album, not a Righteous Brothers–sounding record at all."

Bill stopped, thought for a minute, and replied, "Well, it's damn near righteous."

We had our album title.

I was the house bandleader on The Singing Bee, *a hugely popular TV show on the CMT network. Going into it, I was pretty petrified to be on screen and featured as a performer. Thankfully, producer Phil Gurin allowed me to put a band and a group of studio singers together—all people I had previously worked with in some capacity.*

Being surrounded by familiar faces made the project a lot of fun. What was initially going to be ten episodes turned into fifty over a period of four years. I made some long-lasting friendships with Melissa Peterman, Roger Cain, Beau Davidson, and the other members of the cast and crew, as well as having some great adventures with Bobby along the way. Being in front of the camera and getting recognition out of the studio went a long way to making it possible for me to gain the confidence to start doing my "Evenings with Steve Dorff."

23

Pure Country

I TRULY BELIEVE that the marriage between a great song and the right artist is the key to having a hit.

There is no better example of mine than George Strait's version of "I Cross My Heart." Eight years before George recorded it and made it a country standard, Bette Midler had recorded it. The legendary producer Arif Mardin heard the demo, loved the song, and told me he was going to make it a huge hit with Bette.

Eric Kaz and I couldn't have been more excited. Bette was amazing, Arif was a world-class arranger/producer, and the song was strong. How could we miss?

We missed . . . big time.

To her credit, Bette loved the song, but after singing it several times she just didn't feel like it was the right fit for her at the time. As disappointed as I was, after hearing a rough mix I had to agree.

Losing a Bette Midler cut was pretty devastating. A perfect example of that fine line between glorious success and dismal failure that we songwriters experience all too often. It made me want to invent a career called "songwriter therapy" just so I could attend a few sessions.

I was still passionate about the song, though, and for the next eight years I played "I Cross My Heart" for anyone and everyone who would listen. The universal response was: "Nice song, Steve, but not one of your best."

I even played it for my mother, who of course unconditionally loved anything I wrote. She also said, "Nice song, Steve, but not one of your best."

The mediocre responses made me question myself. Perhaps I was hung up on a song that simply wasn't as good as I thought it was. So I put it on the backburner.

Temporarily.

Cut to me reading the shooting script for *Pure Country*, a film I was hired to score and write a few songs for. The film was to star George Strait as a huge country star named Dusty Wyatt Chandler. Disillusioned by the fabricated glitz and glamour that his career has become, Dusty yearns to return home to his simple country roots. It was a good screenplay by Rex McGee, to be directed by Christopher Cain.

This was a dream project for me to get. As in most television or film projects, the process of picking the composer is highly competitive, and usually quite political. Each of the principal players or executives has relationships with various composers with whom they have worked previously. Gary Lemel, then president of music for Warner Pictures, had really gone to bat for me with legendary producer Jerry Weintraub and Chris Cain. My having had prior success at Warners, and understanding of the mechanics of both the country music and feature film worlds, made me a top candidate in Gary's eyes.

Luckily, my initial meeting with director Chris Cain turned out to be the only one I would need to have.

I was a huge admirer of some of Chris's films. *The River Runs Black* and *Young Guns* were among my favorites and his director's vision and music plan for *Pure Country* were exciting and at the cutting edge for the time.

We had a great meeting at his office on the Warners lot. I got the gig. In reading through the shooting script, I knew that we needed to have certain songs picked to prerecord, which we would then film to. Therefore, the process of song selection had to happen pretty quickly in order to meet the tight production schedule.

George Strait and his record producer, Tony Brown, were picking most of the songs that would be used in the film. I wrote a few things that I thought might work for the project, but in truth, I was not thoroughly familiar yet with what really worked best musically for George. But Tony and George had already picked several really great songs for the film and soundtrack, and I could already tell this had the chance to be a groundbreaking album.

Chris called me one evening and asked me to look specifically at a scene at the end of the script that called for a poignant love song for George to sing to Harley Tucker, the female star of the movie. Nothing they had found yet really fit that moment perfectly, and it was a high priority song that he needed to find ASAP.

So he asked the $64,000 question:

"Steve, do you have anything that you've written that might work there?"

I smiled. It was as if I had been waiting for someone to ask me that question for the last eight years.

The next day, I went to Warners, sat down at the piano, and played "I Cross My Heart."

Chris called Jerry Weintraub and Gary Lemel and asked them to come over to the soundstage to hear the song he thought was the perfect choice for the film's pivotal love song. Within an hour, I was playing the song for the film's bigwigs, and they all felt like it was the song they had been waiting for. They asked me to record a demo. Jeffrey Steele, who is an amazing songwriter in his own right and a fabulous singer, was nice enough to agree to sing the demo for me. And, as he always does, he nailed it.

Chris and I then flew to Nashville to play the song for George and Tony. We first played the demo for Tony at his office at MCA records. George hadn't arrived from Texas yet and Tony was eager to hear the song. Tony listened to the first verse and chorus and stopped the tape. He was concerned that this song was not "right" for George. There were lots of internal and unusual chord progressions and voicings, an odd key change, and a very different-sounding bridge that all added up, in his mind, to a song that sounded more like a Lee Greenwood record than a George Strait record. After all, Eric Kaz and I had originally conceived and demoed it as an R&B-style song with pop changes. Even though Jeff's demo was designed to soften the pop influences, the song was still the song.

Despite Tony's reservations, somehow the country music gods were looking down on us, and when George arrived, he agreed to give the song a go. He immediately owned it with his unmistakable voice and impeccable performance, and Tony, to his credit, made a great record.

The song stayed at #1 for three weeks, and the soundtrack sold over eight million copies: a major milestone for country music from a film.

Unfortunately for Kaz and me, due to strict Motion Picture Academy rules, Bette's recording from some eight years earlier kept us from being considered for an Oscar nomination, which I think we would have easily gotten with that song.

Four million BMI performances later, CMT honored the song by naming it the ninth greatest country love song ever written. The lesson is: don't ever give up on a song you truly believe in.

Sorry, Mom, apparently it *was* one of my best.

It's not often that you're blessed with the kind of working relationship I had with Gary Lemel. Gary was a true music person, a lover of great songs, and a wonderful singer in his own right. Above all else, though, he was a straight shooter and a great executive who had the respect and love from everyone who was lucky enough to get to work with him. Thank you, Gary, for including me in so many fantastic projects!

24

End Zone Suicide

Talk about being at the right place at the right time.

Once again I got a phone call from Gary Lemel at the Warner Bros. lot. He asked me if I could come over late that afternoon and sit in on a screening of a new film starring Bruce Willis, Damon Wayans, and Halle Berry; directed by Tony Scott; and produced by Joel Silver.

It was a private screening for Hank Williams Jr., who had been asked to come in and write the main title song for the picture. Gary wanted me to produce the track on Hank Jr. It certainly sounded like it was going to be a fun star-studded project to work on.

I met Gary at his office and together we walked over to the screening room to meet Joel, who was arguably one of the hottest movie producers on the planet. A few other Warners execs were also invited, and after a few minutes of small talk we all sat down to watch the film. There was one small problem: Hank Jr. was late.

We waited for about twenty minutes, and then Hank and his wife finally came in and apologized for the delay. Joel explained a few things about the movie, which was set fictionally in the pro-football world. Hank Jr. had been riding high with his ABC *Monday Night Football* theme, which was on TV every week, so he was the obvious choice to write the song for this movie.

So everybody thought.

The lights dimmed, and the opening action sequence began with a hard-hitting game in progress during a torrential rainstorm. The way it was shot took you right into the scene as if you were one of the players in the game. It was exciting to watch and, as a longtime football fan, I was immediately hooked.

As one of the plays unfolds, a running back takes a handoff and begins to break away for a long touchdown run. Just as a defensive back from the other team is about to make a tackle, the running back pulls out a gun from under his jersey and starts to shoot the opposing players. As the player scores, he kneels down, pulls off his helmet, and proceeds to blow his own brains out . . . blackout.

It was a riveting opening action sequence that had me sitting on the edge of my seat for sure.

All of a sudden, a rather loud voice yells out, "Turn on the lights, stop the film!"

It was Hank Jr.

Gary and I looked at each other, bewildered. What in the world was going on?

Hank had a big problem with the opening scene and proceeded to tell Joel Silver that because of his affiliation with the NFL, there was no way he was going to be involved in a movie that portrayed pro football in this disgraceful and disgusting manner. He was deeply offended, and he and his wife then left rather abruptly.

We were all quite a bit stunned, and Joel Silver was pretty upset. There were several choice expletives being thrown around the room for a few minutes before Joel, chomping on a cigar and fuming, turned to Gary and said, "Now what in the fuck do we do?" He then looked at me, seemingly for the first time, and barked, "Who in the fuck is he?"

Joel clearly thought I was with Hank Jr. and wanted me out of there. This was becoming a bit of a scary nightmare scenario in itself.

I sunk further into my seat. All I really wanted was to watch the rest of the movie. I was hooked and curious to see where it was going.

Gary explained to Joel that I was the studio's choice to produce the track for the film as I had done for several of Warners pictures, including the Clint Eastwood films.

Joel relaxed a bit, puffed on his cigar and once again said, "Okay, what in the fuck are we going to do for this song we need yesterday?"

I perked up. Writing songs "due yesterday" was my specialty.

"Let's have Steve write it," Gary blurted out.

Excited for the opportunity, I dived in and suggested that we could go in a much more pop direction than Hank Jr. would have done.

Joel quickly warmed to that idea.

"Who are you thinking?" he asked.

Without hesitation I mentioned a few different artists who immediately came to mind, including the Righteous Brothers.

"I love the Righteous Brothers," Joel said. "Can you get them?"

I could.

Gary and I walked back to his office and called Bill Medley straight away. Bill got back to me later that evening and I told him the entire story. He and Bobby were taking some time off from each other, but he said he would love to do it as Bill Medley.

"When do we need to record it?" he asked.

"Yesterday," I told him.

"Okay, well then, send me the song."

"Ummm, It's kinda not written yet." I replied. "But it hopefully will be tomorrow, because we have to record it yesterday."

As soon as I hung up with Bill, I called John Bettis and told him the entire story. The next morning, John emailed me the start of a lyric called "Friday Night's a Great Night for Football." As usual, John nailed it. We got together later that day to finish the song up. I called Gary, who called Joel, and they agreed after reading the lyric and hearing me tell them how I would approach the recording that there was no time for a demo.

"Let's just get in there and do it ASAP," was Joel's mandate.

They were already scheduled to shoot an elaborate and extremely expensive video sequence, with Bill singing the song over the main title credits, to be shown immediately following the opening football sequence.

It's rare to have the kind of trusted relationship I had with both Gary and Doug Frank, who would later take over for Gary when he retired. Both of these guys were so incredibly supportive of me through the years, with so many important projects.

I considered them good friends as well as respected executives, and I loved working with both of them. We booked the session at Conway two days later, which offered just barely enough time for me to put it together. Miraculously, the band came together quickly thanks to Patti Zimmitti, who was contracting for me at the time. J.R. on drums, Neil Stubenhaus on bass, Dean Parks on guitar, and Randy Kerber and Pat Coil on keys. The incredible Mick Guzauski agreed to engineer the tracking date.

Because there was no demo, Bill learned the song on the spot. By the end of the session, he had it down and sang the doors off of it. I had Larry Herbstritt do a great horn chart and we overdubbed brass and backing vocals by the Waters and mixed the next day.

Everybody was thrilled with the end result, and the opening video sequence with Bill came out so great that Tony Scott ended up using it again over the end credits. It was a crazy, intense schedule, but the end result was fantastic.

I asked Gary if he could possibly give me just a little more time on the next one.

25

Everyone Should Have a Larry

LARRY HERBSTRITT had come to California with his partner to make it big.

He was an unknown songwriter from Coudersport, Pennsylvania, who had convinced someone in Snuff Garrett's operation to give him a meeting. Since I was the new guy, about two months into my new digs, I got the appointment.

Larry played me a few songs. I loved the music but wasn't crazy about the lyrics. I suggested to Larry that he and I possibly write a few songs together. This guy had talent, and when I tried to put my finger on what I responded to the most in his work, the answer surprised me: Larry and I were incredibly similar in our musical styles.

Like attracts like.

Larry's songs were crafted in a structure that was a lot like mine: really cool, classically based chord changes. As we got to know each other over a period of several weeks of meetings, it was also apparent that we had a great deal in common in addition to music. Our upbringings were similar, and we had the same taste in films. The only major flaw was our conflicting baseball loyalties. I was a diehard Yankee fan and he was a Pittsburgh Pirates fan. But I still liked him.

Despite our similarities, we had very different personalities. Larry is a pretty soft-spoken guy who doesn't say too much when you first meet him.

I am not.

It wasn't long before we started writing some songs together, along with a lyricist I was working with at the time, Gary Harju. Soon, we had a great run of songs that were being recorded by the likes of Cher, Dionne Warwick, Merrilee Rush, Johnny Mathis, and countless others. Together, Larry and I wrote "I Just Fall in Love Again," which won the Juno Award for Song of the Year for Anne Murray.

We were so musically in sync: I'd have an idea for a verse or chorus musically and he'd massage it . . . or vice versa. We did "Fire in the Morning" for Melissa Manchester, "Cowboys and Clowns" for Ronnie Milsap, and "If I Had You" for Karen Carpenter.

It was a prolific partnership.

Beyond the songwriting, Larry Herbstritt would become a most trusted friend, and a collaborator on many television and film projects over the years. When I started to get busy in scoring for television and film and really needed help with orchestrating, cowriting cues, and conducting the sessions, I turned to Larry. Larry and I had that unexplainable "musical shorthand connection" that is pretty rare and hard to find. He knew my musical style and changes as well as I did, and he was a huge contributor to my successes.

Larry was such a brilliant musical mind, I often farmed out a bunch of my arranging to him . . . we had a musical trust and we talked in a way no one else understood. I could tell him exactly what I was hearing and he knew how to do it. He could interpret my musical thoughts and needs.

It was as if he saw the plasmic bubbles as well.

With Larry, it was a different kind of collaboration than with my other partners. If I had a great chorus idea and was too busy or lazy to write whole thing, I would tell him to "come up with a verse"—and he would. Later, that translated into scoring. When I got busy doing television, I'd have Larry write cues based on themes. He was my principle orchestrator on both *Murder She Wrote* and *Columbo*. I would sketch stuff, play some piano parts, and tell him to expand, giving him a shared writing credit. We co-composed all of the episodes of *Spenser: For Hire* together.

Everyone should have a Larry—someone they implicitly trust. Because I was so busy and didn't feel like I had the time to do it all, I had the luxury of working with a partner who knew my style and exactly how I did things.

Having a Larry is also perfect when you get those unexpected calls out of the blue.

One such call was from Switzerland from the then manager of Greg Lake, of the world famous Emerson, Lake and Palmer. Greg had somehow heard a song of mine that had previously been a country hit for Barbara Fairchild, and later a single release in England for Dusty Springfield. Greg loved the song, was in preproduction for his solo album, and was headed to Los Angeles to record. His manager wanted to know if I would be interested in working with Greg, doing some arrangements for him and conducting the sessions.

It was a no-brainer.

For weeks, Greg and I would meet at the house he had leased up in the Hollywood Hills. Our sessions would last for hours while we went over songs, keys, and mockups of the arrangements, drinking so much tea that I would pee every ten minutes. Larry would often accompany me to do takedowns for some of the arrangements. It was all he could do to keep from peeing in his car one day, from all the tea he consumed.

The best part about this album is that there seemed to be absolutely no budget. We spent so much time demoing, re-demoing, recording, and rerecording than I could have done four albums in the same amount of time.

Suffice to say, Greg was an absolute perfectionist, and he knew exactly what he wanted. One of his ideas was to record the old Diana Ross and the Supremes hit "You Keep Me Hangin' On." We worked up a fabulous arrangement, and I was anxious to finally get the real recording started. Unfortunately, I came down with a horrendous stomach flu the week before we were scheduled to record. Greg had to return to England and wanted to do a session on Memorial Day. I told him that the union scale for the musicians would be double or triple "Golden Time" wages for that holiday.

He told me to go ahead and book the band.

I still wasn't feeling great as the flu seemed to be lingering in my body, but I was excited for the session. The band was spectacular: Chris Squire from Yes on bass; Jeff Porcaro, David Paich, and Steve Lukather from Toto; and, because Greg liked serving tea to Larry Herbstritt so much, we had Larry on acoustic guitar.

We must have recorded the song fifteen or twenty times, each time better than the take before, when I fell off the conductor's podium and passed out.

I woke up at St. Joseph's hospital in Burbank, where I was being treated for severe dehydration from the lingering flu. Larry was by my side.

Greg's version of "Let Me Love You Once" ended up being a solo single that went Top 20; to my knowledge, after some thirty takes with one of the best rock bands ever assembled, "You Keep Me Hangin' On" was never released.

Larry and I would also travel together to London, where I was writing the score to Hugh Wilson's film *Rustler's Rhapsody*. My British music editor informed me two hours before we were getting on the plane that three of the major film sequences had been massively re-edited the day before, and since these hundreds of bars of fully orchestrated music had already been written, Larry and I spent almost the entire ten-hour plane ride cutting and pasting these massive scores together, trying to salvage as much of the music as possible. Of course, this was back before computer editing—and, needless to say, it was a nightmare of a job.

My poor music copyist in London, a sweet man named Vic Frazier, had bags under his eyes for days after having to make all of the noted changes we had given him upon arrival at our London hotel. Of course, Vic had bags under his eyes to begin with when we first met him, so that became a great source of comic relief for Larry and me over the years.

What's also interesting about *Rustler's Rhapsody*, a B-movie western spoof that gained a cult following after not performing well at the box office, is that Milton Brown and I had a hit song with Gary Morris called "Lasso the Moon," and years later, George Strait told me that *Rustler's* was one of his favorite movies. In some strange way, I think having done the music to that movie helped me connect in a much bigger way, creatively, with George when we worked on *Pure Country* together. We would recite different scenes from the movie and laugh, and it most definitely helped to break the ice and let us get to know each other better.

I can't really remember Larry ever getting tired except once—so tired that it affected his work. One of my favorite Larry moments was when I was prerecording hundreds of short song excerpts for *The*

Singing Bee. I hired Larry to do charts. He was working eighteen-hour days in order to keep to an impossibly tedious schedule. We were recording 850 tracks over a ten-day period. Larry was doing hundreds of takedowns for me during a short period of time.

One of the songs we were doing with this amazing band in Nashville was giving us a lot of trouble, as it just wasn't sounding like the original version. Something was obviously very wrong in the chart, and none of us could figure out what the issue was. It took a minute, but the great drummer Paul Leim said he thought the chart might have been written backwards.

Sure enough, Larry was so tired and bleary-eyed that he had somehow pasted the chord symbols reading not only "right to left" (like Hebrew), but also from "bottom to top."

A musical Rubik's Cube.

Larry wrote it backward and they played it backward. That had to be a first, and we still have a good laugh whenever that comes up among the guys in the band, who I still see and work with whenever I'm in Nashville.

Larry Herbstritt is one of the most talented guys I've ever had the pleasure of working with and calling my friend.

Sadly, while writing this chapter, I heard we lost Greg Lake to cancer at the way-too-young age of sixty-nine. His voice was unmistakable, and the time we spent together unforgettable.

26

NASHVILLE

I GUESS I COULD SAY Nashville is my home away from home.

My first ever trip to Nashville, Tennessee, was sometime in 1970. I had a dozen or so songs that I felt could be pitched in the country genre, and because I was signed to Lowery Music as a staff writer, I felt like that would help make it a little easier for me to get in a few doors that normally I wouldn't be able to.

I asked Bill if he would send me there for a week, as a kind of fact-finding trip, to see what Music City was all about. Bill agreed to pay for my hotel and, more importantly, to make a few calls on my behalf to some of his key contacts in order for me to make some appointments. I was a bit nervous to go it alone, so I asked my friend, Mark Yarbrough, to make the four-hour drive with me.

We were on some sort of school break, so off we went to Tennessee.

Most of the first couple of days there was spent just looking around and marveling about how close all of the music companies were in proximity to each other. The entire music business seemed to be on two or three streets, between 16th and 17th Avenues. I made a ton of calls, and most of them went unreturned, but I did get in to see Roger Sovine at BMI and Buddy Killen at Tree Music. Ray Stevens sat with me and listened to a few songs.

It was a great learning experience. Nobody really liked anything I had, or at least didn't think it was "country-sounding." They were right. I returned to Atlanta feeling like the trip had been productive, as I had learned a little bit of how the town worked, and now knew that if I was ever going to get a song recorded there, it better be a "real deal country-sounding song." Nashville was a competitive town, and the songwriters there were universally great.

Back at Lowery's, I made a conscious effort with Milton to target the country market with some of the songs we were writing. Milton was an expert in that genre, having been a diehard country fan his entire life growing up in Alabama. Because I was from Queens, New York, hadn't seen a tree until I was fourteen, and couldn't even spell "country music," I trusted Milton to show me the way. What it boils down to is that I just try to write a good song with an honest message. I still operate with the belief that a great song can be arranged and recorded in any genre, and many of the hits I've had have pretty much proven that.

When I had made my mind up to leave Lowery Music, I seriously considered making the move to Nashville instead of Los Angeles. It was closer, still in the South, and full of music people, but what ultimately pushed me toward California is that I really wanted to write pop songs, and music for film and television. That had always been my dream. I feared that, by moving to Nashville, I would be limiting myself to the world of country music. So, I took that fateful trip to L.A. and never looked back.

Little did I know how Nashville's influence would continue to thread throughout my entire career, even with my move to L.A. For starters, there was no bigger country-music fan on earth than Snuff Garrett. Yes, he was making great pop records, but his Texas roots were steeped in western swing and country classics. He had been a DJ in Texas before moving to L.A., and he had more knowledge of any and every country song than anyone I have ever known.

I suppose that's why when the country-flavored film projects of Clint Eastwood came his way. Snuff's entire slate of production projects began to swing toward the country market. Without realizing or planning it, I had fallen into opportunities from the best of both worlds. With Snuff, I was either arranging or coproducing projects with country megastars like Brenda Lee, Tanya Tucker, Ray Price, Marty Robbins, Dottie West, and Roy Rogers. And with the tremendous record-breaking successes of *Every Which Way but Loose* and *Bronco Billy*, it became much easier for me to go to Nashville and get through many doors that were not previously available to me.

Publishers like Al Gallico and Bob Montgomery were close friends of Snuff's, and I would routinely visit with them when I was in town. I was also starting to have hits with Anne Murray and Lee Greenwood, while other top country artists like Barbara Fairchild, Ronnie Milsap, and Con Hunley were covering some of my songs. All of the important doors were opening, and a lot of my friends and contemporaries, like Jim Ed Norman, Steve Buckingham, and James Stroud, were now running labels and becoming hot producers.

I had also produced hit projects on my own, including Con Hunley, and of course the three-time ACM Duo of the Year, David Frizzell and Shelly West. My years with Snuff, and the many successful country projects I was a part of because of him, would become the bridge to my continued and even greater successes on to the Nashville scene, once I left Snuff and moved on to Warner/Chappell and Chuck Kaye.

At Warners, I had the autonomy to travel to Nashville whenever I needed to. I no longer had to answer to anyone, and I was now doing a lot of cowriting with many top Nashville writers, as well as being in demand for doing string arrangements for artists like Wynona, Reba, Tim McGraw, Clay Walker, Alan Jackson, and Clint Black. *Rustler's Rhapsody* was the first major country-flavored film project I did on my own, putting together a great soundtrack with Randy Travis, John Anderson, Gary Morris, the Nitty Gritty Dirt Band, and Rex Allen Jr., among others. And then along came the brass ring, *Pure Country* with George Strait.

I've been asked so many times, "How have you managed to have the success you've had in Nashville without actually having lived there?"

I guess I've always considered myself to be an anomaly for Nashville.

I never lived there, although many people, and surprisingly even friends of mine in L.A., have thought I did. It's no doubt that the power of film and television exposure helped propel me to some great extent, but I'd also like to think that my songs had that little different spin on the ball that made them special because I did NOT live there. But I have spent a great deal of my career in Nashville, I have some wonderful lifelong friends and associates that I've made there, and I still visit almost every other month to do work there. My son Andrew, a very successful songwriter in his own right, made Nashville his permanent home.

What I can say with certainty is that I have to some degree been a victim of what's known as a "good ol' boy" mentality that comes along with the territory. Even going back to the Billy Sherrill/Bob Montgomery days when I was first starting to visit Nashville, I would be told, "You've gotta be here every day to truly fit in." No matter how much success I had, there was always an air of me being sort of a foreigner, or not truly belonging.

My boys with Clint Eastwood at "Bronco Billy" session.

George Strait at the BMI Awards.

With Anne Murray in Toronto, Canada, recording "I Don't Think I'm Ready for You" from the film *Stick*.

Céline Dion backstage in Vegas.

With my kids Callie, Andrew, Kaitlyn, and Stephen.

Callie and Kaitlyn in Maui.

Andrew and Stephen in Venice, Italy.

Blake Shelton.

Bobby Tomberlin.

Eric Kaz.

John Bettis.

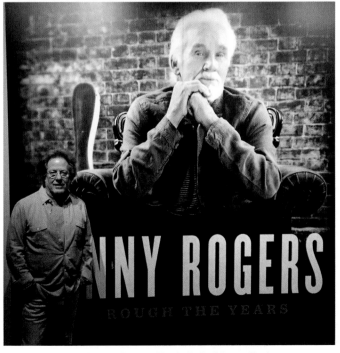

Kenny Rogers Country Music Hall of Fame display.

B. J. Thomas in the studio.

Some of my favorite Nashville musicians.
Left to right: Jimmy Nichols, Eddie Bayers, B. James Lowry, J. T. Corenflos, and Joe Chemay.

Pure Country scoring session at Ocean Way, Nashville.

Some of my favorite L.A. musicians.
Left to right: Dean Parks, Matt Rollings, Leland Sklar, and Vinnie Colaiuta.

In the studio.

Concert in Tokyo, Japan.

Andrew Marshall Dorff.

To be considered a resident part of the music community in Nashville, you really should move there. Trust me, I thought seriously about doing just that several times in the eighties and nineties. It made perfect sense, and many of my close friends who have had tremendous careers in Nashville had moved there permanently from L.A. Over the years, Nashville has changed and grown in so many ways, and as the music community has become much more diverse, that feeling of not being totally accepted has dissipated greatly.

I do have a favorite story that I think perfectly illustrates the prejudice that was sometimes glaring back in the day. One afternoon, we were taking a break from recording some songs from *Pure Country* at Soundstage. Tavern on the Row was a convenient and popular place to grab a quick lunch. As I walked in to the restaurant with a few musician friends who were on the session, I recognized a well-known songwriter sitting with his publisher, with whom I was also mildly acquainted. As I was passing their table, I nodded a quick hello gesture, and he looked up at me and said, in a rather loud and obnoxious tone, "Yeah, they finally do a movie called *Pure Country*, and look who they ask to write the songs."

I just grinned, bit my tongue to stop myself from telling him to go fuck himself, and kept moving . . . but you get the idea!

Great songwriters and artists come from everywhere, and Nashville is also filled with creative energy and a great place to write. One perfect collaboration I enjoyed there was with an Aussie of all people, Troy Cassar-Daley. Every once in a while you meet someone for the first time and there is an instant connection, like you have known them for your entire life.

I got a call from Peter Karpin, who was head of A&R for Sony Australia. He asked me if I would be interested in meeting one of his artists with the idea of possibly doing a project together. Troy Cassar-Daley is a fabulous singer/guitar player/songwriter from Brisbane who has the real deal. He is an exceptional guitar player and has an authentic country style in his singing, like Merle Haggard or Lefty Frizzell. He did not have even a hint of an Australian accent when he sang, which is funny because his speaking accent was so thick. In fact, he has such a thick accent when he speaks it is almost difficult to understand him. Yet when he sings his voice is completely pure.

We both happened to be in Nashville at the same time, so we met and decided to try to write a few songs together. One of the songs we wrote was called "Little Things," which would go on to become a big hit for Troy in Australia. It was undoubtedly the catalyst for Troy asking me to produce his entire album. He had always wanted to record an album in America. Peter Karpin signed off on it, gave us a budget, and we made a beautiful album over the course of a month. Half of it was recorded in Los Angeles, the other half in Nashville. It won the Aria award—the Australian Grammy—for Album of the Year.

Nashville is a melting pot of great musical talent from all over, just as Hollywood and New York are for actors and screenwriters. Certain local organizations, such as the NSAI and the affiliated Songwriters Hall of Fame, might just want to take a longer look at that fact in order to bolster their credibility with the rest of the universe.

I love Nashville, and I have done some incredible work there that I am very proud of. The musicians I have worked with there are amongst the finest in the world. There are still times I wonder what my career would have looked like if I had moved there from Atlanta way back when.

As we all get older, I think we all look down that proverbial "road not taken," but all in all, I'm pretty satisfied with the road I got to take.

27

I Just Fall in Love Again . . .
and Again . . . and Again

I'VE OFTEN WONDERED what the correlation is between my being a hopeless romantic and someone who has spent most of his life writing about love. It's ironic how one of my biggest hits, "I Just Fall in Love Again," has become a real-life, reoccurring episode of my own life.

I still often joke to friends that I think I've probably written about love all these years a lot better than I've actually lived it.

"I Just Fall in Love Again" was a long time in the making. Larry Herbstritt and I had an awesome melody going—a big sweeping ballad with a nod to some classical chord changes in the chorus. I felt like we had an important song. We had one small problem: the lyrics we had come up with were, in a word, terrible, and after doing a demo on the song, I was unhappy with the way it turned out.

There was another writer at Snuff's company, Gloria Sklerov, who had been writing some really beautiful songs. Gloria and I had never written together before, but I really admired her lyrics. Before I gave up on our song altogether, I played it for Gloria to see if she had an idea how to fix it. Gloria loved the melody and agreed that the lyrics were pretty lame. She said she and her partner, the late Harry Lloyd, would love to take a stab at writing a new lyric to our melody.

It was probably the best save I could have ever hoped for.

It was late summer of 1975. I had played many songs for Ed Sulzer, who was heading up A&R for Richard and Karen Carpenter on the glorious A&M Records lot. To say I loved the lot would be an understatement. I was obsessed with this lot, which had so much Hollywood history attached to it, first from being the original Charlie Chaplin movie lot and then as the home of A&M Records: Herb Alpert, Burt Bacharach, Paul Williams, and of course, the Carpenters. A songwriter's dream was to be included on one of their albums.

I had just finished doing a new piano/vocal demo of the song that Gloria and Harry had magically fixed, and I wanted to pitch it to Eddie first. I made the appointment to see him on the famed lot a few days later, and lo and behold, after one listen, I heard the words that every songwriter wants to hear:

"I like it. Let me play it for Richard."

I don't think I ate or slept for a few days, and then I got the call: the Carpenters were going to record the song for their new album. I was beside myself with excitement, as this was without question the most important cut of my career by arguably the biggest recording act in the world at that time. I was invited to the live recording session at the A&M soundstage with some seventy-plus members of an orchestra led by the legendary Peter Knight. Peter had arranged the Moody Blues' classic album *Days of Future Past*, which was one of my all-time favorite albums. His orchestrations were simply incredible, and I remember trying to fight off the tears that were pouring down my face as Karen Carpenter sang "I Just Fall in Love Again" for the first time.

Although the Carpenters never released it as a single, I still consider their recording to be maybe the most perfect recording of anything I've ever written.

A few years later, I got a call from the late, great Dusty Springfield. She heard Karen's recording and told me she was going to put a version of "I Just Fall in Love Again" on her new album. I was thrilled. I couldn't wait to hear her version. But as classic as Dusty's performance was, I was again told a single release was doubtful, for whatever reason.

But I knew the song was great. And I was patient. After all, so far I had had two of the most wonderful female artists on the planet sing it.

Still, a year or so later, I got a call from my good friend Jim Ed Norman in Toronto. He was in Canada producing another one of my favorite artists, Anne Murray.

"Steve, we know that Karen and Dusty have already recorded 'I Just Fall in Love Again,' but Anne would like to give it a try." Anne, like me, was a huge fan of Dusty, and she had heard Dusty's version on her album.

The third time was the charm.

Anne's version went on to become the big hit single that I had always hoped for this song. It was honored with the Juno (Canadian Grammy) Award for Song of the Year, and it stayed at #1 in *Billboard* for three weeks. It has also had the distinction of being recorded by over fifty artists in innumerable languages all over the world, as well as attaining four-million-broadcast status at BMI.

Thanks, Gloria and Harry, for the beautiful lyric!

Back to falling in love.

In reality, I really do love being in love with one person. The trouble is that, since my marriages, I haven't found that one special person who is the "girl of my dreams." I have come very close to that special person a few times since my second divorce, but there always seemed to be something that got in the way of it being the *happily ever after* that

I've always written about. Because, at my core, I am an eternal optimist who still believes in true love. I have, indeed, fallen in love again and again. Even in my sixties, I believe "the one" is still out there. And I will keep writing about her until I find her.

As far as my past loves, I admittedly keep trying to squeeze all of these fabulous girls into one song, kind of a retrospective, like Jimmy Webb did so perfectly in his song "Name of My Sorrow." It'd be tough to top that masterpiece, though.

The truth is, I really have nothing bad to say about the women I was in these relationships with. I have learned a great deal of valuable life lessons, rode the rollercoaster, and took away some amazing experiences which gave me some equally amazing songwriting material. Some of my favorite songs—and what I personally consider to be my best work—came from these romantic rollercoasters of love, heartbreak, pain, joy, disillusion, hopefulness, forgiveness, and regret.

There was one woman in particular who was the impetus for a lot of these songs. It still upsets me a little when I think about her. It's pretty tough to have a great relationship when there's no reciprocity from the person you're emotionally giving everything of yourself to. I fell for her hard, and I deeply believed we were something special. It took me a while—much longer than I thought it would—to get over that one. I haven't quite pulled all of the toxic shrapnel out of my back. Some people just don't come as they advertise themselves to be.

Oh well, at the end of the day I got a few really great songs out of the deal.

My collaborators have been invaluable to me during my repeated times of love and loss. Bobby Tomberlin stayed up all night with me writing a song called "If Only." Milton Brown helped me tremendously with his haunting lyric to "Everything I Touch Turns to Blue."

One day at lunch while I was blabbering with Eric Kaz about how I never got closure with this one person, he started scribbling on a napkin. The next day, Kaz emailed me a lyric called "Face-to-Face."

I called him immediately.

"Where did this come from?"

"Out of your mouth, at lunch yesterday."

I never did get my closure with that person, but wow, did we ever come up with an amazing song. I can't help but wonder if she knows it was written about her. Perhaps if she reads this book she will. Perhaps she won't. It's okay, because the music is in the world, and the experience made me a stronger writer.

Love often does.

As far as the rest of the women, I'm pretty sure they know who they are: the magnificent, complicated, and passionate women about whom I've written a lot of these songs. If and when they read this, I hope they smile and know that for that period of time that I was with them, I was loyal, and I truly cared about them more than they will ever know.

28

ELVIS

———

As THANKFUL and grateful as I am for all of the wonderful artists who have graced my songs with their voices, there are a few who I would have loved to have heard sing one of my songs.

My sister Sherry was definitely one of those crazed screaming teenage girls who cried every time she watched Elvis on TV. Because I was nine years younger than Sherry, I really wasn't into the Elvis craze or fifties music in general. I was too busy listening to Al Jolson, Jimmy Durante, and theater songs.

Coincidentally enough, about a year or two before Elvis passed away, Felton Jarvis, who was producing Elvis at the time, put a song of mine "on hold" for Elvis. He told me he loved the song and would be playing it for Elvis soon. That was about as close to an Elvis Presley cut that I would get. I did tell my sister about it, and she screamed over the phone as if I had brought Elvis over to her house for dinner.

I've worked with many artists and producers over the course of my career who knew Elvis well and loved telling stories about him. B. J. Thomas, Bill Medley, Chips Moman, Mac Davis, and many of my studio musician friends had great stories about the King. Still, I felt as if I had somehow been out of sync personally with the Elvis era. Sure, I knew all of his hits, but I couldn't recite all of his movies or discography like I could with the Beatles . . . or Burt Bacharach.

———

In 2005, I received a call from my agent asking me to take a meeting with the director Jim Sadwith, who had done the successful Frank Sinatra miniseries for television. He was finishing up a four-hour miniseries for CBS called *Elvis*, and was looking to hire a composer to score the project.

I gladly took the meeting in Santa Monica. As was the norm, there were several composers still being considered for this high-profile project, but I was told they had to make a choice quickly, as the network had moved up the delivery and airing dates.

I had a nice thirty-minute morning meeting with Jim; answered all of his questions as they related to my musical approach, schedule, and so on; and left to head back to meet my friend for lunch at Art's Deli in Studio City. My agent, Cheryl Tiano, called me in the car and asked me how the meeting went. I told her I felt good about it, but I had no idea whether or not I would get the gig.

Later that afternoon, Cheryl called again.

"I have good news and bad news."

"Okay, let's have the good news."

"You got the job."

"Then what could be the bad news?"

"You got the job."

She proceeded to tell me that the postproduction schedule had been moved up by a month to accommodate the network wanting to air the miniseries over two nights in early May. It was mid-April, which meant I had to write and record the entire score in about fourteen days—and I hadn't even seen the first frame of picture yet. Now I understood what Cheryl meant by the "bad news" part of the equation.

I got to look at the first two-hour assembly of the movie ("Part 1") the following day. I was really blown away by Jonathan Rhys Meyers's portrayal of Elvis, and I was not surprised at all when he eventually won a Golden Globe for his performance. Randy Quaid, who went on to win the Emmy for his portrayal of Colonel Tom Parker, was equally incredible. All of a sudden I was getting a crash course in Elvis the best way possible—by seeing his history unfold, as told beautifully by Jim Sadwith and Patrick Sheane Duncan.

Jim and I were on the same page in terms of our musical approach to the miniseries: sparse, solo instrumentation that sounded realistic for the period. That would help a lot in terms of not having to spend days orchestrating. I would come up with the main character themes for Elvis, Priscilla, and the Colonel, and then fill in the dramatic sequences with period-sounding incidental music. We didn't use any of the Elvis hits. This was focused more on his biographical rise, from his high-school years through his international superstardom.

For expedience of time, I decided to record all of the love themes and sadder dramatic sequences in Los Angeles, with Jim Cox on acoustic piano and synths and George Doering playing acoustic and gut-string guitars. John Guess engineered. Jim Sadwith and I were loving the intimate feeling of the score. It was working well.

The more rhythmic sections and rockabilly style sequences had to be authentic, and I felt that going to Nashville would be the best way to accomplish that. We had an awesome band: Paul Leim on drums, John Hobbs on keys, Joe Chemay on bass, and Brent Rowin and Biff Watson on guitars. Brent played that Jerry Reed–style rockabilly as well as anyone. I also had Jelly Roll Johnson play the harmonica, as that was the thematic sound I used for Colonel Tom Parker.

Once again, we somehow beat the killer deadline, spending sixteen-hour days in the studio and finishing the project barely on time. It was an amazing project, and one that could only have been accomplished with the extraordinary talent of the outstanding musicians and John Guess's great mixes.

Now I had my Ph.D. in Elvis, and I had become a huge fan after all.

29

MICHAEL LANDON, MURPHY BROWN, AND DOLLY PARTON

IF THERE WAS ONE TV show I never missed as a kid growing up, it was *Bonanza*. God, I loved everything about that show, right down to the Cartwrights' Chinese cook, Hop Sing. Every Sunday night at 9 p.m., right after *The Ed Sullivan Show*, I would switch the channel from CBS to NBC and wait for that killer theme music by David Rose. Once, on a ski trip to Lake Tahoe, I dragged Nancy across the lake from where we were staying just so I could see the set where they filmed the exteriors for the Ponderosa Ranch.

I was in the middle of lunch one day when Sam Schwartz called me and asked me to put together a CD of music for a two-hour movie/pilot being directed by and starring Michael Landon.

"*The* Michael Landon? How fast do you need it?"

Sam explained that they wanted to hear something right away, so I ran home and put together a sample CD of various scoring cues I had done, and messengered it over to Michael Landon's people. The next morning, Sam called and said that Michael Landon wanted to meet me at his office on the Culver City lot at 2 p.m. I was beyond excited, if only just to get to meet Little Joe Cartwright after all the years of watching him on *Bonanza*.

I arrived at Michael's office, and his longtime secretary offered me a coffee and took me in to meet him. There he was, handsome as ever—great tan, long hair, and a youthful smile. He got up and shook my hand, smiled, and couldn't have been nicer. He told me about the movie he was just finishing up for CBS, a drama called *Us*. I believe it was his first project for any network other than NBC, where he had done *Little House on the Prairie*, *Highway to Heaven*, and of course *Bonanza*. CBS had all but guaranteed him a slot on the fall schedule, but it wanted the two-hour movie as the kickoff.

David Rose, the composer for every show Michael had ever done, had recently passed away, and Michael was looking and listening for someone who could take the reins and work as closely with him as David had done. Not an easy task. Michael then started to tell me about a family vacation to Hawaii that he had just returned from, and how he needed to get the postproduction rolling.

"When are you available to start?" he asked.

I just looked at him. "What? Who? Me?" I was tongue-tied.

"Yes. You. I loved your music. You're the guy. I just wanted to meet you before we got going."

I was in shock . . . this was one of those "pinch-me" moments.

"Um, I can start right now, sir."

He wanted to score the film in two to three weeks' time, whenever I was ready, but he wanted to listen to my main theme as soon as I had it written. I was so excited, I think I started humming something to myself in the car on the way home that actually became the jumping off place to what would be the theme, which was called "Us."

Michael came over to my house in Studio City one day to hear me play it for him on the piano. He was wearing jeans and a tight cutoff black T-shirt, and I thought Nancy was going to pass out as he walked through our kitchen and kissed her hello. Michael loved the theme, made a few suggestions, and then said, "Let me know when and where you want to record."

Two weeks later, we were at Evergreen Studio in North Hollywood with a forty-five-piece orchestra, recording all day. Michael was in the control room, giving me the thumbs-up on every cue. It was maybe the most enjoyable, stress-free day in the studio I have ever had.

Michael had a screening for cast, crew, and CBS and Sony execs in a packed room on the lot. The movie was fabulous, and everyone, including me, thought we were in for another classic long-running Michael Landon series.

Michael was leaving the next day for a ski trip to Sun Valley, Idaho. That was the last time I would ever see him.

It was reported that, while skiing, Michael was experiencing terrible stomach pains and had to be hospitalized. A few days later, it was announced that he had been diagnosed with terminal pancreatic cancer.

It just took the wind out of me when I heard that. I was devastated. It was much more than just music. In just a few months I had become friends with one of my boyhood heroes.

I called Michael a few weeks later just to leave a quick message that I was thinking about him. To my surprise, his wife Cindy answered the phone. I asked her to send my best wishes and prayers along to Michael for me, and she said, "Hold on, he's right here and would like to say hello."

Michael got on the phone and sounded terribly weak. He wanted to apologize for it looking like the series wasn't going to go because of his illness. Can you imagine? I told him to get well, rest up, and we'll do another one. I could tell he had been crying, and he said he had to go.

We were on the phone maybe all of forty-five seconds. Cindy took the phone back and thanked me for calling.

Michael Landon died four days later. It was an absolute honor to get to know him and work for him. He was a good man, and one of the most loyal people I have ever met.

There's something to be said about loyalty in this business.

Hopefully, when you do a good job on a movie or television show, you get asked back by the studio or production team for their next project. I had enjoyed that kind of relationship with Gary Lemel and Doug Frank at Warners for years.

In 1988, I had the theme songs to four hit network shows, all running simultaneously. *Growing Pains* was rockin' along on ABC, *Just the 10 of Us* was debuting, and *Spenser: For Hire* and *My Sister Sam* were both ending their respective successful runs. I was also doing a few pilots and several TV movies in my spare time.

With all of the various meetings, writing, and recording that needed to be done weekly on all of these shows, it left me little time to do much else, let alone get any sleep. But I loved it. It was a crazy schedule every composer dreams about.

Diane English was wrapping up *My Sister Sam* after two seasons on CBS, and there was rumor of a new, exciting project she had been developing for the '88 fall season. It was a show called *Murphy Brown* and would star Candice Bergen as a sarcastic, dedicated, and ambitious news reporter on a TV show set in Washington, D.C.

The buzz on this show was incredible.

Diane asked me to come in for a meeting to discuss the music. The overall musical tone of the show would be set in the world of Motown. Murphy would be an R&B fanatic, and most of the episodes would be written around the many great Motown-era standards. The challenge for me was to come up with something original that had the flavor of R&B yet still said something fairly specific about the show. John Bettis was once again my go-to guy for this one. After reading the pilot script, he naturally came up with the perfect title, "Like the Whole World's Watching."

I didn't want to do the traditional tracking/solo-vocal approach, and we ended up with a song that had this great groove under it. I was hearing more of a "group sound" to make this really stand out. Maybe even an a-cappella treatment?

I had recently heard a vocal group out of Nashville who were signed to WB Records called Take 6. These six guys had the most incredible sound I had ever heard, with intricate and sophisticated harmonies and vocal arrangements that were totally fresh and unique. I was able to get their contact information, and they agreed to meet with me and listen to the song.

We met in L.A., and I spent a few minutes showing them the song at the piano. They loved it, had a few ideas arrangement-wise, and within half an hour—within minutes of learning it—they completely made it their own. They had transformed what was basically a pretty simple tune into this incredible, mind-blowing ear-candy event.

I was in awe of their collective true genius. Rather than demo it, I called over to Diane's office and asked if I could come over and show her the song.

"How are you going to show it to me?" she asked. "There is no piano here."

"I don't need a piano, just sixty seconds of your time."

Somewhat intrigued, she told me to come over after lunch.

Diane was mildly surprised when, a few hours later, what looked like a full basketball team walked into her office with me.

"This is Take 6, and here's what we've come up with for *Murphy Brown*."

This was a highly unusual presentation scenario, but it went over like gangbusters. Diane made the guys sing it several times for everyone in the office she could find. She kept pulling in members of her staff, as well as people from all over the building. She then called Harvey Sheppard, the chairman of Warner Bros. Television, and asked if we could drop by his office for sixty seconds.

Fifteen minutes later, we were all crowded in his office, where Take 6 was performing the song for Harvey and his staff. The reaction we were getting was unbelievable. Granted, having these amazing guys singing something live, in such a unique song form, was the major selling point, but I think the song was great, too.

Murphy Brown was a brilliant, groundbreaking television show that ran for ten years, becoming one of the longest-running sitcoms in history. Take 6 went on to record a full version of the theme song, which John and I expanded. It was one of the first recordings the band did with instrumental accompaniment. We used the sixty-second a-cappella version to begin the piece, and then the guys did an insanely brilliant arrangement with orchestra to finish it.

It is one of the best records I have ever been a part of, and am so proud to have gotten to work with the brilliant guys in Take 6.

Other than the work that I've done with my longtime collaborators, I have enjoyed writing a song or two with a variety of great songwriters. One of my favorite people I have gotten to work with is Allan Rich. Allan is one of the sweetest, most down-to-earth men I know, as well as being an unbelievably talented guy with words.

Most of his success as a songwriter has come from his longtime collaboration with my friend Jud Friedman. The two of them have written many big hits together. Allan and I first met while he was out visiting L.A. from New York. He attended some BMI-sponsored songwriting expo panel that I was speaking on. We briefly talked afterward, and he told me he was thinking about moving to Los Angeles. I just had this feeling about Allan, so I told him to call me when he was settled, that I'd love to hear what he was doing.

Our first session together was pretty much classic Allan Rich.

He came out to the house and seemed a bit nervous. By his own admission, Allan has this quirky, change-your-mind-every-ten-seconds nervous energy about him. It's part of what makes him great. Looking a bit anxious, he started to read me a few lyric ideas, and nothing was really hitting me. He then apologized, and said, "I have this other one, but you're going to hate it. I wasn't even going to bring it to you. I'm embarrassed."

"Don't be silly, let me hear it."

He began to read a lyric called "Dump the Dude."

I fucking LOVED IT!

I think we wrote the song in thirty minutes. We also wrote a really cool song that day called "Black Mercedes." I demoed both songs the following week. Somehow Dolly Parton heard "Dump the Dude" and recorded it for a pop album she was making in Los Angeles. It was quite an honor to have an amazing songwriter in her own right, like Dolly, do our song.

There's something uniquely commercial about Allan's lyrics that I love. We've gone on to write several other fantastic songs together, one of which, "Make It Christmas," is a personal favorite of mine, and "I'd Know How to Love You Now," which I know is a big hit just waiting to happen.

Allan and I have yet to have a big hit single together, but I have no doubt we will.

I have had the great fortune of getting to work with Dolly Parton on several occasions. She is one of the sweetest, most genuine superstars I have ever met. I was asked to arrange and conduct a few really great records for her. Steve Buckingham was producing an album with Dolly that included a fabulous version of Cat Stevens's classic "Peace Train." Dolly's vocal, along with the backup vocals from the singers from Ladysmith Black Mambazo, was simply incredible.

I was asked to put an orchestra on the track in Los Angeles. Engineered by the incomparable Al Schmidt, this track was simply an amazing work of art. For the animated film Annabelle's Wish, *Dolly performed a beautiful version of "Silent Night" and a song that Marty Panzer and I wrote called "Something Bigger Than Me." Dolly's immense talent is as stunning as that of anyone I've had the pleasure of working with.*

30

FROM CHARLES MANSON TO FATS DOMINO

IN SIXTY-ODD YEARS, I have collected a lot of songs, a lot of friends, and a lot of stories. Some of which makes sense to put in this bag of my life; others are simply part of the grab bag of my cumulative experiences.

Here are a few stories, beginning with Charles Manson. Because who wouldn't want to start with Charles Manson?

The FBI Crashes My Session

From time to time, I would have friends drop in on sessions I was doing, sometimes invited and sometimes not. Usually, these were people I knew, or were friends of the artists I was working with.

I will never forget the time I was doing a Fender Rhodes overdub on a track at Criterion Studios in Hollywood. The engineer interrupted what I was playing by pushing the talkback button down and asking me through my headphones if I could come into the control room. I asked him if there was something wrong.

"There are two men here who need to speak with you for a moment," he said.

I walked back into the control room to see two rather large guys dressed in identical navy-blue suits. At first I thought they were some dudes trying to impersonate the Blues Brothers, but other than that I had no idea who they were.

One of them politely apologized for interrupting what I was doing as he pulled a badge out of his jacket pocket. This made me a bit nervous, and I started going through a list of things in my head I might possibly have done wrong. He introduced himself and his partner as FBI agents and asked me for my ID.

Now I was getting really nervous and immediately felt guilty, my mind racing with possibilities of what I had absolutely done wrong. Upon proof that they were talking to Steve Dorff, they asked if there was a place where we could speak in private for a few minutes. I thought I was hosed.

As we walked toward the piano in the studio, I was picturing myself in a prison for doing God knows what.

"Is everything okay?" I asked. "Did I do something wrong?"

They asked me if I knew, or had any contact with, a Charles Manson.

"*The* Charles Manson?" I gulped. "Absolutely not. Why?"

They went on to explain that my name was included on a list of twenty-five or so names recovered at the ranch where Manson was holed up during his murder spree.

I was now completely freaked out.

In fact, the house that was targeted by the murderers belonged to record producer Terry Melcher. Sharon Tate and the other victims had been renting the house from Terry, and they just happened to be at the wrong place at the wrong time. Manson's clan was simply told to murder everyone in that house. Chances are that Terry Melcher was on that same list and was the target to be murdered.

The agents went on to explain that they had found threatening letters to people on this list, and wanted to know if I had received one. Apparently, old Charlie, in his relatively spare time from being a full-time psychopath, considered himself a great songwriter. He had sent cassettes of his songs to various record producers and publishers. I had absolutely no knowledge of ever receiving such a tape, as we had a strict "no unsolicited material" rule at our office. Any tapes of songs that came in the mail from unidentified sources were never opened. They were simply tossed into a big box for recycling in the mailroom.

The two agents thanked me for my time and gave me their cards in case I had any more information to share. They apologized again for interrupting my session, shook my hand, and left.

I had to sit down and digest. I could have been on Charles Manson's hit list. It was pretty scary that I might have been associated in the slightest way with this horrific madman.

I was shaken up for days.

Luis Miguel: *Un Te Amo*

Luis Miguel was arguably one of the biggest recording stars on the planet.

The Mexican star had sold over one hundred million records around the world, mostly to Latin-speaking audiences. I must confess, however, that before Shari Sutcliffe called me to ask if I'd like to write a string arrangement for him, I had never heard of him. Shari had been contracting a new album project that Luis was recording in Los Angeles, and had suggested me to his producer as someone new to possibly work with on the album.

Luis listened to some string charts I had done and said he had a particular song in mind for me to work on with him. He asked Shari to set up a meeting so we could get acquainted. It would just be a meet-and-greet—something simple, to see if we were compatible. To prepare for the meeting, I picked up a few Luis Miguel CDs and listened to a whole lot of songs in Spanish over the next two days.

The meeting was set for 7 p.m. at a bungalow Luis was staying in at the Beverly Hills Hotel. I didn't expect the meeting to last longer than half an hour, so I had made dinner plans afterward at 8:30. As I prepared for the quick meet-and-greet, I threw a pad of staff paper in my bag, just in case I would need to take some notes.

Thank God I did.

When I got to the hotel, I used the valet parking, telling the valet I wouldn't be terribly long. I found the reception desk and asked for Luis's bungalow number. The concierge informed me that "one of Luis's people" would be out shortly to escort me to his place.

A few minutes later, one of his entourage came out to meet me, shook my hand, and said, "Follow me, please."

I trailed him to a posh bungalow hidden in the back of the hotel's lush grounds. As we approached, I could hear music blasting and the voices of several people emanating through the door.

As soon as I entered, I felt like I was in a James Bond film. I was greeted by a dozen of the most beautiful women I had ever seen in my life. Behind them were a few guys and, of course, Luis Miguel himself.

The Latin American idol had star quality. He was magnetic as he stood and introduced himself. He kissed me on both cheeks, greeting me like we had known each other for years. He told me to grab a drink and some food from the enormous buffet and join the party.

I quickly cancelled my dinner reservations. Clearly this was to be more than a little meet and greet.

Luis's suite of rooms was gorgeous, the wine and champagne was flowing, and there was enough food for a small wedding reception. Over the course of the next hour, Luis introduced me to several people while his gorgeous harem kept my wine glass filled. After the requisite small talk and niceties, he finally put his arm around me and said, "I want you to hear this beautiful song I am going to record, and you are going to do the arrangement for me, yes?"

It was more of a gentle command than an actual question, but I was thrilled. I didn't know that getting the job was as simple as Luis liking me.

"Great. Do you have a tape or demo of it for me that I can hear?"

He shook his head and pointed to an electronic keyboard in the living room.

"No, I will sing it for you."

There were at least a dozen people still milling about, and the only thing they all had in common, other than being ridiculously good-looking, was that they were exceedingly loud. And the stereo was blasting.

"Uhh, do you think we can turn the stereo down just a bit so I can hear the song clearly without any other music getting in the way?" I wondered.

Luis was charmed that I would even ask and did not turn down the stereo. Instead, he started to sing in my ear, a capella. It was a Spanish song called "Un Te Amo."

Unable to understand Spanish, I had absolutely no idea what the song was about and, more importantly, I didn't know the chord changes, tempo, or structure of the song.

Luis seemed to think I could easily jump in. "Come, play it along with me at the keyboard."

"Sure . . . uh . . . okay." I stalled and I grabbed my music paper. I tried to feel what the changes should be under the melody he was singing, as best as I could . . . especially considering that I had never heard the song before, and still had no idea what it meant. He sang it for me a few more times, and I recorded him on a little handheld tape recorder I also happened to have in my bag.

All in all, it was a fascinating first-time meeting with a true superstar who wanted me to write an arrangement for a sixty-piece orchestra of a song I had never heard before in a foreign language I didn't understand, from a handheld tape recorder with people screaming, laughing, and partying in the background.

No problem.

I woke up the next morning, called Shari, and told her about our "meeting."

"Welcome to my world," she chuckled.

The tracking session was set a few days later, with an incredible band that included Robbie Buchanan on keys, J.R. on drums, Nathan East on bass, and Dean Parks on guitar. Robbie was great at straightening out some of the changes I had missed because of the tape with some wonderful substitution chords. Luis's scratch vocal was incredible, and for the first time I was hearing this beautiful song the way it was intended to be heard.

I went home and wrote the orchestra arrangement, which we did at Ocean Way in Hollywood the following week. The record turned out beautifully.

There was no doubt why Luis is one of the greats. The album was called *33*, and like all of his albums it was a huge worldwide success. And, yes, it was one of the most beautiful songs I've ever gotten to arrange.

Blast from the Past

Sometimes it really is a matter of simply being at the right place at the right time.

One early evening I was meeting a friend at the bar in Shutters on the Beach, a nice hotel in Santa Monica. While sitting at a table in the rather plush lobby, having a glass of wine, I noticed a familiar face walk right past me. He happened to look over, and as he did we both yelled at each other at the same time. It was the director Hugh Wilson, whom I had worked with some fourteen years before on *Rustler's Rhapsody*. Hugh had moved to a beautiful farm in Virginia, and it had been at least ten years since we had seen each other.

We made a bit of small talk, catching up with what we were both up to, and he told me he was getting ready to shoot a new movie called *Blast from the Past* that he thought I'd be perfect to do the music for. He told me to call him the next day to get a script, and we would chat more about the project.

To this day, I still wonder if I really would have gotten to do the film if I hadn't been sitting there, but some things in this business often do come down to just plain fate.

I called Hugh the next day and he had a script delivered to me. It was a charming, funny, and somewhat zany story starring Brendan Fraser, Alicia Silverstone, Christopher Walken, and Sissy Spacek—a phenomenal cast. I was thrilled to have the chance to be a part of this project, and to get to work with Hugh again. There was one small problem: the studio, New Line Entertainment, wanted another composer.

I've heard the story a few different times from several different people who were involved in the project. Apparently, when Hugh was told that the studio had chosen another composer for the film without his approval, he sat in his production trailer on set and vowed not to come out and direct the film until a deal was made for me to compose the music for his movie. Needless to say, the studio caved.

Loyalty in this business is special, and Hugh Wilson more than stepped up for me. I had a wonderful experience scoring this movie, and getting to work with my friend Steve Tyrell, a great artist himself, who did the song supervision.

We went then almost immediately into production on Hugh's next film, *Dudley Do-Right*, at Universal, also starring Brendan Fraser.

Hugh had a way of making everybody who worked on his films feel special. He's a comedic genius whom I feel privileged to have worked with.

Jack Gold and Andy Williams

One of the most memorable stories of my career came from a pitch meeting that I had the first year I was in Los Angeles. Jack Gold was a staff producer at Columbia Records. He produced Johnny Mathis, Andy Williams, Barbra Streisand, Vicki Carr, and countless other major artists at Columbia. The acts that he produced were not songwriters, however, so he was always looking for great songs to record.

Getting a meeting with Jack was not easy. He had his favorite publishers and writers that were his go-to regulars, and new guys like me usually had to just drop songs off with a receptionist in the hope that he might listen. Fortunately, I was good friends with Bo Goldsen, whose dad, Mickey, was a close friend of Jack's. Bo was able to get me a face-to-face with Jack, and I came prepared. It was my first time getting to see the hallowed halls of Columbia Records, with pictures of all the great artists, past and present, hanging everywhere, and gold records displayed on every other available wall. It was impressive.

A secretary showed me into Jack's office, where he was seated behind an enormous desk. I nervously reached out my hand to shake and thank him for seeing me. He just looked at me and said, in a quiet voice, "Sit down." No one had bothered to tell me that Jack suffered from Parkinson's disease, and on his bad days he would not be in good spirits.

This was one of his bad days.

He asked me how I was liking California, who I was writing songs with, had I gotten any songs placed yet . . . those kinds of questions. He spoke quietly, and because of the trembling he was experiencing it was hard for me to understand a lot of what he was mumbling. I told him I was a big fan of his records and had a few songs that I hoped he would love.

He stared at me, reached out his shaking hand, and motioned to me to hand over the demo to him. I had 45 rpm dubs with me. These were vinyl discs, album-sized, with little holes in the center.

As I started to hand him the first song, Jack started shaking pretty violently. I didn't know whether to yell for help or put the disc on the player for him. I was freaking out, but I didn't want to show that to him, so I handed him the disc. He fumbled with it for what seemed like an hour but was most likely thirty seconds, until he finally got the hole to go over the peg on the stereo. He then reached for the needle arm and scratched the shit out of the demo a few times before finally getting it to the beginning of the song.

Holy Jesus. By now I was having a complete panic attack!

He looked at me sternly and told me to relax. The intro of the song started . . . but something was wrong! Five seconds in, I realized his turntable was playing at 33 1/3 rpm and not 45. Jack was now relaxed with his eyes closed, listening to my song at the wrong speed.

"Holy shit," I thought. "This can't be happening. Surely he knows that this is playing at the wrong speed?"

The vocalist was now singing, twenty seconds into the first verse, and I was about to either scream, "IT'S THE WRONG FUCK-ING SPEED!" or climb over his desk to change the speed on his turntable.

A split second before I did both, Jack opened his eyes, smiled at me for the first time, and said, "Yes, something wrong?"

"Mr. Gold, I'm sorry but the demo is playing at the wrong speed," I said, exasperated.

"If it's a great song," he shot back, "it'll hold up."

A beat, and then he started laughing.

He totally got me! No one bothered to tell me that he ALSO had this incredibly wicked sense of humor.

He knew how green I was, and he was having fun fucking with me. After that, he asked me to put the remaining two songs on the player for him, and we listened to them at the right speed. He even put one of the songs on hold for an artist he was working with.

In the end, he didn't cut it, but Jack saw me often, and whenever I felt like I had a great song, his door was always open. He recorded four or five of my songs over the years with Johnny Mathis, Andy Williams, and Susan Anton.

He was a one of a kind!

Speaking of one of a kind: my mom had two musical superheroes that she watched on TV religiously every week. I think she made me watch as well. Perry Como and Andy Williams could do no wrong in her book. When I got a call from Jack Gold to meet with him and Andy, I scrambled to find an Andy Williams album that he might autograph to his biggest fan, Elaine Dorff.

Jack was not doing as much production as he used to and had left Columbia due to his declining health. I had been doing quite a bit of arranging and now production, and Andy was looking to record some new material for his next album. Jack thought we would be a good fit to go into the studio and record a few things.

At the last minute, Jack called and said he couldn't make the meeting, and for me to just handle it directly with Andy. We met at a nice bistro in Beverly Hills for lunch. Andy was with his brother, Don Williams, who was managing him at the time. Don and I sort of knew each other through Ray Stevens, whom he also managed. Like me, Ray was a former graduate of Lowery Music University.

Coincidentally, Claudine Longet—Andy's former wife who had been involved in the shooting scandal years before—had recorded a song of mine for her album.

I didn't bring that up.

There was a lot of incestuous stuff going on here.

I didn't bring that up, either.

The lunch meeting was great. Andy knew of my work and was anxious to do something "new and contemporary," as opposed to the covers of other people's songs that crooners like him were primarily known for. We agreed to meet in a week and go over some songs that I would put together for him to hear.

And, yes, I got the autograph for my mom, and she was thrilled!

Sandy Pinkard and I had been doing some writing at the time, and he had a lyric that I really liked called "Every Time I See Maureen." I wrote the music for it in a Beach Boys style because I thought Andy's beautiful bell-tone high voice would sound great with close backing harmonies. I found a few other songs that I loved and we scheduled our song meeting.

Andy came over to the house one Saturday and we sipped tea and listened. He loved "Every Time I See Maureen" but asked me if I would change the title from "Maureen" to "Laureen," the name of his current girlfriend.

That was his only request? Done!

Andy picked three other songs for us to do, and we set the session for the following week. We tracked at A&M Studio B with some great players: Bill Cuomo, George Doering, Ed Green, and Joe Chemay. Joe put together a great Beach Boys–sounding vocal group to emulate that type of Brian Wilson harmony to back Andy.

Andy wanted to redo all of his lead vocals once I had the track completely finished. He had to go to New York and told me he would sing when he returned from his trip. I overdubbed some strings and put together a nice comp mix for him to hear while he was in New York.

Andy called me after hearing the finished tracks and told me he was going to stay in New York longer than he had originally planned, and could I fly in to New York and do his vocals there? Of course I would, especially since Columbia Records would be footing the bill and putting me up in a suite at the Plaza Hotel.

I arrived in New York and got to meet the famous Laureen at dinner with Andy. She was very pretty and very young . . . another story for another day! Andy sang his heart out the next day at a beautiful Sony-owned recording studio that was converted from a church. The sound was awesome. We ended up finishing three of the four songs that day.

Andy Williams was a legendary performer. I was so proud to get to work with him and have him sing a few of my songs. "Every Time I See Laureen" was included on his soundtrack to *Oliver's Story*. It was also released as a single, but it never really cracked the charts. It didn't matter. What mattered to me was getting the opportunity to work and become friends with him. He would later introduce me to the Osmonds, who would also go on to record a few songs of mine.

Annabelle's Wish

One of my favorite projects came at the perfect time. I was asked to a meeting about an animated Christmas movie that was being developed by the Ralph Edwards Production Company, about a baby calf who desperately wants to be one of Santa's reindeer.

I had never done an animated movie before, and there were unique challenges that came along with the project. Since there were no "live actors" in the film, much of the orchestral score had to be written to character storyboards, as opposed to film. It was a musical, and several songs that moved the plot forward had to be written, too, as well as the score.

My experience in writing for musicals with John Bettis made him the perfect choice to write the lyrics for the project. Randy Travis was the story's narrator. I had known and worked with Randy before, too, so John and I cowrote a few of the songs with him as well.

Because of non-union budget constraints, I recorded the score in Salt Lake City, Utah, with members of the Salt Lake City Symphony Orchestra. It was a fun couple of days. I took my engineer, Rick Riccio, with me, as well as Larry Herbstritt, who did the orchestrations.

Rick and I decided to try to fit in a couple of hours of skiing at Deer Valley while we were there. Halfway down the mountain, we got caught in a pretty nasty squall storm that came out of nowhere. Rick's face looked like the Abominable Snowman's. My nose felt like it was not a part of my face but completely frozen off. It was all we could do to get down the mountain without killing ourselves and back to the hotel to get ready for the second day of sessions.

I was pretty amazed at the sound we got at the studio, an old church converted into a full-blown, state-of-the-art recording facility.

The orchestra, which was comprised of 75 percent women, was

exceptional. While it's not unusual to have many wonderful women playing in the orchestra, it's not too often there is a full-blown brass section comprised of women. It was really fun, and they played great.

With Randy Travis, Beth Nielsen Chapman, Dolly Parton, Alison Krauss, Nanci Griffith, Kevin Sharp, Jerry Van Dyke, and Cloris Leachman singing the songs, the soundtrack album turned out to be fantastic. John and I wrote a beautiful lullaby called "Tiny Dreamer (Callie's Song)," sung by Nanci Griffith, which we dedicated to my one-year-old daughter, Callie. To this day, nineteen years later, Callie still always looks at the closing credits to make sure her name is listed in the song titles.

Both of my daughters, Callie and Kaitlyn, still have their *Annabelle's Wish* Christmas stockings, which they hang every year, and I love that they, as well as my boys, will be able to watch and share this holiday movie with their families for the rest of their lives.

For me, that was the greatest Christmas gift I could ever ask for.

Vintage Jukebox: My '53 Seeburg

In 1979, I received a rather large check in the mail from BMI.

Up to this point, I had gotten many quarterly checks from BMI for amounts generally in the $50–125 range. I was always happy and excited to get that extra mailbox money.

When this particular check came, however, I opened up the envelope and did a double take. There were far too many zeros in it. There had been a mistake.

"I think BMI screwed up," I said to Nancy as I showed it to her. "This is way too much for just the first quarter of earnings, don't ya think?"

Nancy's dad saw the check and immediately exclaimed, "I get checks like that all the time in the mail. It's a scam, no one ever wins."

Obviously she thought it was a *Reader's Digest* check or something.

I knew it had been a particularly good quarter. *Every Which Way but Loose*—both the film and the Eddie Rabbitt record—had been enormous hits. The single was the all-time highest first week entry in *Billboard* history, debuting at eighteen. Still, I had no idea how good of a quarter it actually was.

Suffice it to say, we were happy to learn that BMI had not screwed up, and that those zeros were in fact real. I immediately called Milton in Mobile to see if he had gotten an identical amount. He had, and he was still peeling himself off the ceiling.

One of my longtime dreams was to have an antique jukebox in my house that had nothing but my songs on it. It was a pretty tall order indeed, but first I had to have the jukebox. It was a purchase I could only legitimately make with the rare occasional "fuck you" money. And, all of a sudden, I was flush with a few thousand extra "fuck you" dollars.

I knew exactly where I was going to spend my surplus. There was a store in Van Nuys I had always wanted to go to but had never dared to step foot in. It was called Jukebox City.

As soon as the check cleared, I headed over. It was a cool store, owned by a guy who found and restored these beautiful machines into mint condition.

I was a kid in a candy store!

As I was looking around the showroom, I saw the one that had my name on it: a vintage 1953 Seeburg, the first model they made to play 45s. It was exactly like the one used on the opening credits of the TV show *Happy Days*. It was in mint condition, with color wheels and improved speakers.

They wanted $2,500 for it, and I bought it on the spot.

It took me about six years, but eventually I was able to fill it with fifty 45 rpm singles that I had written. Of the one hundred songs total on the jukebox, I had written eighty of them. Now, in full disclosure, some of them were B-sides, some were lousy versions of mediocre songs, but I had fulfilled one of my dreams!

Fats Domino

There's only one Fats Domino, and what a hoot it was to get to arrange a song for this legendary performer.

"Whisky Heaven" was a song that Fats was set to record for the film *Any Which Way You Can*. Fats had insisted on using his band for the recording, so I was asked to fly to Las Vegas, where Fats was performing, to record the track. Fortunately, we found a fairly good studio there, and along with a few great players who I brought with me from L.A. as insurance, we set out to prerecord the song that Fats would sing in the movie, on camera.

Having been told that Fats had a great five-piece horn section, I wrote out a fairly simple brass arrangement for them that we could record there as well. To say that his band was a bit ragged by "session player standards" would be an understatement. Fats was a beautiful soul, and his band were all really great guys, and excited for the chance to be on the record. The only slight problem was that they were terribly out of tune with each other.

Luckily, we were able to get a track done thanks to the ringers I had brought along from L.A. The horn section was a different story. I passed out the parts that I had written for the two trumpets, trombone, and tenor and baritone sax. They all looked at me like I was crazy. One of them had his music upside-down on his music stand, but he didn't realize it.

None of them read music.

For the next two hours we cobbled together a brass overdub, mostly three or four bars at a time, as we improvised parts that I had to sing to them. Miraculously, we got it done enough so I could head back to L.A. and try to figure out how to make it all work as a finished product without Clint Eastwood killing me.

Long story short, after returning to L.A. I overdubbed almost all new parts over the existing parts, salvaging what I could, and replacing the out-of-tune stuff. Fats's vocal was great, and the finished product was pure Fats Domino.

The upside-down trombone part still makes me laugh.

31

Hold

An interesting concept in the music-publishing world is the "hold."

This is when a recording artist or producer likes one of your songs, has the intention of recording it, and wants to take it off the market so that no other artist or producer will have access to it.

It is equally exhilarating and frustrating.

For a songwriter, there's nothing quite like getting that phone call that informs you that an artist has put one of your songs on hold—or, even better, that they are actually recording one of them. I guess, for me, about the highest honor I can be paid is when a great recording artist, or anyone, for that matter, chooses something I've written above the thousands of other songs that get submitted for any project.

It goes without saying that getting a song recorded, especially by a top-tier recording artist, is almost a miracle in itself. Having a hit single . . . maybe the odds are equal to be getting hit by lightning. My collaborator Eric Kaz and I said once in a bout of frustration, "Let's face it, we songwriters live miracle to miracle." We looked at each other, and of course a day later wrote a song called "Miracle to Miracle."

I've had songs of mine put on hold for various periods of time, ranging from twenty-four hours to two weeks. Who the artist or producer is will often be the deciding factor as to how long one should honor that hold. Once you grant someone a firm hold on a song, you've essentially made the decision to not show that particular song to anyone else. If the person who has requested the hold ends up not recording the song, then you've wasted valuable time, and have missed other potential opportunities for getting that song recorded by someone else. It can be a tricky situation, as I have found it to be on several occasions. For one thing, it is unfair for a writer to put a song on ice for any period of time without any compensation.

In one instance, I had a brand new song cowritten with Eric Kaz called "Hypnotize the Moon." Eric and I were excited about the demo we had just done and were anxious to start the process of getting it out there. We were getting quite a bit of great feedback from people who were hearing it.

Then came THE call.

A respected producer called me from Nashville and said he had heard the song, and would love to record it with hit country artist Ty Herndon. He thought it would be a smash for him, and he just needed a few days to get it to his artist, who was on the road performing. He asked if he could put a hold on the song until he had the chance to play it for Ty.

I, of course, said okay. I called Eric to tell him the good news, and we agreed to stop showing the song to anyone else until we heard back from the producer.

A week went by and we heard nothing. I felt like we had a really good song, and I was reluctant to wait too much longer for a confirmation that they were going to record it, but I also knew that schedules of performing artists can often be hectic, and a possible Ty Herndon record was certainly worth waiting a little longer for. I finally heard back and was assured that they were going to go into the studio to begin recording his new album, with our song included on it, within the next month. Ty was excited about the song and eager to record it.

A month passed. Then two. Eventually, I decided to check in and see how the project was going.

Word was that Ty had recorded the song, and, according to the producer, it had come out "Fantastic!" He went one step further to tell me it was likely to be either the first or second single from the record. I couldn't wait to hear it, and I was getting pretty jazzed at the possibility of having a hit. The release date of the album finally arrived a few months later. I asked my assistant to run over to a record store to pick up the CD. When I got back from a lunch appointment, the CD was on my desk. I immediately undid the wrapper and looked at the back cover to see where "Hypnotize the Moon" was on the track list.

I kept scanning up and down and couldn't find it.

Was I going blind? I opened the accompanying booklet and looked for our song. There were twelve songs on the CD, and "Hypnotize the Moon" was not one of them. Just a little bit pissed, I called the producer in Nashville and delivered a rather long rant.

"What happened to our song? I thought we were going to have a single. You kept this song on hold for EIGHT MONTHS, and then it didn't even make the album, after you told me it came out fantastic?"

There was a moment of dead silence. Finally, he spoke.

"We didn't feel like in the end we really hooked it. We would like to try cutting it again for the next album . . . can we put it on hold?"

Was I going deaf? Did he really just ask to keep the song on hold indefinitely?

"I don't think so," I said definitively. "I'm not going to hold this song for another year, only to be disappointed if you fail to hook it again. Thanks but no thanks."

Never again, I muttered to myself. I truly believe that a hold on a song should be treated like a short-term rental. Put a non-refundable deposit down for a certain amount of time; if you record the song, the fee is returned; if you don't, like in this particular incident, the writers and publishers keep the deposit for their trouble. Easy as that.

Fortunately for Kaz and me, there was a happy ending to this story. Within a few days I sent the song to a few other producers I had heard were looking for material for upcoming projects. My friend James Stroud, who was producing hit artist Clay Walker, heard the song and played it for Clay; a week later they were in the studio recording "Hypnotize the Moon" for his new album. And boy, did they ever "hook it."

The song came out as the first single from his new album, *Hypnotize the Moon*, and went to #1.

As far as honoring holds would go, never again will I let a song be put on hold for an unreasonable period of time, unless I have assurance that the song gets recorded and released.

Lesson learned.

32

My Own Best Publisher

Our songs are our children.

I haven't gotten to write nearly as many songs with Paul Williams as I would have liked, but the dozen or so that we have written together include some really good ones, with a few "hits waiting to happen."

Paul, like so many of the classically great lyricists, has a style and language all his own. The depth of what he says in a song, and how he says it, is incomparable and unique to him.

Paul and I were introduced to each other by Chuck Kaye, who was running Irving/Almo Publishing on the A&M lot. Chuck suggested that we try to schedule a writing session because he thought we could do some great things together. We met for lunch one day at a sushi restaurant in Studio City, and of course, being a huge fan, I had to ask him as many questions about his career as I could possibly think of.

Finally, we got around to talking about the role of a great publisher. I had always admired Chuck as a great publisher—someone who could pick up the phone and get almost anyone to listen to a song he was excited about. I really missed that in my career. While I was at Snuff Garrett's, I never really had someone who would function in that particular role. I was always the one who, after writing and demoing a new song, would work for days and weeks trying to get the song placed and recorded.

Paul then gave me a piece of advice I have never forgotten, and that I guess I instinctively knew all along.

"Steve, we will always be our own best publishers. The writer puts a piece of his heart and soul into every song he writes, and 24/7, he lives and breathes the songs he creates. Our songs are our children!"

A publisher, for the most part, is an agent for many writers and many more songs, and although they may love certain songs more than others, and be dedicated to trying to get them cut, there's just no way that he or she can possibly feel as emotionally attached over a long period of time.

I took Paul's advice to heart, and I still continue to pore over my back catalog of songs, knowing that a truly great song has no expiration date.

A great example of that is a song I cowrote with Gary Harju that the late Dottie West recorded called "The Woman in Love with You." Dottie did a lovely performance of the song on an album that Snuff and I coproduced. It was never released as a single. Some eleven years later, I was home in bed with the flu and could do nothing but lay around listening to songs. Somehow, I ended up revisiting that one, as I had always loved the melody and what the lyric said.

I had the idea to change a few lines and re-demo it for a man to sing. Gary suggested a line change for the man to sing, *"Don't always wear the white hat,"* and I immediately thought of George Strait for this "brand new" eleven-year-old song. George heard it, loved it, and we had our third #1 record together.

Once again: never give up on a song you really believe in!

As for Paul Williams and me, in addition to a song called "Double or Nothing," which we wrote as a duet for Kenny Loggins and Gladys Knight for the *Rocky IV* movie, we have written some wonderfully poignant songs together, of which I am extremely proud.

I will continue to not give up on them, either.

I must say that, after leaving Garrett Music, I did start to enjoy having a staff of song pluggers at Warner/Chappell after Chuck Kaye, who had left Irving/Almo to take over as CEO, brought me over there. I also loved the writer/publisher connection I had with Ira Jaffe, both at Famous Music and then later for a brief time at NEM. Ira was a great song man, and he could smell a hit as soon as he heard one.

I often debated with my son Andrew the value of going back through one's catalog with the idea of resurrecting good songs that might have fallen through the cracks and might not have gotten recorded when they were new. With all of the songs being written and demoed weekly in Nashville alone, it seems like the shelf life of a great new song is lucky to be three or four days. The volume of new songs being written is staggering.

For me, a big year of writing songs might total sixty. Today, in Nashville, young writers have told me they are turning out 250–300 songs per year. In many respects, the business has become a "throw enough shit on the wall and some of it is bound to stick" scenario.

In fairness to the major publishers who are servicing twenty-five to fifty songwriters each, it's seemingly impossible to service that many songs to the select few artists, producers, and record company A&R people who are looking for material. There simply aren't that many projects, so the odds of getting even a great song cut become pretty slim.

Factor in the reality that a lot of artists or producers write their own songs, and the odds get dramatically slimmer still for the independent or staff songwriter. Hence, my song written with Eric Kaz . . . we live "Miracle to Miracle."

It's been a rare occurrence for me that a brand new song, freshly demoed, gets recorded right away. Unfortunately, lightning in a bottle like that just hasn't been my career's MO. That's why I am constantly going back through my catalogs, listening and rethinking songs I truly believe in.

"I Cross My Heart" and "The Man in Love with You" were both #1 records for George Strait. There were also eight and eleven years old, respectively, before George recorded them. Over the years I've had dozens of my songs recorded years after I wrote them. It just takes a lot of belief and perseverance.

One such example happened just this week.

In 1996, Kent Blazy and Kim Williams, two amazing songwriters from Tennessee, came out to Los Angeles to write with me for a few days. I think we wrote about six songs in three days. It was a marathon. These guys were quick with fresh ideas and even better at executing those ideas. One of the songs we started that week was an idea called "Lay Down and Dance." It was a fun, up-tempo song that I eventually recorded with Troy Cassar-Daley.

I always thought it was a better idea than a baked song.

Kim and Kent had stayed friends, and they remained in contact with me over the years.

About a year ago, Kent called me to tell me the tragic news that Kim Williams had suddenly passed away. I was heartbroken. Kim was one of the nicest and most talented guys you could ever meet. We had just written a couple of new songs together a few months prior to his passing.

Kim and Kent both had a longstanding association with the great

Garth Brooks. Garth was looking to do a new album project, and Kent was sending him some songs, one of which was our twenty-year-old relic "Lay Down and Dance."

Garth absolutely loved the title, and the song's meaning. He just didn't think the music or lyric were quite as relevant as they needed to be. He suggested we start from scratch and give the song a complete facelift, to make it more "Garth." He recommended bringing in one of his favorite cowriters, Victoria Shaw, to help out, and help out she did: I just received a call that "Baby, Lay Down and Dance" will be included on Garth's new ten-CD retrospective collection, as well as being the first single release from his forthcoming new album.

I continue to mine the old catalog for the hidden gems that, for some reason, haven't yet had their time to shine. Thanks, Paul, for the early on great advice!

33

SHERRY, NANCY, AND MOM

THE YEAR 2008 is one I would love to forget but surely never will. Within the space of five months, I lost two of the most important women in my life.

My first wife and my mother.

In 2005, Nancy was complaining of blurred vision, and had experienced a few episodes of temporarily losing her peripheral vision. She had just finished getting her master's degree in psychology, and was working on her doctorate. I told her I thought it was probably just a case of her eyes being tired from all of the heavy reading and papers she had to write. She went to the eye doctor, who after doing a full evaluation recommended possibly seeing a neurologist, as the loss of peripheral vision was a bit troublesome to him.

After several exams and evaluations, a CT scan revealed a tiny dot in the occipital lobe, or vision center of the brain. The doctor was almost certain it was nothing to be alarmed about, simply a small lesion. Over the course of the next six months and a few more episodes of vision distortion, another CT scan and MRI were ordered, and we got the dreaded news: it was in fact a small tumor, and that small dot had grown significantly. Nancy would need to have a biopsy to determine exactly what we were all facing.

Glioblastoma was the last thing any of us had wanted to hear. I had never heard that term before, but it sure didn't sound good. Over the course of the next few years, the regimens of chemo treatments, radiation, and a new trial drug that actually shrunk the tumor by 85 percent gave us tremendous hope that Nancy would beat this thing.

She fought hard, but the disease fought harder.

After almost three years of what was the most difficult and gut-wrenching experience of my life, we said goodbye to Nancy shortly after midnight on February 19, 2008. She was only fifty-nine years old.

My boys were devastated at their loss of their mother, and I was, too. My daughters Callie and Kaitlyn had come to love Nancy so much in their young lives, and they too were heartbroken. Nancy had many close and valued friends who were shattered by her loss.

Everyone loved her.

Even though deep down I knew it was increasingly inevitable, her passing left me with deep unresolved sadness. Months before her death, Nancy came to my house and we cried together and shared stories, apologies, regrets, and hopes. She asked me to take care of our boys and my girls, whom she loved as if they were her own. Her love for Callie and Kaitlyn was a shining example of giving that she showed Stephen and Andrew. It has enabled my four children to love and accept each other as true brothers and sisters. That is the greatest gift that Nancy could ever have given to me.

Her passing also left me with a new unexpected challenge of being my boys' only parent. She was an adoring mom who took such good care of them, always planning every holiday and family event. I regretfully never realized how much credit she deserved for doing all she did for our sons. The saddest part for me, personally, was that after six long years of dedicated study, a brilliant thesis, and hundreds of hours spent helping people as a clinical psychologist, Nancy had received her hard-earned doctorate, and was on the verge of what would have been, no doubt, an important career of helping so many children and families. I am so proud of her accomplishment, proud to have known and loved Dr. Nancy Dorff (the first doctor in my entire family history), and proudest of her for being the best mom to our sons.

At the time of Nancy's passing, my mom had just celebrated her ninety-fourth birthday. Other than osteoporosis, she was in pretty good shape. Her mind was sharp, and she could carry on full and intelligent conversations with the nurses and friends residing in the assisted-living facility where she was in nearby Camarillo, California. I would normally try to get up to see her at least every few weeks when I was in town and not traveling.

I had just gotten back from a trip to Nashville and drove up one afternoon to visit. We had lunch together, I caught her up on what the kids and I were up to, and then she whipped my butt in a game of Scrabble before I kissed her and said goodbye. I remember laughing with the nurses about how well she was doing and how much energy she had.

Three days later, at about nine in the morning, I received a call from one of the nurses who told me my mother wasn't waking up.

"What do you mean, she's not waking up? Is she alive?" I asked.

The nurse explained that her vitals were starting to shut down, and because they have seen this time and time again in people my mother's age, it was most likely that my mom was not going to wake up.

I jumped in the car and shot up there in about thirty minutes. By the time I arrived, Elaine Dorff had already passed away peacefully in her sleep.

Ironically, it would have been my dad's ninety-fifth birthday.

My sister Sherry, ever the optimist, would later say, "Mom was giving Dad a birthday present."

It was an unbelievably sad drive back home for me, flooded by memories of things I hadn't thought about in years. I was much closer to my mom than I was my dad. I was a lot more like her in so many ways. In spite of the years I struggled with her drinking, I loved her very much. She and my grandma (her mother, Gertie) were always there for me, and had been the solid foundation of my upbringing. My mom never stopped telling me I could do anything I put my heart and mind to, and she gave me that all-important high self-esteem that would help me navigate the ups and downs of this life.

Losing my mom was hard. Losing my sister was harder.

Even though we lived on opposite coasts, Sherry and I had stayed close throughout our lives. We would speak on the phone at least once a month, never miss a holiday or birthday call, and generally would keep up with each other fairly regularly regarding our mom, and dad, when he was alive.

There were a few years in there where we drifted. Sherry, like both my parents, was unable to stop drinking once she started. She was in total denial about it, and I frankly couldn't deal with speaking to her on the phone when I could tell from her first slurred word that she had had way too much to drink.

Once, when Sherry was visiting me in California, I was going to an event and she asked if she could open a bottle of wine and have a glass while I was gone. I came home a few hours later to four empty bottles, and I was uncomfortably thrown back in time to when both of my parents would do the exact same thing. Only this time, I wasn't eight or ten; I couldn't run to my room, bury my head in the pillow, shut the world off, and visit the orchestra in my head.

Sherry and I had a series of serious "Come to Jesus" conversations about her health, and how she desperately needed to get help for her alcoholism. Thankfully, she started to attend AA meetings back in New York, and she was finally on the right path to staying away from her demon in the bottle.

I was unbelievably proud of her.

A few years ago, Sherry was on vacation in Vegas when suddenly her face began noticeably swelling up. She felt no pain but had some shortness of breath. She went to an emergency room and the doctor there said she should probably get examined when she got home, as he couldn't really diagnose without a full MRI or CT scan.

Upon arriving home, Sherry went in for tests that showed a fairly large tumor on her lung. It was small-cell lung cancer, commonly caused from smoking. Sherry had been a heavy smoker since she was a teenager.

Sherry's only daughter, Lizz, was due to have her first child, a beautiful little girl named Ella Gaffney. I truly believe that Ella added a year onto Sherry's life. Sherry fought and fought through round after round of chemo and radiation treatments. She lived to be a grandma to that little girl.

On May 17, 2016, my big sister peacefully passed away.

My entire immediate family growing up was gone.

It has been a difficult adjustment, not having Sherry here. In some strange way I feel like an orphan, even though I have my kids to see or speak to every day. Sherry knew me longer than any other human being on the planet, from the first day I was born. I miss her terribly.

Tina Shafer—a talented singer/songwriter from New York—and

I had written a beautiful, poignant song about her brother's passing many years ago. I don't think I ever truly appreciated the depth of Tina's lyric until Sherry passed away. It's one of my all-time favorite songs that I have written, and it has never been recorded.

It doesn't matter. I have started playing "The Backyard Sky," in Nancy, Sherry, and Elaine's memory.

Each one of these beautiful women taught me so much about strength, courage, perseverance, and unconditional love.

May God rest their souls.

In their own way, each of these women shared deeply my passion for music, and they never stopped supporting and encouraging me to follow my dream—especially the dream of writing a Broadway musical.

34

BROADWAY, HERE I COME

The Josephine Baker Story

IT FEELS LIKE I've been writing about Josephine for 119 years. But Josephine would have never happened without *Lunch*.

Despite the personal debacles surrounding *Lunch*, we decided to do a concept CD to keep the show alive. We went to various artists we knew, and they all agreed to sing. Faith Prince, Carol Burnett, Davis Gaines, Kim Carnes . . . all said yes. The show had a short run, and the CD could be purchased at various music stores around the country.

Cut to twenty years later.

I got a call from Tony Award–winning producer Ken Waissman, whose hits included *Grease*, *Agnes of God*, and *Torch Song Trilogy*. He wanted to know if I'd write the score for a show called *Josephine: The Josephine Baker Story*.

"Of course I'd be interested. How'd you decide on me?"

"Bob."

"Bob? Who is Bob?"

I racked my brains. For the life of me I had no idea who Bob was . . . especially a Bob who could convince a Tony-winning producer to blindly hire me.

Bob worked at the famed (and now closed) Colony Records on Broadway and 47th. The store was an institution in New York City and boasted one of the nation's biggest collections of sheet music, vinyl, theatrical songs, and all forms of music memorabilia. Ken Waissman was at the store checking out when Bob, a cashier with long stringy dirty black hair, asked him, "What are you listening to these CDs for?"

"I'm looking for the next great composer-lyricist team to write the next great musical for me."

"Oh. Okay. Well, you forgot one then. *Lunch*."

Bob went to the back of the store, in some discarded, cobweb-filled corner, and pulled out our CD. Now, Colony Records supposedly stocked anything that's ever been performed anywhere, any time in the world. That's how driven they were to have everything possible.

Somewhere over the course of the next three days, Ken was meeting with Ellen Weston, *Josephine*'s book writer, and they listened to Davis Gaines sing "Time Stands Still," which I cowrote with John Bettis. She looked at Ken and said, "These are the guys."

It helps to be at the right place at the right time.

It's essential to be good at what you do.

This combination breeds success . . . plus, it's always helpful to have a Bob in your corner.

Yet, because of the *Lunch* debacle, John Bettis and I swore it would be a long time before we'd tackle another theater piece.

Never say never.

Before *Josephine* came along, we had a few "can't say no" projects. The first was in 2001, when Rick Hawkins approached us with a project based on the life and love of George Burns and Gracie Allen. It was called *Say Goodnight*. John and I both loved the whole idea and didn't hesitate before saying, "We're in."

Rick wrote a fabulous book and John and I began to write some really terrific theatrical songs. To this day, I think some of the songs we wrote for *Say Goodnight* are some of our best. We did a workshop reading, and that's about as far as that one went because Frank Gorshin, a top comedian/impressionist most notable as the Riddler from Adam West's *Batman*, decided to do a one-man show on Broadway called *Say Goodnight Gracie*.

The timing sucked. We were dead in the water with our show.

Pure Country is a musical based on the movie that I did all the music for. Rex McGee, who wrote the screenplay, came to John and me one day and said, "Let's do a musical." Again, we said yes. We've toiled with this one for nine or ten years. But we've hung in because we think it's a great show, especially for Middle America. I'm not sure if it will ever go to Broadway, but it could easily sit down in places like Nashville and Vegas. We opened at the Lyric Stage in Dallas in June 2017 for the show's premiere run.

Josephine was our fourth stab at writing a stage musical and, without question, our best chance of going to Broadway. We've written over sixty songs for this show; we've had readings and workshops. We had six different Josephine Bakers playing the title role until we landed on the spectacular Deborah Cox—that rare triple threat who finally brought Josephine to life. And we are closer than we have ever been to a Broadway opening.

But it hasn't always been easy.

The war stories about our musicals are no different to most others. There are a lot of talented writers with a lot of strong opinions. And with so many cooks in the kitchen, it's nothing short of a miracle that we were able to do a standing-room-only run at the prestigious Asolo Repertory Theater in Sarasota, Florida, in the spring of 2016.

As of this writing, we are aiming to go up in New York in 2018.

Fun fact: Colony Records was located in the same historic Brill Building where Carole King and Gerry Goffin, Mike Leiber and Jerry Stoller, and Barry Mann and Cynthia Weil wrote some of the undying hits of the sixties. And before Herb Bernstein, Bill Lowery, and Snuff Garrett came into my life, it was the same building where I had first started knocking on doors. Unfortunately for me, I was a decade behind the glory of the Brill Building.

35

Evenings with Steve Dorff

Although I am a pretty good piano player, I have never considered myself a singer, nor did I ever want to "perform" in public.

That changed when Bobby Tomberlin convinced me to be "the face" of my songs.

Paul Williams had actually encouraged me first, but I wasn't ready at the time. Now, in my sixties, I do the occasional *Evening with Steve Dorff*, where I sit behind the piano, sing and play my hits, and tell the stories behind them. These began after Bobby Tomberlin first encouraged me to play a few shows with him, and I discovered that audiences love to hear the behind-the-scenes stories almost better than hearing the familiar hit songs done by a random pianist singing George Strait's hit song.

I now love doing it, but in the beginning, I had to be pulled kicking and screaming to do it.

Yes, I could sit down at a dinner party with friends or family and play a few of my hits without causing myself too much anxiety, but I never really had the desire to actually play in front of hundreds of people I didn't know. Then Bobby and I started doing some *Writers in the Round* in Nashville and at a few songwriter festivals that were sponsored by BMI.

To be honest, I was never a fan of playing "rounds" with more than one other writer. In the first place, being a keyboard player, it has often been awkward to be squeezed between several guitar players. Secondly, the kinds of songs I write don't really fit musically with a lot of the situations I've been put in, which are organized by people that either don't care about that sort of thing or can't really tell the difference. Lastly, if the chemistry isn't right between the respective writers, it can prove to be a train wreck of an evening.

That has happened one time too many for me. I've noticed that some writers tend to make these performances a sort of one-upmanship fest—a contest or competition to see "who has written the biggest hits," replete with sarcasm and the occasional verbal snark toward the other participating writers.

This didn't go over too well for me when I experienced a rather cocky songwriter, who had had a few hits, trying too hard to make himself shine over Bobby and me. He was a fool to think he could get away with that with me, because for every hit he played, I played a bigger one. He ran out of recognizable songs long before I did, and he came across like a redneck ass-clown with his total lack of class and humility.

It was embarrassing not only for Bobby and me but for everyone else at the venue.

When I perform, the one thing I have definitively learned is that unless the audience is a "listening audience," the show doesn't work. Perhaps the worst experience I've had, that taught me that lesson in spades, was a show I agreed to do with Bobby at a place called Puckett's in downtown Nashville. We might as well have been a hired garage band playing covers. The rowdy, obnoxious audience totally ignored us and just kept eating, drinking, and talking.

I looked at Bobby and simply said, "Never again." After that I told him I would only consider doing shows that included guest performances by close friends, where our music had at least something in common with their music.

There is a little place in North Hollywood called Kulak's Woodshed. The best way to describe the room would be a surreal bedroom on an acid trip: books, birdcages, wall-to-wall posters and pop art, a queen-sized bed in the middle of the room, and clutter everywhere. A beautiful baby grand Yamaha piano is squeezed between all of this, with film camera operators and a full-view TV screen that receives emails from viewers watching you play live. On a busy night it might hold fifty people maximum.

Bobby and I decided to book an evening there, and we had a blast. The place was packed, and as Bobby and I traded stories and songs, everyone had a really great time. Paul Kulak, who owns the venue, makes these incredible DVDs of the performances, and the sound in there was surprisingly stellar.

The best thing about these shows, for me personally, was discovering that I could get out and play in front of people who really appreciated the experience of hearing songs they knew and loved performed by the people that wrote them. I also realized that I could be somewhat funny and entertaining when telling the crazy stories of how the hits happened, and that fine line between glorious success and dismal failures. For the first time ever in my career, I was actually having fun playing. My confidence in these situations had been greatly restored. Maybe Bobby and Paul were right? I figured it might be a good time to branch out a bit and make people more aware of the person behind the music.

I eventually started to play a few BMI events solo for my friend Dan Spears, who coordinates events with corporate sponsors and radio executives, with the goal of educating these people about what performing rights societies actually do for the writers and publishers that they represent. After doing a few of these shows by myself, and feeling like I had a good handle on what was becoming fun and easier for me, I was ready to attempt a full-on two-hour *Evening with Steve Dorff*.

What could I lose? Except my sanity, self-respect, and newly found confidence.

Ideally, I wanted to play somewhere other than Los Angeles or Nashville. A friend who books these types of shows in Florida suggested a venue in Fort Lauderdale called the Bonnet House. This place was a historic home and museum, built on several acres of a botanical wonderland. The setting for my show was outdoors on a beautiful November evening, with a full moon over the ocean. They sold three hundred tickets to the show. Some of the guests included friends I had gone to school within New York City, now transplants who had moved to Florida for the winters. I hadn't seen some of these people in over forty years. I also had friends from my college days at Georgia who lived in Florida. It was a great reunion of sorts, and the show itself was well received.

I have since done about twenty shows as I try to keep as normal a "home schedule" as possible, since my daughters both live with me full-time. Some of my more memorable *Evenings* were at the Cutting Room in New York City and Bogie's in Westlake, California, where I had lots of friends and songwriting fans in the audiences.

To this point, my favorite show was one I did recently in Danbury, Connecticut, at the Palace Theater. It was just one of those seamless performances where everything I said and played seemed to flow naturally and without any hiccups. As I hopefully get the opportunity to do more of these, I realize that there is a certain intimacy between myself and the audience that comes with what I do, and that is necessary to make the performance enjoyable for everyone by being as open and authentic as possible.

I have grown to love performing, and these evenings give me a great platform from which to do so. It's become both a challenge and great fun to help educate the average listener to the fact that there are just plain old songwriters in the world whom nobody has heard of, who write the hit songs heard on the radio for big-name recording artists to sing and perform. Not being the face of my songs has its advantages and disadvantages: being told "I'm one of the greatest songwriters that no one has ever heard of" gets under your skin after a while.

It's not really an ego thing, either. It's more the frustration that most people simply do not recognize the fact that there are people like me who, while we are not in the spotlight, contribute greatly to the world of music by writing the soundtrack to people's lives.

When I began playing in a few clubs, at the urging of friends and associates, I was amazed at how many audience members had absolutely no clue that I wrote "that Barbra Streisand song" or "that Kenny Rogers hit." Yes, Barbra, Kenny, and all the rest are the "faces" of my songs, but I like to think of myself as the heart and soul behind them.

I discovered that when people finally "get it," they are fascinated by the stories and situations behind the creation of these creations.

The usual three questions I get are:

1. What comes first, the words or the music?
2. How long did it take to write that one?
3. Did you have the artist who made it a hit in mind when you wrote it?

These are all excellent questions that are pretty easy to answer.

1. Depends on who I am writing with, and it varies from song to song.
2. Anywhere from twenty minutes to a year.
3. Ninety-nine percent of the time . . . No.

The toughest question that I get is, "What's your favorite song that you've ever written?"

That is an impossible question to answer. Yes, I have some that I think are maybe my best work in terms of craft, but a lot of those have never been heard, aren't the most commercial, or might not ever get recorded. Some of my most successful songs are ones I don't consider to be even close to my best.

Much to my surprise, I've been asked after a show or performance, "Do you have a CD I can buy?" I got to seriously thinking, "What are my best songs?" Isn't that a purely subjective thing, depending on who the listener is, and what their individual tastes are in music?

A few years ago, I was in the process of re-demoing a few older songs that I felt could use a facelift, in terms of their presentation. I was happy with the way some of these songs were coming out, with little production value, and a simpler and more straightforward approach to the demos. I started to think about making a CD for myself, including the twelve songs that I consider to be, not my favorites per se, but my "completely subjective choices of what I think constitute my best work."

Okay, shoot me, I said it . . . I guess they might be some of my favorites.

I wanted the project to reflect who I am personally to anyone who might listen to it. I chose songs that were emotionally tied together in one piece, and that told a somewhat autobiographical story about the guy who, along with his talented cowriters, wrote these songs.

I called the CD *It's Personal.*

The fact that I was going through a tough breakup at the time that cut awfully deep most definitely influenced the types of songs I included. I even wrote two new songs that were totally inspired by my search for understanding why "*love does what it does,*" one of my favorite lines from a song I wrote with Susan Ruth. Completing this project took me six months, and it was the best therapy I could have ever asked for. I also finally had a CD I could sell at my performances the next time anyone asked me if I had one.

And, now, I'll have a book as well.

It was actually at one of my shows that I met my literary agent, Michelle Zeitlin, who introduced herself to me after seeing the show and encouraged me to put these great stories and memories down on paper. I remember thinking, "Wait, I'm not old enough to write a book. I'm not nearly done yet . . . I hope."

After all, the time to write a book is after you've experienced most of the journey, hopefully getting that emotionally taxing Ph.D. in life, when you can recognize the distinction between those dreaded three-word phrases "paying your dues" and just plain "getting screwed over." I've certainly experienced both. The passage of time certainly has a way of tempering the perception of how things really happened, and it has put things in their proper perspective.

Funny how that works.

AFTERWORD

My guess is that I saved tens of thousands of dollars in time and therapy when I made the conscious decision early on in my life that performing in front of people, trying to be a Billy Joel or an Elton John, was just not in the cards for me.

Yes, I put out a few records that were god-awful, and I played in a few bands in high school, but I was able to identify the fact that I was NOT a great singer, and I really wanted to stick to what I thought I did best . . . writing songs. I truly have loved being that "behind the scenes" guy, maintaining my anonymity, and being able to walk past the obnoxious paparazzi at great restaurants without them giving me a second glance.

In my opinion, being a songwriter who has had a successful career doing what he is passionate about is an award in itself. Most people assume that having written a #1 song is the pot of gold at the end of the rainbow. Yes, having "hits" on the radio is obviously what we all hope to accomplish. The royalty income stream is also nice, as it is indicative of the amount of success derived from the songs and music we've written.

But there is more. There is so much more.

Maybe it's because I never really considered myself to be a "musician," per se, that I have the highest regard and admiration for the amazing musicians I've gotten to experience my musical journey with, both in and out of the studio. It is truly an honor to get to work with and call my friends these musical magicians who have added so much of their talents to making my music sound so good.

I can honestly say that being in the studio with these extraordinary musical geniuses, helping me to create and expand what started in my heart and my head, has been the single most gratifying and fun part of the entire process of making music for me. I hate to leave anyone out, as I've been so blessed to work with so many great players. The list of the greats I've watched play my music over the years is staggering. I do wish, though, to single out some of the people who influenced early on and continue to influence today how I approach my arrangements, production, and even sometimes the writing.

Not being a guitar player yet relying so much on guitars in so many of my scores and arrangements, I needed to find players with great musical instincts, which is that intangible quality that is so rare and hard to find. Both George Doering and Dean Parks have contributed so much to the world of recorded music, and I am so grateful for and honored by the amazing work they have done with me on so many projects.

The foundation of any rhythm section is the bass and drums, and, ironically, almost every session I've ever done starts with my determining who is playing those instruments before any of the others. I have been so blessed to experience the best of the best, but John "J.R." Robinson, Jeff Porcaro, and Paul Leim lay it down as well as anyone who has ever played the drums. Any combination of one of these guys with either Leland Sklar, Neil Stubenhaus, or Joe Chemay on bass is about as deadly solid as it gets.

I used to think I was pretty good myself on piano and keys until I got to work with virtuosos like Randy Kerber, Randy Waldman, Michael

Omartian, and more recently Matt Rollings and Jimmy Nichols. These guys can play anything from classical to jazz to rock, country, blues, and funk.

It's been this writer's dream come true to have had these amazing talents perform my music.

I also honor the memory of Jimmy Getzoff, who was my first concertmaster when I started doing sessions in L.A. Jimmy was a consummate violinist; he always put beautiful string sections together for me, and he cared about the music as much as I did. He was a sweet man and a dear friend.

Maybe the greatest ears of any musician I have ever worked with belong to Gayle Levant, harpist extraordinaire. Gayle has been a dear friend, a regular on any orchestra date I have ever done or will ever do, and always the most trusted musical ears in any room. I can't tell you how many times, on various sessions, Gayle would come over to me on a break and whisper something like, "Check bar 65 in the second trombone part. He should be playing a G natural instead of a G-sharp." And she would be right. Her ability to take a simple chord chart and make it sound like Stravinsky has always made me smile. There's something very special about a glissando when it's played by Gayle.

A couple of truly great and meaningful experiences for me were when I got to work with two of my boyhood idols, Peter Matz and Don Sebesky. I actually hired Peter to orchestrate a musical piece that I wrote with John Bettis for Warner Bros. Studios' seventy-fifth anniversary. It was sung beautifully by Michael Crawford, and Peter's textbook arrangement was classic Peter Matz at his best.

Years later, I would ask Don Sebesky to orchestrate big-band renditions of two Christmas classics for a Rodney Carrington

Christmas album I was producing. It was certainly one of the most fun sessions I have ever experienced. Both of these musical giants inspired me so much throughout my life, and it was a kind of a full circle moment in both instances to have a chance to work with them.

I can't forget the engineers—the guys who make everything sound so good. Again, I've gotten to work with some of the very best, but John Guess and Rick Riccio were always there when I needed them. They solved any problem and contributed greatly to each and every project they worked on with me.

Recently, I have been working with a number of talented new artists and writers that I am quite sure will, in the near future, break through to become tomorrow's hit-makers. Sam Bailey, who won *The X Factor* in the UK, is one of the most powerful vocalists I have ever worked with. Dylan Chambers is a young, brilliant artist/writer from L.A.; Robyn and Tiago are a unique duo from London; and Brent Loper is a bright new country artist from Mobile, Alabama. All of these artists and others have thankfully given me the opportunity to create new music with them, and to give me more reasons to keep doing what I love to do most.

Thank you to everyone mentioned and everyone unmentioned. I could not have done it without you, and I plan to continue to celebrate and share and utilize your skills until I stop writing, which will probably be when I stop breathing. Which brings me to the question I have been asked repeatedly in the last decade: "What else is there for you to accomplish and when are you going to retire?"

Retirement is not a word in my vocabulary. I feel as if every day poses a new challenge, whether it be reinventing myself musically for the thousandth time or just trying to write that one more great song that I haven't dreamed up yet. I believe that when you run out of goals, that's when your career is over. There are those awards I haven't won, the *James Bond* movie that I've yet to be asked to score, the marquee on Broadway that has yet to put my show's name on it, and the ultimate honor, as far as I am concerned: the Songwriters Hall of Fame.

Every day I wake up to believe that these goals are within reach, and that motivates and inspires me to continue to do what I do.

My girls are older; they love having the house all to themselves with their friends when I'm gone for a short time, as long as I keep money on their ATM cards. I enjoy traveling a bit more, seeing new places, and also seeing a part of the business that was foreign to me for so long from the other side of the piano. I've gotten to meet many new people that I never would have crossed paths with, and, who knows, maybe in the near future I'll meet my next ex-wife.

Again, retirement is not and never will be a part of my vocabulary. I still love writing a song when I have a fresh idea both musically and lyrically, I still love working with great artists and musicians in the studio, and, more than ever, I still enjoy sitting at the piano and getting back in touch with what set me on this journey in the first place. After everything I've been able to accomplish to this point of my career, as an arranger, producer, and composer, I am most proud of the fact that over four hundred artists from all over the world—almost fifty of them hall-of-famers—have honored me by singing songs I have written.

I think my mom and dad were proud, although my dad's validation came much later than I would have wanted it to. Still, it resulted in me encouraging my kids, from a young age, to absolutely and unabashedly follow their dreams. And they know that I will support them in any and every way that I can. Unconditional support makes a difference.

My uncle Norman, the youngest of dad's three brothers, is also proud. He is now a spry ninety-two years old, and the only living uncle I still have. Every time I see him, he asks me the same question:

"What is it you do again Stevie?"

I always give him the same answer:

"Uncle Norman, I make shit up."

I sincerely hope that somewhere along the way I touched some people's hearts and helped them get through whatever they might have been going through in their lives. Music can be a wonderful escape and salvation, as it was for me. God put the gift of song in my heart, and I hope that maybe my music made things a little bit better for people when they most needed to hear it.

Most of all, I'll just keep waiting for the phone to ring to hear those words I'll never get tired of hearing:

"Hey, Steve, we just cut one of your songs!"

ACKNOWLEDGMENTS

To Stephen, Andrew, Callie, and Kaitlyn: where and how do I begin to tell my children how much they have meant to me in uncountable ways, and how they continue to inspire me every day of my life? Four totally individual and unique personalities, and yet the commonality of all having beautiful hearts. I so appreciate the special individual relationship I have with each of you. Without you in my world there would be no music, and no way I could ever be the person I am. Whether you know it or not, and I'm quite sure you do, being your dad has been the greatest gift, and most beautiful privilege, this life could ever have given me. I love you all so much, and wish all beautiful things for you always.

To Nancy: thank you for being the person you are, and for being there for me throughout the tough times when I was trying to find myself. You are very much alive in all of us.

To Lori: it means more than you know that we can be good friends and have each other's backs. Thank you.

A very special thanks to all of the talented musicians and recording artists who have honored me by performing my music over the years, and to the songwriters who have shared their talents with me in those many rooms where these songs came to be.

For Snuff: thank you for the belief you had in me from the beginning, all of the many doors you opened, and for giving me a platform to shine. R.I.P.

To my dear friends, and family, too numerous to mention: thank you for the contributions you've made to my life.

Hey Colette . . . I could never have accomplished this without you. You made every part of this daunting process fun, and pushed me to remember things about my journey that I had either forgotten or didn't want to revisit. Thank you!

To Backbeat Books: thank you for encouraging us to share this story. We hope it gives insight to other songwriters and creative people in the arts as to just how tough yet rewarding the struggle and journey can be.

To Michelle Zeitlin: thank you for your passion, patience, and chutzpah. We could not have done this without you.

To all of the contributors listed in this book and to the contributors who are not: Thank you. Thank you for everything. Special thanks to: Elaine Dorff, Henry Dorff, Sherry Gaffney, Gertrude Masse, Francis Dorff, Sharon Freedman, Bob Freedman, David Freedman, Zac Freedman, Dylan Freedman, Brooke Purdy, Hannah Hope, Kim Everett, Jen Prince, Jhenn Webberly, Max Purdy, Scout Purdy, Doug Purdy, Kerry Hart, Maureen Lewis, Sean Hanish, Alfred Molina, Francesca Ferrara, Vanessa Waters, Jade Sealey, Nickella Moschetti, Susan Ziegler, Tegan Summer, Mariana Marron, Myra Stevenson, Mark Hudis, Robyn Peterson, Miriam Von Freedman Troy, Moses Von Freedman Troy, Dippy Troy, Diane Troy, Sydney Bossert, Rebecca Eisenberg, Matthew Friedman, Deb Gallagher, Sue Stahl, Savannah Bloch, Briana Carman, Erica Steinlein, Christian Kennedy, Sundeep Morrison, Stephanie Stockton, Rebekah Burcham, Diana Dezube, Clair Colburn, Emilie Petrone, Ellen Braithwaite, Elan Smolar Eisenberg, Ari Smolar Eisenberg, Harrison Prince, Lyle Prince, August Prince, Gordon Prince, Ginny Hanson, Sally Flanzer,

Jerry Flanzer, Joan Gottlieb, Michael Gottlieb, Karen Tenkoff, Claudia Horwitz, Carrie Clifford, Rooney Troy, Rachel Crowl, Tania Nolan, Danny Lippin, Rick Zieff, Margaret Nagle, Sailene Ossman, Jennifer Lee, Stefanie Vaimakis, Alli Steinberg, Merzy Eisenberg, Russ Eisenberg, Julie Eisenberg, Glen Sperling, Curtis Smolar, Carina Eisenberg, Adam Gascoine, Jill Gascoine, Amy Handelman, Steve Cassling, Christopher Cain, Clint Eastwood, Hugh Wilson, John Hughes, Eric Kaz, John Bettis, Linda Thompson, Allan Rich, Marty Panzer, Don Passman, Milton Brown, Margaret Brown, Bo Goldsen, Maribeth Derry, Jim David, Paul Williams, Chris Ledesma, Jim Ed Norman, Shayne Fair, Lenny Roberts, Rick Riccio, John Guess, Doug Rider, Michael Woodrum, Greg Reneau, Sandi Naidoo, Shari Sutcliffe, Debbi Datz, Glen Datz, Dominic Mantuano, Warren Wiebe, Patti Zimmitti, Jay Landers, Bobby Tomberlin, Terri Bjerre, Bruce Phillips, Joe McGuire, Don Stalker, Peter Svenson, Bruce Hinton, Frances Preston, Ron Anton, BMI, Don Blocker, Bill Lowery, Ira Jaffe, Gary Lemel, Cotton Carrier, Doug Frank, Michael Gorfaine, Sam Schwartz, Cheryl Tiano, Roxanne Lippel, Yale Farar, Herb Bernstein, Brad Mallie, Dr. Issac Adatto, Maxine, and Julia and Oren Waters.

ANDREW MARSHALL DORFF

DECEMBER 16, 1976–DECEMBER 19, 2016

ON DECEMBER 19, 2016, I received a phone call that every parent dreads and no parent should ever get. My son Andrew Dorff passed away tragically in an accident while starting his vacation in the Caribbean.

A life cut way too short, but a life so fully and well lived. Andrew spent every waking minute loving what he did. He loved love, he loved playing with words and writing songs with people he considered his heroes, his fellow songwriters. He loved Nashville, and he very much considered it home. He loved his Universal Music family, and all of the many friends he made in the Nashville community.

Most of all, he loved his brother, and he loved his two little sisters, and I know how much he loved me. He told me two or three times a day for forty years.

I couldn't be more proud of all of his musical accomplishments, but I am so much more proud of the genuine person Andrew was. Genuine, sweet, generous, honest, caring, and loving. I will forever miss his amazing sense of humor; his weekly analysis of the NFL games on Sunday; discussing the endless differences between men and women, even though he seemed to have a much better handle on women than I ever did; and, of course, the many talks we had about songs and music.

At a young age, somewhat in the shadows of his big brother and dad, Andrew Dorff stepped out from those shadows and found the

---

light . . . and, with his own voice, he created a body of work that will live on for decades to come. For forty years I've had the honor of being Andrew's dad. He has brought me nothing but love and joy, and he was simply the best brother, friend, and son that any person could ever hope for.

I like to think that Andrew was an angel loaned to all who knew him and loved him for those forty years. His bright light will forever shine in every heart he ever touched, and I will carry his love in my heart for the rest of my days.

DISCOGRAPHY AND ACCOLADES

STEVE DORFF SONGS AS RECORDED BY:

Aaron Neville
"A Little Thing Called Life"
The Tattooed Heart

Al Caiola
"Infinity Blue"
Infinity Blue

Alison Krauss
"The World from Way Up Here"
Annabelle's Wish

Amanda Marshall
"This Could Take All Night"
Tin Cup

Andy Williams
"Every Time I See Laureen"
Oliver's Story

Anne Murray
"I Just Fall in Love Again"
New Kind of Feeling

Anne Murray
"I Don't Think I'm Ready for You"
Heart Over Mind

Anne Murray
"You Set My Dreams to Music"
Somebody's Waiting

Anne Murray
"If I Ever Fall in Love Again"
(w/ Kenny Rogers)
Greatest Hits Vol. II

Barbara Fairchild
"Let Me Love You Once Before You Go"
Mississippi

Barbra Streisand
"I'd Want It to Be You"
(w/ Blake Shelton)
Partners

Barbra Streisand
"Higher Ground"
Higher Ground

Barbra Streisand
"It Must Be You"
A Love Like Ours

Beth Neilson Chapman
"In the Moment You Were Mine"
You Hold the Key

Bill Medley
"Friday Night's a Great Time for Football"
The Last Boy Scout

Billy Dean
"Once in a While"
8 Seconds

Billy Joe Royal
"Summertime Skies"
Summertime Skies

B. J. Thomas
"As Long as We Got Each Other"
Growing Pains

B. J. Thomas
"Expression of Faith"
Back Forward

B. J. Thomas
"Skyline"
Lunch

B. J. Thomas
"We Almost Had It All"
Best of B. J. Thomas

Brenda Lee
"Ruby's Lounge"
L.A. Sessions

Cactus Brothers
"I'm Gonna Right a Great
Country Wrong"
Pure Country

Carol Burnett
"Perfectly Alone"
Lunch

Carpenters
"I Just Fall in Love Again"
Passage

Carpenters
"If I Had You"
Lovelines

Céline Dion
"Miracle"
Miracle

Chad Everett
"You Set My Dreams To Music"
Chad

Charlie Rich
"I'll Wake You Up When I Get Home"
Every Which Way but Loose

Cher
"Pirate"
Cherished

Christopher Cross
"Swept Away"
Back of My Mind

Christopher Cross
"Is There Something"
Best of Christopher Cross

Clay Walker
"My Heart Will Never Know"
If I Could Make a Living

Clay Walker
"Hypnotize the Moon"
Hypnotize the Moon

Clint Eastwood
"Barroom Buddies"
Bronco Billy

Clint Eastwood
"Beers to You"
(w/ Ray Charles)
Any Which Way You Can

Con Hunley
"Oh Girl" (Producer)
Oh Girl

Crystal Gale
"There's No Love Like Our Love"
(w/ Gary Morris)
What If We Fall in Love?

Cymarron
"Start Again"
Rings

David Frizzell
"You're the Reason God Made Oklahoma"
(w/ Shelly West)
Any Which Way You Can

David Frizzell
"I'm Gonna Hire a Wino to Decorate
Our Home"
The Family's Fine, But This One's All Mine

David Frizzell
"Another Honky-Tonk Night on
Broadway"
The David Frizzell & Shelly West Album

Davis Gaines
"Time Stands Still"
Lunch

Davis Gaines
"I'll Love You Back to Life"
Against the Tide

Dionne Warwick
"Easy Love"
No Night So Long

Dolly Parton
"Dump the Dude"
Rainbow

Dolly Parton
"Silent Night"; "Something
Bigger Than Me"
Annabelle's Wish

Donny Osmond
"Echo of Your Whisper"
Four

Dorsey Burnette
"It Happens Everytime"
Dorsey Burnette

Dottie West
"Woman in Love With You"
New Horizons

Dusty Springfield
"Let Me Love You Once Before You Go"
Let Me Love You Once Before You Go

Dusty Springfield
"I Just Fall in Love Again"
Living Without Your Love

Dusty Springfield
"As Long as We Got Each Other"
Growing Pains

Dusty Springfield
"You Set My Dreams to Music"
Something Special

Eddy Arnold
"If Only"
Yes

Eddie Rabbitt
"Every Which Way but Loose"
Every Which Way but Loose

Engelbert Humperdinck
"Definition of Love"; "True Love at Last"
Definition of Love

Eric Carmen
"As Long as We Got Each Other"
(w/ Louise Mandrell)
Tonight You're Mine

Faith Prince
"I'm No Angel"
Lunch

Gary Morris
"Lasso the Moon"
Rustler's Rhapsody

George Howard
"Spenser: For Hire"
A Nice Place to Be

George Strait
"I Cross My Heart"; "Heartland"
Pure Country

George Strait
"The Man in Love with You"
Easy Come, Easy Go

Gladys Knight
"Double or Nothing"
Rocky IV

Glen Campbell
"Any Which Way You Can"
Any Which Way You Can

Glen Campbell
"Any Which Way You Can"
It's the World Gone Crazy

Greg Lake
"Let Me Love You Once"
Greg Lake

Jackie Wilson
"Where There Is Love"; "Love Changed
Her Face"
This Love Is Real

Jennifer Warnes
"As Long as We Got Each Other"
Growing Pains

Jermaine Jackson
"Take Good Care of My Heart"
(w/ Whitney Houston)
Jermaine Jackson

Joan Kennedy
"Higher Ground"
Higher Ground

Joe Diffie
"The Way It Never Was"
Mi Amigo

Joe Odom
"Angel Child"
If You Knew Her Like I Do

John Anderson
"I Ride Alone"
Rustler's Rhapsody

John Travolta
"You Set My Dreams to Music"
Can't Let You Go

Johnny Mathis
"Never Giving Up on You"
Different Kinda Different

Judy Collins
"Liberte"
Portrait of an American Girl

Katrina Elam
"Dream Big"
"Love Will Still Be There"
Pure Country 2: The Gift

Kenny Loggins
"Double or Nothing"
Rocky IV Soundtrack

Kenny Rogers
"Through the Years"
Share Your Love

Kenny Rogers
"I Want a Son"
Love Will Turn You Around

Kenny Rogers
"After All This Time"
They Don't Make Them Like They Used To

Kenny Rogers
"If I Ever Fall in Love"
Something Inside So Strong

Kim Carnes
"Waiting for the Pain to Go Away"
Kim Carnes

Kim Carnes
"Skyline"
Lunch

Kuh Ledesma
"One World"
Night And Day

Laura Turner
"You're Where I Belong"
Soul Deep 2

Laurie Beechman
"I Never Danced with You"
Lunch

Lee Ann Womack
"Love Will Still Be There"
September Dawn

Lee Greenwood
"Don't Underestimate My Love for You"
Streamline

Lee Greenwood
"Someone"
If There's Any Justice

Leon Raines
"Kind of Gray"

Lorrie Morgan
"The Heart That Jack Broke"
Girls Night Out

Louise Mandrel
"As Long as We Got Each Other"
(w/ Eric Carmen)
Tonight You're Mine

Marcia Hines
"Maybe It's Time to Start Calling
It Love"
Live Across Australia

Mark Holden
"Let Me Love You Once Before You Go"
Let Me Love You

Mary MacGregor
"Seashells on the Windows, Candles
and a Magic Stone"
In Your Eyes

Maureen McGovern
"Stop Me (If You've Heard This
Song Before)"

Mel Tillis
"Coca Cola Cowboy"
Every Which Way but Loose

Melissa Manchester
"Fire in the Morning"
Melissa Manchester

Melissa Manchester
"Higher Ground"
If My Heart Had Wings

Melissa Manchester
"Why Fall at All?"
Lunch

Menudo
"Like a Cannonball"
Reaching Out

Merrilee Rush
"Easy, Soft, And Slow"
Merrilee Rush

Merle Haggard
"Barroom Buddies"
Bronco Billy

Merv Griffin
"Whoever You Are"

Michael Crawford
"She Used to Be Mine"
A Touch of Music in the Night

Michael Johnson
"Don't Let It Go to Your Heart"
A Walk Across Texas

Michael Rupert
"Lunch"
"A Man Like Me"
Lunch

Nanci Griffith
"Tiny Dreamer"
Annabelle's Wish

Neil McCoy
"It Shoulda Happened That Way"
Neil McCoy

Nitty Gritty Dirty Band
"I Break Horses, Not Hearts"
Rustler's Rhapsody

Oak Ridge Boys
"A Feeling Like That"
Front Row Seats 2

Pamela Myers
"He'll Never Know"
Lunch

Pat Coil
"More Than the Eye Can See"
Just Ahead

Paul Davis
"Thank You Shoes"
Ride 'Em Cowboy

Randy Travis
"Friends Like Us"
Annabelle's Wish

Ray Charles
"Beers to You"
(w/ Clint Eastwood)
Any Which Way You Can

Ray Price
"You've Been Leaving Me for Years"
Master of the Art

Ray Vega
"Even More"
Even More

Reba McEntire
"Angel's Lullaby"
Reba

Rex Allen Jr.
"The Last of the Silver Screen
Cowboys"
Rustler's Rhapsody

Richard Carpenter
"Lunch Concerto"
Lunch

Ringo Starr
"You Never Know"
Curly Sue

Rodney Carrington
"Camouflage and Christmas Lights"
Make It Christmas

Ronnie Milsap
"Bronco Billy"; "Cowboys and Clowns"
Bronco Billy

Ronnie Milsap
"Hate the Lies—Love the Liar"
Inside

Roy Head
"Fire in the Morning"
In Our Room

Roy Rogers
"Hoppy, Gene, and Me"
Happy Trails to You

Russell Smith
"Honky Tonk Freeway"
Honky Tonk Freeway

Shelly West
"You're the Reason God Made Oklahoma"
(w/ David Frizzell)
Any Which Way You Can

Shelly West
"Another Honky-Tonk Night on
Broadway"
The David Frizzell and Shelly West Album

Shelly West
"Somebody Buy This Cowgirl a Beer"
Red Hot

Smokey Robinson
"Driving Through Life in the
Fast Lane"
Essar

Susan Anton
"Listen to My Smile"
Listen to My Smile

Suzy Bogguss
"You Never Will"
Something Up My Sleeve

Sylvie Vartan
"Easy Love"
I Don't Want the Night to End

Take 6
"*Murphy Brown* TV Theme"
The Sounds of Murphy Brown

Tanya Tucker
"Somebody Buy This Cowgirl a Beer"
Live

The Swingin' Medallions
"Rollin' Rovin' River"
Rollin' Rovin' River

The Tams
"How Long Love"
The Best of the Tams

Think Out Loud
"After All This Time"
Think Out Loud

Tom Jones
"You Set My Dreams to Music";
"Dallas Darlin'"
Tender Loving Care

Troy Cassar-Daley
"Little Things"
True Believer

Turner Rice
"When Love Runs Out"
*When Love Runs Out / A Woman
Ain't a Woman*

Ty Herndon
"Her Heart is Only Human"
Living in a Moment

Vanessa Williams
"Higher Ground"
The Sweetest Days

Warren Wiebe
"13 Steve Dorff Original Demos"
Original Demos

Whitney Houston
"Take Good Care of My Heart"
(w/ Jermaine Jackson)
Whitney Houston

Willie Nelson
"You've Been Leaving Me for Years"
All-American Cowboys

HALL OF FAME OR FUTURE HALL OF FAME MEMBERS WHO HAVE RECORDED STEVE DORFF SONGS

Kenny Rogers	Ringo Starr
Dolly Parton	Cher
George Strait	Dionne Warwick
Anne Murray	The Carpenters
The Oak Ridge Boys	B. J. Thomas
Roy Rogers	Tom Jones
John Anderson	Engelbert Humperdinck
Willie Nelson	Randy Travis
Merle Haggard	Alison Krauss
Ronnie Milsap	Dusty Springfield
Chet Atkins	Jackie Wilson
Dottie West	Smokey Robinson
Glen Campbell	Blake Shelton
Eddie Arnold	Charlie Rich
Tanya Tucker	Charlie McCoy
Ray Price	Christopher Cross
Brenda Lee	Kenny Loggins
Porter Wagoner	Johnny Mathis
Garth Brooks	Andy Williams
George Jones	Mel Tillis
Bill Medley	Ray Charles
Whitney Houston	Reba McEntire
Barbra Streisand	Take 6
Céline Dion	The Osmonds

PLUS

- Over one hundred other recordings by notable artists
- Over four hundred songs recorded in total
- Twelve #1 hits
- Ten Top 5 hits
- Nine #1 hits from motion pictures (the most in country music history)
- Eight songs with over three million BMI performances
- Forty-two BMI Awards
- Three Grammy nominations
- Six Emmy nominations
- The American Music Award for "Every Which Way but Loose"
- Twenty-eight motion picture scores
- Sixteen television themes and scores
- *Josephine* heading to Broadway in 2018

INDEX